Becoming a Poet

David Kalstone

Edited, with a preface, by Robert Hemenway

Afterword by James Merrill

Farrar Straus Giroux

New York

BECOMING
A POET

Elizabeth Bishop

with Marianne Moore

and Robert Lowell

Library of Congress Cataloging-in-Publication Data
Kalstone, David.
Becoming a poet : Elizabeth Bishop with Marianne Moore and Robert
Lowell / David Kalstone ; edited with a preface by Robert Hemenway ;
afterword by James Merrill. — 1st ed.
1. Bishop, Elizabeth, 1911–1979.   2. Bishop, Elizabeth, 1911–1979—
Correspondence.   3. Moore, Marianne, 1887–1972—Correspondence.
4. Lowell, Robert, 1917–1977—Correspondence.   5. Poets,
American—20th century—Biography.   6. Poets, American—20th
century—Correspondence.   I. Hemenway, Robert.
II. Title.
PS3503.I785Z75   1989   811'.52—dc19   88-37645

First printing, 1989

Grateful acknowledgment is made to Grand Street, in which the chapter
"Trial Balances" was published in an earlier version.

For Charles and Ferne Kalstone

Contents

Preface

At his death, David Kalstone had all but completed a draft manuscript of this book. He intended to include an introduction of some fifteen pages, with the title "Prejudices," but wrote no more than the first few lines. They begin:

The protagonist of this book is Elizabeth Bishop. I had once planned a more general book about the generation of poets who came of age after World War II, especially Robert Lowell and Randall Jarrell, who completed a shifting and admiring triangle with Bishop in the years when they were establishing themselves as young writers. But the anomalies of Bishop's experience, her intense difference as a poet, eventually took over my book. We write and rewrite literary history. It becomes increasingly clear, the more we know about Elizabeth Bishop, that she makes us describe poetry in a different light . . .

The draft of his preface goes little further, but there is an account of the "more general" book Kalstone first had in mind in a manuscript written a year or two before:

It has to do with the emergence of a distinctive generation of American poets in the years 1935–65. Both biographical and critical, based on newly available letters and archival material, it shows how a tissue of valued personal connections supported a poetry both intelligent and open to unruly private energies. The book is concerned with the way these poets encountered one another in work and in person, their relationships with older poets (Moore, Ransom, Tate, Williams), and the degree to which they assimilated "an elaborate, scrupulous and respected literary criticism" in the pioneering quarterlies of the 1930s and '40s. *Becoming a Poet* grew out of an earlier and more specifically analytical book, *Five Temperaments* (1977), which included close discussions of the work of Bishop and Lowell, among others. If there is a common thread in these works, it has to do with the continuing process of revision in a poet's career—not just single poems, but the symbolic writing down of a life.

The present book is and is not the *Becoming a Poet* that Kalstone once described. All the elements of his original conception are here to some degree, but the focus is sharper, the range less extensive. As he acknowledges, the book that he intended to write became possessed in the course of its writing— almost, it seems, in spite of its author—by Elizabeth Bishop, who proves here to be someone whose authoritative presence is not entirely familiar to us, a poet who is no longer the "Miss Bishop" of Adrienne Rich's youth. A main thread of Kalstone's projected study was to have been an account of the ways in which a postmodernist generation defined itself and set itself apart from its modernist predecessor, but only a few traces of this historical preoccupation remain. Elizabeth Bishop, that stubborn fact, got in the way. As she herself would say, she was half in, half out of her generation—nor could she be fitted readily into any generation; she was one of a kind.

I think of two things in particular that set Bishop apart. For her, to a degree unusual among her close contemporaries, the poem was an artifact—something made, something composed—before it was a medium of expression. Her work on a poem might take years, but when it was done it was done. ("After a poem is published," she told an interviewer in the 1960s, "I just change a word occasionally. Some poets like to rewrite, but I don't.") The volume called *The Complete Poems*, published when she was fifty-eight, was simply the collection of those poems she had finished so far, those that were complete; not more than one or two of her reviewers caught on. And her choice of predecessors, of "influences"—of the tradition within which she worked—was highly personal, touched only rarely by literary fashion or transitory enthusiasms or the temper of the time. Bishop's own pantheon—much too strong a word— had few of the names to be found on the lists her male contemporaries were fond of making. Hers constituted a congenial and unpretentious but quite exclusive gathering that stayed remarkably stable from her college days on. Among its members were George Herbert and Charles Baudelaire—"two of my favorite poets (not best poets)," as she wrote to Anne Stevenson— together with Marianne Moore, Gerard Manley Hopkins, Gesualdo, Max Jacob, Anton Chekhov, William Cowper, St. Teresa of Avila, Joseph Cornell, Charles Darwin, Sydney Smith, Anton Webern, and Paul Klee. And, of course, Robert Lowell. Good company. Writers, artists, composers whom she loved; she required no other sanction. If you were setting out to define a postmodern generation—its predecessors, its principles—what on earth was to be done with her? And yet there was no leaving her out. Bishop was altogether of her time, if not of her generation, and she was a master.

It may well have been Kalstone's encounter with Elizabeth Bishop's "intense difference" through the abundant, particularizing medium of her letters—what he elsewhere in his notes calls "those startling detailed presentations of the world which were her way of assimilating herself to the felt strangeness of life"—that brought about his abrupt and salutary change in direction. In the unfinished manuscript that he left—it was perhaps a year away from completion—one can see the shock of the encounter with Bishop still at work, can feel the tension between old prejudices (to use his word) and new recognitions. What we have is quite far from his original intent and quite surprising: an exacting (though informal) inquiry into the workings of friendship between poets and the steady growth of an extraordinary mind. And although it can hardly have been altogether what he meant to give us, I see David Kalstone's book as an excellent *vade mecum* for writers—a guide to becoming a poet—for he offers a paradigm that has much to say about how writers ought to (and, alas, how they sometimes do) behave. In going at their work, in going about the business of living.

Becoming a Poet, then, is neither the book its author first intended nor the one he might finally have written. Nor is it a verbatim reproduction of his manuscript. It could not be. A great many small acts of editorial judgment have necessarily intervened between the drafts he left and these pages, but those of us who have worked on the book have sought to keep the voice and the emphases his from beginning to end. David Kalstone had succeeded in completing at least one draft of all but the introduction and the final chapter by the time of his death and had rounded off two of his chapters for publication in *Grand Street*. There were a few gaps, and the notes, along with the verification of facts and quotations, had yet to be done. But in the main his book had taken on its final form. At the outset of our work on the manuscript, we had an assortment of drafts in various states and stages. For the most part these were type-scripts, written in Europe and in this country on a number of different machines, often heavily revised in pencil or pen and bearing occasional marginal comments by Kalstone and others. And there were the *Grand Street* pieces, which did not corre-spond exactly to the chapters on which they were based but drew on material from other chapters as well and had been substantially reworked for periodical publication. There were also computer printouts that turned up later, some of them improved drafts of the typescript versions and others with brand-new material, including nearly all of one chapter. And there were several hundred 5×8 note cards, dating from the author's first researches, that had his transcriptions from letters, draft manuscripts, and periodicals, along with observations jot-ted down as he read.

Out of these I drew together a rough manuscript, collating the various drafts and reconciling them as much as possible with each other. I typed up a first version of the end notes and appended my own notes and queries, suggesting revisions that might be made in the text. James Merrill and Richard Poirier, the author's literary executors, read this draft and my comments, as did J. D. McClatchy and Pat Strachan, then Kalstone's editor at Farrar, Straus and Giroux. We quickly found ourselves in agreement that, although it might be possible to rewrite Kalstone's text, making it more polished and at times more precise, the outcome could no longer be called his nor would it be in his distinctive voice. What had to be done was to turn this somewhat daunting palimpsest into a book that was David Kalstone's own.

And so, although I had no choice but to act in the author's stead and make a number of minor emendations as I carried the rough drafts through to a finished one, I have made few changes in substance or in style—fewer, certainly, than Kalstone himself would have thought necessary. There are passages here he would have cut, for he meant to have a finished manuscript that was somewhat shorter than this. There are other passages that he would have reworked, I'm sure, but I've not made the attempt, nor have I tried to fill the few gaps he left with more than a phrase or two to smooth a transition. Where errors of fact caught my eye, I corrected them. If I could not correct them without revising the text substantially, I let them stand. Now and then I've added a sentence or two in clarification, usually in the notes, drawing on Kalstone's own note cards or on passages from the letters. But I've let the book retain the spontaneity of Kalstone's drafts, and along with that come some of a draft's imprecisions and inflations. David's book was hardly meant to be the final word on its subject; much of the way, indeed, it offers the very first. And I find the freshness of the writing here a delight.

The end notes were prepared with the invaluable help of Kerry Fried and Claudia Rattazzi at Farrar, Straus and Giroux. Kalstone's original drafts bore brief indications of the sources of most of the quotations from letters and manuscripts. Every effort has been made to locate these sources, and to verify them, wherever possible, against the originals. For the frequent instances in which Kalstone, during his research, drew on manuscripts or periodicals for material that has since been published in book form—the prose of Bishop, Moore, and Lowell and the letters of Jarrell—we have used and cited the published text.

Among those David Kalstone would have thanked for their help and their critical advice during his writing of the book are Svetlana Alpers, Frank Bidart, John Malcolm Brinnin, Maxine Groffsky, Elizabeth Hardwick, Anthony Hecht, J. D. McClatchy, James Merrill, Richard Poirier, and Pat Strachan. He would have expressed his gratitude to the National Endowment for the Humanities for their support of his research during the calendar year 1981, to the John Simon Guggenheim Foundation for their grant of support from July 1985 to June 1986, and to Alice Methfessel, Elizabeth Bishop's literary executor; Marianne Craig Moore, literary executor for the estate of Marianne Moore; the Lowell Estate and its executor, Robert Silvers; Lisa Browar, formerly Curator of Rare Books and Manuscripts at Vassar College, and the staff of the Vassar College Library; Patricia C. Willis and her colleagues at the Rosenbach Museum and Library, Philadelphia; Rodney Dennis, Curator of Manuscripts, together with James Lewis, Curator of the Reading Room, and the members of the staff of the Houghton Library, Harvard, particularly Melanie Wisner; and Holly Hall, Head of the Olin Libraries Special Collections of the Washington University Libraries, St. Louis. The publishers and I would like to add our thanks to his, and to say that we are most grateful to Charles and Ferne Kalstone, the author's brother and his sister-in-law, whose steadfast and persistent encouragement has done much to further this book's publication.

Robert Hemenway

*One of the strange things about poets
is the way they keep warm by writing
to one another all over the world.*

—VIRGIL THOMSON

Elizabeth Bishop
and Marianne Moore

1 / From the Country to the City

Among the manuscripts that Elizabeth Bishop left unpublished at the time of her death in 1979 was the long memoir
of Marianne Moore that has since appeared in her *Collected Prose*,
a piece that she had been working on intermittently for a number
of years. She had, of course, written to and about Moore all
her adult life—from the time they first met in 1934, when
Bishop was twenty-three: a great many letters, tributes in the
form of a poem and three essays, informal talks about Moore
and her work, anecdotes saved and polished over the years, tales
told out of school. That critics linked their names both flattered
and irritated, amused and puzzled the women—seemed an evasion of what mattered most, the stubborn particular. So, when
yet once again a magazine, this time French, spoke of Moore's
influence on Bishop, the younger woman wrote to her old
friend:

Everyone has said that—I was going to say, all my life—and I
only wish it were truer. My own feeling about it is that I don't show
very much; that no one does or can at present; that you are still too
new and original and unique to *show* in that way very much but will
keep on influencing more and more during the next fifty or a hundred
years. In my own case, I know however that when I began to read

your poetry at college I think it immediately opened up my eyes to the possibility of the subject-matter I could use and might never have thought of using if it hadn't been for you. —(I might not have written any poems at all, I suppose.) I think my approach is so much vaguer and less defined and certainly more old-fashioned—sometimes I'm amazed at people's comparing me to you when all I'm doing is some kind of blank verse—can't they *see* how different it is? But they can't apparently.

And Moore, looking back at Bishop's letter a few years later and with an equally polite and generous irritability, wrote her:

As for indebtedness, Elizabeth, I would reverse everything you say. I can't see that I could have "opened your eyes" to subject matter, ever, or anything else. And a stuffy way of appraising us by uninitiate standards blankets all effort with impenetrable fog! I roam about in carnivorous protest at the very thought of unimaginative analyses. Alexander Pope to the rescue!

Even allowing for Bishop's deferential tone and for Moore's playful archness, the two women show a healthy respect for the distance between them and for the complex of feelings we call "indebtedness." Moore, who had had no tutelary older poet in her own life, must have sensed Bishop's talent and independence from the start. Her role in Bishop's emergence as a poet is more mysterious than any simple comparison of texts could suggest. In a relaxed moment at the close of her memoir, Bishop writes:

I have a sort of subliminal glimpse of the capital letter *M* multiplying. I am turning the pages of an illuminated manuscript and seeing that initial letter again and again: Marianne's monogram; mother; manners; morals; and I catch myself murmuring, "Manners and morals; manners *as* morals? Or is it morals *as* manners?" Since like Alice, "in a dreamy sort of way," I can't answer either question, it doesn't much matter which way I put it; it *seems* to be making sense.

Moore is taken up in an alliterative blur of childhood associations with the remote Nova Scotia village where Bishop grew up: the coiling initial letters that fascinated Bishop in her beloved grandfather's Bible; his old-fashioned village lessons in behavior revisited in one of a planned series of poems on "manners"; and beneath it all the unspoken fact of Bishop's childhood: an absent mother. Thinking about Moore would have been in part like recognizing fragments of her Nova Scotia life "through the looking-glass." What must it have been like, for example, for a young woman who had not seen her mother since she was five to know an older poet who was inseparable from hers? And to have met Moore in the very year that Bishop's own long-absent mother died? The apartment at 260 Cumberland Street in Brooklyn where Moore lived with her mother was "otherworldly," Bishop says in her memoir—"as if one were living in a diving bell from a different world, let down through the crass atmosphere of the twentieth century." The young writer always left there feeling happier, "uplifted, even inspired, determined to be good, to work harder, not to worry about what other people thought, never to try to publish anything until I thought I'd done my best with it, no matter how many years it took—or never to publish at all." Moore's world was in part a vanished sustaining maternal world transposed into another key; it nourished Bishop's writing life, yet could be contradicted with impunity. It was as if Bishop had in Moore both a model and a point of departure, an authority against which she could explore, even indulge, her more anarchic impulses.

Bishop, who for most of her life shied away from other literary figures, said that her seeking out Moore was the one time, the only time, that she ever deliberately tried to meet a "celebrity." Like her later friendship with Robert Lowell—the other great literary attachment of her life—Bishop's "apprenticeship" to Moore had rich emotional dimensions. When, years after, she thanks Moore for opening up subject matter which she, as a young poet, might never otherwise have thought of using, Bishop is talking about a complicated, instinctive affinity.

Their friendship began in the spring of 1934, when Bishop was a senior at Vassar. She first heard of the poet from her "more sophisticated" school and college friend Frani Blough—though she "perhaps pretended," Bishop said later, that she already knew Moore's name. When she found some of Moore's poems, she was "astounded." There was no copy of Moore's *Observations* on the shelves of the Vassar library, so Bishop tracked down the poems in early issues of *The Dial* and *Poetry* and began a determined study not only of the verse but of reviews of Moore's work and of Moore's reviews of other poets. From *The Hound and Horn* (October–December 1932) she copied out in longhand "The Jerboa." She took notes on T. S. Eliot's review, in *The Dial* for December 1923, of the English edition of Moore's *Poems*, briskly marking apropos Eliot's praise of "Those Various Scalpels": "Even then they picked on the one which seems more obvious . . . I'll take 'Jerboa.' " (So, it turned out, would Eliot in 1935.)

Almost by accident Bishop discovered that Miss Fanny Borden, the Vassar librarian, knew Moore, had known her from the time Moore was a child, and in fact had the only copy of *Observations* at Vassar. Bishop, in telling how she met Moore, always dwelt on Miss Borden, as if she were an appropriately eccentric, somewhat gothic herald to the story: the tall, thin librarian, almost inaudible, who rode a chainless bicycle, was a niece of *the* Lizzie Borden, a fact that some felt had had a "permanently subduing effect" on her personality. Miss Borden offered to introduce Bishop to Moore, and it was arranged that the two would meet one Saturday afternoon in March outside the third-floor reading room of the New York Public Library, at the right-hand bench. (Evidently not all Miss Borden's protégées were given the same treatment; Moore met some of them at the information booth in Grand Central Station, from which she could, if she were bored, easily scuttle away "to catch a train.") Bishop arrived early; when she saw "a tall, eagle-nosed, be-turbaned lady, distinguished-looking but proud and forbidding," she was needlessly alarmed, fearing that this might be the poet. Fortunately, Moore herself was less intimidating. They sat on the library bench and talked. Bishop, years later, didn't remember about what, only that she "loved her immediately." That day she invited Moore to go to the circus on the next Saturday but one, and before long she would send Moore Father Lahey's life of Gerard Manley Hopkins and write to ask her if she might be interested in an excellent new book on tattooing.

The Moore Bishop met was forty-seven, her red hair mixed with white, her eyes pale blue, her "rust-pink eyebrows frosted with white." She wore a braid drawn in a loose crown just above the forehead, a style of the 1900s she never bothered to change. Bishop observed, a year or so later, that the small pointed face and "delicately pugnacious-looking jaw" made her look like Mickey Rooney! It was an odd moment in the older poet's life. She had ceased being editor of *The Dial* in 1929. It had been almost ten years since she had published a book of poems, and the royalties on *Observations* up to that point totaled fourteen dollars. In *The Hound and Horn* Yvor Winters had remarked, in 1931: "Miss Moore, indeed, seems to have exhausted the possibilities of her style and to have abandoned writing." (Moore's *Selected Poems*, with an introduction by T. S. Eliot, was to appear in 1935.) After their first meeting, Bishop (with some of the exaggeration of youth) noted down that she found Moore "poor, sick, her work practically unread I guess" but "amazing." Moore was "very impersonal," spoke just above a whisper, but "she can talk faster and use larger words than anyone in New York . . . She really is worth a great deal of study." What would surprise any reader of their correspondence is an unexpected parity between the older woman and the younger from the very start. Of course it was four years before Moore invited her to call her by her first name, something Bishop celebrated in electric capitals: DEAR MARIANNE. Her tone with Moore is always respectful, grateful, thoughtful, but from the very beginning also bold—a "flicker of impudence," Moore said.

Aside from some detailed exchanges about Wallace Stevens, Bishop seems uninterested in Moore's modernist connections. Rather, what attracted her were the older poet's

manners and mannerisms, her fusion of old-fashioned domesticity—the kind Bishop knew with her aunts and grandparents
during her early childhood in Nova Scotia—with forthright
notions about writing and style. Moore herself had insisted on
the connections between the odd self-enclosed, self-nourishing
speech of her family and the language of her poems. In the
discreet Postscript to the *Selected Poems* ("All dedications are
dowdy," Ezra Pound had told her) she alluded to her mother:

Dedications imply giving, and we do not care to make a gift of
what is insufficient; but in my immediate family there is one "who
thinks in a particular way"; and I should like to add that where there
is an effect of thought or pith in these pages, the thinking and often
the actual phrases are hers.

Mrs. Moore had been an English teacher at a girls' school and
spoke very slowly in "Johnsonian sentences." Bishop found her
extreme precision enviable and thought she could detect echoes
of Marianne's own style in it: "the use of double or triple negatives, the lighter and wittier ironies—Mrs. Moore had provided
a sort of ground bass for them." In letters to the two women
she took care to point out some of the effects. She could hear
Mrs. Moore saying the last sentence of "The Wood-Weasel"
(Only / Wood-weasels shall associate with me"). And "Propriety" has the effect of a dialogue, and "I think I hear a maternal
note" at the end.

Bishop got to know the mother and daughter well in 1934
and 1935; she'd moved to New York after Vassar and went
often to see them in the fourth-floor apartment on Cumberland
Street. The apartment was full of emblematic animals and presented (as Marguerite Young has said) an "anarchic order":
when you pulled the lamp chain, you discovered a beetle-sized
baby ebony sea horse in your hand. Mrs. Moore, in her seventies, was "very serious—solemn, rather—although capable of
irony, and very devout." Her face was pale, her eyes large and
a pale gray, and there was almost no white in her hair. Each
time Bishop left the Moore apartment, Mrs. Moore followed

her to the hall, took her hand, and said a short prayer. She could be, Bishop said, "over-fastidious." She burned in the furnace a copy of Mary McCarthy's *The Company She Keeps*. Moore once told Bishop with her "serious, severe look" that a certain accomplished writer whom she'd known for years was never invited to the house: "He *contradicted* Mother." "Her manner toward Marianne was that of a kindly, self-controlled parent who felt that she had to take a firm line, that her daughter might be given to flightiness or—an equal sin, in her eyes—mistakes in grammar."

Both Marianne and her mother "corrected" many of Bishop's stories and poems between 1934 and 1940. "I should say, in candor," Marianne remarked in her comments on Bishop's story "The Sea and Its Shore," "that most of the pencilled interpolations on these two pages of suggestions were 'contributed,' and that Mother is a rabid advocate of the power of suggestion versus statement and wishes you need not say just at the end that he was drunk. She thinks the study is a marvellous satire on life; let alone writing."

On the whole, Bishop must have found Moore's own poems and letters more provocative, more daunting than the "corrections." "Why had no one ever written about *things* in this clear and dazzling way before," Bishop was to remark of Moore's work. "Although the tone is frequently light or ironic the total effect is of such a ritualistic solemnity that I feel that in reading her one should constantly bear in mind the secondary and frequently sombre meaning of the title of her first book: *Observations*." As Eliot said of the *Selected Poems*, "For a mind of such agility, and for a sensibility so reticent, the minor subject, such as a pleasant little sand-coloured skipping animal, may be the best release for the major emotions . . . We all have to choose whatever subject-matter allows us the most powerful and most secret release; and that is a personal affair."

――――

Bishop was a keen observer before she met Moore; learning that this could be a way of life identified with a way of writing was another matter. Every detail of the letters Bishop would send from Europe and Key West was carefully "inspected." Each of the many gifts elicited an elaborate description: of seeds of the papaya, "the necks set so they stand up like seed-pearls on stiff silk." Bishop's postcards provided, Moore would write her, "a veritable course of study." And the younger woman wrote from Mallorca of these careful responses: "I'm afraid that I can't really have made this trip at all until I've lured you into commenting on every bit of pictorial evidence I can produce." The Moores' habit of scrutiny, appropriating the exotic to their self-contained world, was challenging, intriguing, amusing— and must also have posed something of a conundrum. It was tied to a life that was already, even in the 1930s, becoming valetudinarian. Mother and daughter, in a manner worthy of a Victorian ménage, found themselves bound to one another by illnesses, a tie that in the 1940s became acute. Marianne's letters are ringed with care and tribulation. Pleasures are always framed by trouble; going to see Eliot's *The Cocktail Party* is "well worth the struggle." Moore is constantly in awe of Bishop's travel and casts her in a role that is in a way intimidating; apart from visits to Marianne's brother, John Warner Moore, in Virginia, the Moore women always seemed too ill or beset to travel. Bishop, on the other hand, was in these years almost always on the move. After Vassar she settled in New York for almost a year; then, in July 1935, set out on her first trip to Europe. She traveled in Spain and North Africa, lived in France until the summer of 1936. She returned to France in 1937; and then after a series of yearly trips to Florida, bought, with her friend Louise Crane, a house in Key West, her first real "home" since her childhood. Even afterward she was always traveling: yearly trips north; Mexico in 1942. The regular letters and gifts she sent the Moores obviously meant a great deal to them. Theirs was a life of ingestion, of collecting rare specimens, to which Bishop added countless shells, duck feathers, decorated eggs, small carved animals: "Each object is full of ideas and of beauty and has livened us more than I can tell you, in our degradation of after-illness." Alongside the Moores' life of domestic economy and effort, Bishop felt herself something of a truant. Moore wrote her during the same illness, in 1936: "To be snakes in alcohol is abhorrent to us and you must efface the image of us; and when you have come back help us by example to have leisurely habits and better health." Bishop, who was traveling in Spain and Morocco, chose to take "leisurely habits" as a reproach, and assures Moore (and herself) that she will be at home and at work in June. The pattern repeats itself through the early 1940s. Moore can write, for example: "I am in bad repute with Mother anyhow for pursuing with childlike curiosity, as I do, every Robinson Crusoe-like thing the torrid zone can produce." Bishop, who shared the older poet's "childish curiosity," must also have sensed in Moore's predicament the pressure behind such absorption and scrutiny. Randall Jarrell, contrasting the two poets a few years later, thought that Bishop was "less driven into desperate straits or dens of innocence, and [took] this Century of Polycarp more for granted."

If Moore opened the young poet's eyes to the subject matter she might use, Bishop also seemed to be testing herself against the older poet—a mixture of disobedience and dependence. Almost from the start there was a useful tension between them that had to do with the ways the two women lived, the resemblances that triggered or accentuated differences. Bishop once said of herself that having no family to rebel against had made her passive. In a curious way, her identification with Moore helped liberate her; she adopted Moore's methods but learned to use them in different ways.

———

For a young poet of twenty-three, Bishop's admiration of Moore's style is surprisingly cool and independent. Like all really deep influences, this one took a long time to absorb. She wrote in her notebook sometime in 1934 or 1935:

Miss Moore's "architectural" method of conversation, not seemingly so much for the sake of what she says as the way in which it is said: indifferent subject matter treated as a problem in accuracy, proportion, solidity, balance. If she speaks of a chair you can practically sit on it when she has finished. It is still life, easel painting, as opposed to the common conversational "fade-out."

Bishop is intrigued, perhaps a little stiff, with the idea of "indifferent subject matter." Her notebook entries of 1934 and 1935 are only in part descriptive exercises:

the soft combed and carded look of the flames in the gas oven

the rain came down straight and hard and broke into white arrow heads at the tips

These last mornings the street-sprinkler goes around about 9:30. The water dries off very rapidly but very beautifully, in *watermelon* patterns—only wet-black on grey, instead of darker green on lighter green.

Her observer's instinct, clear in passages like these, cuts across a more deeply rooted inclination, an interiorizing interest. When, not long after, the passage about the street sprinkler finds its way into a poem ("Love Lies Sleeping"), it is with a psychological and subjective cast that Moore would not have been likely to give it. As with so many of Bishop's poems of this period, "Love Lies Sleeping" (first called "Morning Poem") is set on the edge of waking:

> Along the street below
> the water-wagon comes
>
> throwing its hissing, snowy fan across
> peelings and newspapers. The water dries
>   light-dry, dark-wet, the pattern
>   of the cool watermelon.
>
> I hear the day-springs of the morning strike . . .

The accuracy is of a very special sort, less after the fact, less explicit visually than the notebook entry (no colors, no adverbial stage directions). Instead, the rhythm ("light-dry, dark-wet") suggests an impression only just gathering before she finds an image for it. The protagonists of many of these early poems ("The Weed," "The Man-Moth") have trouble accommodating the claims of the world. The precision of a passage such as this one is colored by the effort of "coming back to life." Hence the provocative "hissing" and the eventually comforting context as the water wagon's "snowy fan" turns human discards—the peelings and papers—to wholeness, "the pattern / of the cool watermelon." The frailty of human arrangements and recognitions is one of the subjects of "Love Lies Sleeping," and one of its most haunting images is of the mind just barely reassembling the world but pleased with its own ingenuity:

> From the window I see
>
> an immense city, carefully revealed,
> made delicate by over-workmanship,
>   detail upon detail,
>   cornice upon façade,
>
> reaching so languidly up into
> a weak white sky, it seems to waver there.
>   (Where it has slowly grown
>   in skies of water-glass
>
> from fused beads of iron and copper crystals,
> the little chemical "garden" in a jar
>   trembles and stands again,
>   pale blue, blue-green, and brick.)

Bishop sometimes expressed the wish that she "could recover the dreamy state of consciousness" she lived in then, in her twenties, "at the time I was writing the poems I like best." Among her notebook entries of 1934–35 are many that, if not directly indebted to surrealism, show a mind disposed to absorb its lessons and eager to move from observation to symbolic resonance:

The window this evening was covered with hundreds of long, shining drops of rain, laid on the glass which was covered with steam on the inside. I tried to look out, but could not. Instead I realized I could look into the drops, like so many crystal balls. Each bore traces of a relative or friend: several weeping faces slid away from mine; water plants and fish floated within other drops; watery jewels, leaves and insects magnified, and strangest of all, horrible enough to make me step quickly away, was one large long drop containing a lonely, magnificent human eye, wrapped in its own tear.

The monitory eye wrapped in its own tear seems an appropriately riveting image for Bishop's writing at the time: the odd combination of observation and alienation that makes her early poems, especially, different from Moore's. She had, by the time she discovered Moore's work, an already matured metaphysical taste. She was drawn to the Elizabethan and Jacobean poets; she had read and reread them. George Herbert was—and remained—one of her favorite poets. (She recounts in her notebook a dream during this period in which George Herbert appears to her. They discuss the difference between his work and Donne's, and touch upon Miss Moore's, which is said in the dream to beat Donne's but not his. "This may have been subconscious politeness on my part," Bishop notes. "He had curls and was wearing a beautiful dark red satin coat. He said he could be 'useful' to me. Praise God.") When she was in her teens someone gave her an edition of Gerard Manley Hopkins's poems; she already knew by heart the passages from Hopkins quoted by Harriet Monroe in her anthology *The New Poetry*, which a friend had given her one summer at camp.

Clearly her attraction to Moore's style in some ways puzzled her; she puts it rather soberly in her notebook:

It's a question of using the poet's proper material, with which he's equipped by nature, i.e., immediate intense physical reactions, a sense of metaphor and decoration in everything—to express something not of them—something I suppose, spiritual. But it proceeds from the material, the material eaten out with acid, pulled down from underneath, made to perform and always kept in order, in its place. Sometimes it cannot be made to indicate its spiritual goal clearly (some of Hopkins say, where the point seems to be missing) but even then the spiritual must be felt. Miss Moore does this but occasionally, I think, the super-material content of the poems is too easy for the material involved—it could have meant more . . . Genuine religious poetry seems to be about as far as poetry can go—and as good as it can be.

Despite the serious and schooled tone, the issues are deeper, less dispassionate than they seem. Hopkins was not only a favorite poet but to Bishop's eye and ear a great observer in his prose. In this notebook, with Hopkins as with Moore, what engages her attention is the mysterious relation between the observed and what it "spiritually" signifies. Even these two poets to whom she is so drawn are not judged fully or continuously successful in linking the two worlds. The problem is addressed abstractly but it reflects more personal preoccupations. Many of her best poems of the 1930s are concerned precisely with divided lives and can be read as versions of seventeenth-century poems about the soul trapped in the body. Sometimes the predicament is comic. Her Gentleman of Shalott accepts with a shrug being half mirror, half man. More often the versions are troubled, as with "The Man-Moth" and "The Weed," poems whose protagonists only reluctantly reenter the waking or everyday world. The gap between the observed world and the unknown, the psychic one, is something that disturbs Bishop in her early work, and something that only long experience helped her overcome. Thirty years later she is able to speak as if there were no conflict.

There is no "split." Dreams, works of art (some), glimpses of the always-more-successful surrealism of everyday life, unexpected moments of empathy (is it?), catch a peripheral vision of whatever it is one can never really see full-face but that seems enormously important. I can't believe we are wholly irrational—and I do admire Darwin! But reading Darwin, one admires the beautiful solid case being built up out of his endless heroic *observations*, almost unconscious or automatic—and then comes a sudden relaxation, a forgetful phrase, and one *feels* the strangeness of his undertaking, sees the lonely young man, his eyes fixed on facts and minute details, sinking or sliding giddily off into the unknown. What one seems to want in art, in experiencing it, is the same thing that is necessary for its creation, a self-forgetful, perfectly useless concentration.

As critical discourse, this is somewhat evasive. But as a self-portrait—using Darwin as her mirror—it helps us see a Bishop considerably more abandoned, more at ease, and confident in her habits of observation. "Sliding giddily off into the unknown" is very different from feeling, thirty years before, that the material world must be "eaten out with acid, pulled down from underneath."

For the protagonists of "The Man-Moth" and "The Weed" the claims of the world come almost as a physical shock, embodied, say, in the rushing of the subway and the poisonous third rail of "The Man-Moth" and, in "The Weed," in the rushing waters where the weed grows "but to divide your heart again." "The Weed" takes place, as did "Love Lies Sleeping," on the edge of dreaming and waking. It is the poem in which Bishop most sees the world through George Herbert's eyes. But unlike Herbert's "The Flower," for example, "The Weed" is a dream of grim release which substitutes for heavenly joys a sense of the wild persistence of life. The call to the physical world is involuntary and takes the speaker back not so much from a world of grace as from a prized state of withdrawal, static and final:

> I dreamed that dead, and meditating,
> I lay upon a grave, or bed,
> (at least, some cold and close-built bower).
> In the cold heart, its final thought
> stood frozen, drawn immense and clear,
> stiff and idle as I was there . . .

Bishop experiences these glacial comforting states often in the early poems and stories. Here change intrudes as a psychic explosion, "prodding me from desperate sleep," in the form of a weed that divides her cold heart's "final thought." From the "immense" clarity of this moment the allegorical scene becomes more animated: a flood of water, then two, divide the heart, but now into "half-clear" streams. The strangest moment in a very strange poem is that when, in a few drops of water shaken from the struggling weed into her eyes, she sees

> (or, in that black place, thought I saw)
> that each drop contained a light,
> a small, illuminated scene;
> the weed-deflected stream was made
> itself of racing images.
> (As if a river should carry all
> the scenes that it had once reflected
> shut in its waters, and not floating
> on momentary surfaces.)

The few drops falling upon her face are like tears, and they contain the most precise, arrested visions of the world the speaker permits herself. ("Illuminated" suggests not only "lit" but also bedecked and pulsing with the illuminist's meaning, a moment of arrested glory for the "racing images.") But the overriding impression of the poem is the calmness, almost the indifference, with which the speaker undergoes both the trance-like state, close to death, and the nervous gaiety with which the weed draws her back to life. Physical vision seems tied to separateness and loss, and somehow to guilt. Awareness is a state to which the speaker only reluctantly abandons herself.

"The Weed," written in the summer of 1936, is obviously related to the dreamlike notebook entry of 1934 in which, on the window coated outside with raindrops and inside with steam, Bishop has a hallucination in one of the drops of a "lonely, magnificent human eye, wrapped in its own tear." The image is unusual enough, though the mixture of alertness and withdrawal it implies is probably not so unusual in a young poet. ("I tried to look out, but could not," Bishop says.) And where many young poets would have been crippled or confused, Bishop was able, at that early stage of her writing, to make successful and moving poems of this disposition. There are finally no ways to explain that distancing power and clarity of the language. As Bishop herself once said, all criticism of poetry must sooner or later mention the poet's "gifts." But an early notebook exposes more of the dividing impulses and the exceptional intelligence of the young woman behind the poems. Her vivacity is as remarkable as her reserve.

The notebook, which dates from 1934–35, shows Bishop just out of Vassar, spending some of the summer off the Massachusetts coast on Cuttyhunk Island and then settling down in New York in late July for what was to be a year of writing, seeing Marianne Moore, reading at the New York Public Library (copying out lyrics from sixteenth- and seventeenth-century masques), and going to concerts, operas at Lewisohn Stadium, museums. But above all reacting to the city itself: "I think that it is in the city alone, maybe New York alone, that one gets in this country these sudden intuitions into the *whole* of contemporaneity . . . you catch it coming toward you like a ball, more compressed and acute than any work of 'modern art.'" Still, when it came to writing about New York, the excitement seems transposed into an equally wondering but more sinister key. "The Man-Moth" dates from that first stay, "Love Lies Sleeping" and "From the Country to the City" from a second stay after Bishop returned from her first trip to France; the three are placed together in *North & South*. Both "The Man-Moth" and "Love Lies Sleeping" contain figures running

[18

counter to the city's rhythms—the man-moth, except for his infrequent romantic ascents, is buried underground in the rushing subways; the lone lover at the end of "Love Lies Sleeping" is, when morning comes, one

> whose head has fallen over the edge of his bed,
>   whose face is turned
>   so that the image of
>
> the city grows down into his open eyes
> inverted and distorted. No, I mean
>   distorted and revealed,
>   if he sees it at all.

Bishop said that she had always assumed that the man at the close of the poem was dead. It is only to his "inverted" vision that the city is *revealed*.

A figure effectively dead turns up in the notebooks, in New York material that Bishop would adapt for "The Man-Moth." She had observed a woman in the subway about whom everything had died—her face dead white, her clothes, her handbag—except her eyelashes. Bishop remembers that in a dream her friend Margaret Miller "had looked into the inside of a small mask someone had pulled from his face, and caught in it all around the eyeholes were the little hairy eyelashes. The woman's face made me think of that—its expression was a concave one, like an empty interior expression, and its only markings were the little eyelashes." The woman's eyes were shut, and the lashes seemed like those on a sleeping doll. "It is rather strange the way the eye is surrounded with inhuman stuff—hair grows, I've heard, even on the dead." The incident contributes obliquely to "The Man-Moth," a kind of morbid counterpart to the man-moth himself, who has, on rare occasions, the capacity to escape and make his romantic ascents to the surface of the city, each one a doomed foray. We know that a newspaper misprint, *manmoth* for *mammoth*, prompted the poem: the idea of a doomed spirit trapped in a subway rider's form, sitting always backward, racing under the city streets (in the world of the third rail "running along silently, as insincere as poison," she wrote in her notebook). In the conditional clauses of the poem's last stanza she transforms her own notebook observations of the deadened woman on the subway into a glimpse of residual purity and spirit:

> If you catch him,
> hold up a flashlight to his eye. It's all dark pupil,
> an entire night itself, whose haired horizon tightens
> as he stares back, and closes up the eye. Then from the lids
> one tear, his only possession, like the bee's sting, slips.
> Slyly he palms it, and if you're not paying attention
> he'll swallow it. However, if you watch, he'll hand it over,
> cool as from underground springs and pure enough to drink.

The observer's curiosity and effort is rewarded by extracted signs of life, but as in her windowpane hallucination, as in "The Weed," there is a link between vision and tears. The man-moth closes his eye and emits a tear; the speaker in "The Weed" sees her "illuminated scenes" in drops that suggest tears. The dead protagonist of "Love Lies Sleeping" *sees* the city through inverted open eyes, head fallen over the side of the bed (an inverted image, as in Newton's *Opticks*, which Bishop had been reading at the time). These poems allow her simultaneously to be a keen observer—the figure who "tells" the poems scrutinizes every detail to extract her meaning—and yet to identify with figures absent, withdrawn, practically lifeless. It is a curiously suspended state and one she becomes aware of at moments of crisis in her life.

In journal entries made on her first trip to Europe, aboard the *Königstein* in late July 1935, Bishop records a series of such disorienting experiences. One evening she sees patches on the waves: "These are *men on rafts*, poor wretches clinging to a board or two . . . I am *positive* I see them there, even a white body, or the glitter of their eye-balls rolled toward us." Twice at dinner she is overtaken by an awful awful feeling of deathly physical and mental *illness*—something that seems "after" me. It is as if one were whirled off from all the world and the interests of the world in a sort of cloud— dark, sulphurous gray—of melancholia. When this feeling comes I can't speak, swallow, scarcely breathe. I knew I had had it once before, years ago, and last night on its second occurrence I placed it as *"home- sickness."* I was homesick for two days once when I was nine years old; I wanted one of my Aunts. Now I really have no right to home- sickness at all. I suppose it is caused actually by the motion of the ship away from New York—it may affect one's sense of balance some way; the feeling seems to center on the middle of the chest.

Readers who know a poem Bishop wrote about her child- hood almost forty years later—"In the Waiting Room"—will recognize the collocation of feelings: the sense of being engulfed, drawn under the waves or literally whirled off the globe, losing one's grip of discrete particulars and having to reassemble the world anew. Whether the childhood illness she refers to in her notebook (she says she was nine then) is the same one she recounts in her poem (in which she says she was seven), the circumstances are similar, and this notebook entry made when she was twenty-four marks the moment when she begins to understand the vertigo and connect it with loss. Of course, and typically, she veers away from homesickness, says she has no "right" to it, and lays the cause to seasickness and moving away from the familiar New York. But are they indeed so different? The fainting spell of "In the Waiting Room" occurred very soon after the seven-year-old Bishop was moved away from her maternal aunts in Nova Scotia to live with her dead father's family in Worcester. "I wanted one of my Aunts," she says of the attack at age nine. Disorientation and the threat of aban- donment are very close in her mind, and the notebook entry suggests that she is beginning to connect her observer's powers with a constant and urgent need to fend off the something that was "after" her; that reconstructing the world was a way to combat or express what in 1935 she identifies as "homesickness"—a homesickness particularly remarkable because at this stage there is no *image* of home attached to it.

We are accustomed to thinking of Bishop's lively clarity, her openness to the world—attitudes she had mastered in her later poems—and forgetting that these blithe strengths were the product of tensions and fears. Her commitment to the *illusion* of physical presence—her hallmark—was hard won. She observed because she had to. This is another reason why Marianne Moore's entrance into her life was particularly important. While Bishop was commenting in poems and stories on her own sense of absence or half-presence in the world, she was in fact involving herself with a poet who was *all eye, all presence*. Moore's secure bravado in dealing with the physical world was something Bishop instinctively valued, though she only gradually absorbed it into her writing. It was not simply the *fact* of her response to Moore, but the miraculous and instinctive timing of it that mattered.

——

The young woman who felt when she sailed to Europe in 1935 that she had no right to homesickness spent much of her life overcoming it. Anne Stevenson, the author of the first full-length book on Bishop, is quite right in saying that Bishop's poems are not conventional travel poems and have much more to do with re-establishing the poet's own sense of place. Bishop was to remark that she always liked to *feel* exactly where she was, geographically, on the map. A whole train of displacements had marked her youth, and the plain facts that set them in motion are recorded in several chronologies Bishop was asked to prepare for publication and in the autobiographical stories she was eventually able to write once she had settled in Brazil. She advised Stevenson to print this entry: "1916. Mother became permanently insane, after several breakdowns. She lived until 1934." Bishop went on to say: "I've never concealed this, although I don't like to make too much of it. But of course it is an important fact, to me. I didn't see her again." The shattering reserve of that comment (down to the careful comma before "to me") is a warning to critics. Bishop never traded on her losses. At least one of her close friends from the Vassar years—Louise Crane—was unaware that Bishop had a living mother until her own mother told her that Gertrude Bishop had died. One of her college advisers, who knew that Bishop was "on her own," found her "in a perfectly polite and friendly way, very reticent . . . When I opened a door, she would turn the talk to her work, about which she was intelligent and resourceful." And one of her professors spoke of her as "an enormously cagey girl who looked at authorities with a suspicious eye and was quite capable of attending to her own education anyway." Long before she ever wrote directly about her childhood, Bishop seemed aware of the fact that she would in one way or another do so. A notebook entry written just before sailing to Europe in 1935 reads:

A set of apparently unchronological incidents out of the past have been reappearing. I suppose there must be some string running them together, some spring watering them all. Some things will never disappear, but rather clear up, send out roots, as time goes on. They are my family monuments, sinking a little more into the earth year by year, boring [?] silently, but becoming only more firm, and inscribed with meanings gradually legible, like letters written in "magic ink" (only 5 metaphors).

The little self-protective parenthesis at the end suggests that for the moment these were feelings best distanced as a *literary* problem. That she understood even earlier the need to "place" her childhood is suggested in a very grown-up essay she did as an undergraduate. "Dimensions for a Novel," written for Miss Rose Peebles's class in modern fiction and subsequently published in the *Vassar Journal of Undergraduate Studies*, suggests that Bishop was an attentive reader of Proust or that some of the novels she had read prodded her to at least an intellectual grasp of how personal loss enters into one's writing:

If I suffer a terrible loss and do not realize it till several years later among different surroundings, then the important fact is not the original loss so much as the circumstance of the new surroundings which succeeded in letting the loss through to my consciousness.

Or again:

The crises of our lives do not come, I think, accurately dated; they crop up unexpected and out of turn, and somehow or other arrange themselves according to a calendar we cannot control.

The essay presents itself as a kind of literary preparation for releases that were to come later. It draws on a reserve of patience, a faith in the indirection that will allow urgent feelings to appear, the slow reordering of sensibility in which events are understood not chronologically but in a new psychically accurate or revealing formation. "The process perhaps resembles more than anything the way in which a drop of mercury, a drop to begin with, joins smaller ones to it and grows larger, yet keeps the original form and quality."

When the young Bishop said that the important thing was not so much one's original loss as the new surroundings that admit it to consciousness, she seemed to anticipate the ways in which she would slowly, obliquely absorb, through her writings, feelings too painful to face head-on. In certain surroundings—Key West after 1938, Brazil after 1951—she would be stimulated by circumstances that reminded her of Great Village, in Nova Scotia, where she passed her early childhood, of the intimacies and improvisations of village life, and of the parentless years she spent there, and only when she was living in Brazil would she be able to write directly about the losses of her childhood.

Bishop had come to Great Village with her mother after the death of her father. Gertrude Bulmer Bishop was twenty-nine when her husband died, only eight months after the birth of their daughter and only child. They had been married three years, and the family always felt that the shock of his early death (he was thirty-nine) brought on the series of breakdowns his wife then suffered. (Bishop herself believed that, though there was no history of insanity in the family, her mother had shown signs of trouble before.) For the first five years of her life the young child was effectively in the care of her mother's parents and her aunts, the youngest of whom was only twelve years older than she. Her mother was hospitalized most of the time: first in McLean's sanatorium outside Boston and then, after a final breakdown, in a mental hospital near Dartmouth, Nova Scotia, for the last eighteen years of her life. Despite the efforts of her husband's family, who did everything possible to support her and who tried to arrange for her return to the United States, she could not, having lost her American citizenship after her husband died, be brought back to McLean's. Her daughter never saw her again.*

"Although I think I have a prize 'unhappy childhood,' almost good enough for the text-books—please don't think I dote on it," the poet wrote in a biographical note to Anne Stevenson. There were many comforting aspects in the part of her childhood she spent in Great Village. She adored her grandfather. He had been a tanner and a small-scale farmer, was "sweet-tempered, devout, and good with children. He was a deacon of the Baptist church and when he passed the collection plate he would slip me one of those strong white peppermints that say (still, I think) CANADA on them." She was treated very well by her grandmother and her aunts, and by the Bishop grandparents, who visited Nova Scotia several times, once in

---

*Writing to Anne Stevenson in 1964, Bishop had this to say of her mother's long stay in the Nova Scotia hospital: "She did receive the very best treatment available at that time, I feel sure . . . The Bishop family spared no expense . . . That generation took insanity very differently than we do now, you know . . . The tragic thing was that she returned to N.S. when she did, before the final breakdown. At that time, women became U.S. citizens when they married U.S. citizens—so when she became a widow she lost her citizenship. Afterwards, the U.S. would not let her back in, sick, and that is why she had to be put in the hospital at Dartmouth, Nova Scotia (across the harbor from Halifax). My Bishop grandfather tried for a long time to get her back in the U.S. One always thinks that things might be better now, she might have been cured, etc. . . . Well—there we are. Times have changed. I have several friends who are, have been, will be, etc. insane; they discuss it all very freely and I've visited asylums many times since. But in 1916 things were different. After a couple of years, unless you cured yourself, all hope was abandoned—"

the relatively unfamiliar motorcar, complete with chauffeur. There were obviously many mysteries in her childhood—her mother's unexplained disappearances, whispered conversations and evasions—and much of these early years must have been spent in parsing out unfinished sentences and interpreting unexplained scenes. Her childhood seems unusually marked, too, by early and remembered deaths: her young cousin Arthur, and the mysterious playmate Gwendolyn, a doll-like pampered creature whose death and disappearance she recalled in a story written in Brazil.

To an unusual degree the child's attention was deflected outward, toward the village itself, its rhythms and familiar figures. Whether the village represented external stability and safety, or whether the child's losses prodded her to scan everything habitually for clues and meanings, the smallest details of Great Village life remained with her: the tanner's pits, the blacksmith's shed behind their house, the dressmaker, the milliner, the routine of taking the cow to graze. Great Village, once a shipbuilding town, was years behind the times: no electricity, no plumbing. It looked like a small New England village, with elm trees, white houses, and the Presbyterian church at the center. (There were two churches, the Presbyterian and the Baptist.) The surrounding farm country around the head of the Bay of Fundy was rich with dark red soil, birch trees, blue firs. The Bulmer family used oil lamps and made yeast in the barn from hop vines. Grandmother Bulmer was a famous butter maker. They had a buggy with a fringe, a wagon, and a sleigh. The aunts all sang or played the piano, and it is from them that Bishop dates her early love of music as well as her lifelong pleasure in hymns. She went for a short time to the village school (one took one's bottle of water and a rag to clean one's slate) and to an infant Sunday school.

The decisive shock of her early life must have come when she had to give up the reassurances of Great Village and her mother's family to live in Worcester, Massachusetts, with the more solidly established Bishop grandparents. Not that they were unkind; her grandfather John Wilson Bishop had been and continued to be extremely generous. He was a successful builder and a contractor for public buildings, and his firm built the Boston Public Library and the Museum of Fine Arts. A self-made man, a native of Prince Edward Island, he had run away from home when he was twelve with a box of carpenter's tools, "made millions," and married well. The Bishop decampment with car and chauffeur must have been a sensation in Great Village. They wired the local hotel for room and bath—when, as Bishop points out, there wasn't a bath in town.

The Bishops were horrified to see the only child of their eldest son running about the village in bare feet, eating at the table with the grown-ups and drinking *tea*, and so I was carried off (by train) to Worcester for the one awful winter that was almost the end of me. 1917–1918.

In Worcester she began to suffer the severe illnesses—bronchitis, asthma, symptoms of St. Vitus' dance, persistent eczema sores—that plagued her until her late teens. Her painful shyness began in those years, she says in a letter to Anne Stevenson, and she adds that, although her Bishop grandparents were very loving, the next generation made her "suffer acutely." Her worried grandfather arranged—and paid—for her to live with her mother's sister Maud, married and childless, near Boston. By the time she arrived—in May 1918—she couldn't walk and had to be carried up the stairs by the Bishops' chauffeur. Her aunt proved a dedicated nurse in the years following, when Bishop was able only fitfully to go to school and spent most of her time "lying in bed wheezing and reading." She began writing poems then, when she was eight.

An unfinished story about her life with her Aunt Maud, "Mrs. Sullivan Downstairs," suggests that, apart from her illnesses, that period, like the earlier one with her maternal relatives, had a certain comfort about it and continued, later in life, to exercise her curiosity. She remembered every dish and stick of furniture, her aunt's sewing machine, its table piled high with *National Geographics*. They played the piano together and sang hymns and patriotic World War I songs. (She had begun piano lessons at her Grandfather Bishop's suggestion and continued to study music for years, taking a course in keyboard literature from Ralph Kirkpatrick at Vassar and clavichord lessons from him for a time when she lived in New York.) When she was eight they lived in one of the suburbs north of Boston and from the top of one of its hills could see the tower of the Boston Customs House. They were the only Canadians in a neighborhood with many Irish and many more Italians, who lived as they had in Sicilian villages—kept goats, treaded grapes, and made their own wine. Downstairs in the two-family house (the kind with big back porches called piazzas on each level) was a Mrs. Sullivan, twenty-one years old with several children, who had bright red hair. The young asthmatic child would spend hours downstairs with her in a kitchen "smelling of cabbage and urine."

When Bishop was thirteen she was at last well enough to attend a sailing camp for girls near Wellfleet, where she continued to go for five summers. At sixteen, she entered the Walnut Hill boarding school in Natick, near Boston. Frani Blough, who was one of her closest friends at the school and at Vassar, remembers her as a "most remarkable girl":

She looked remarkable, with tightly curly hair that stood straight up, while the rest of us all had straight hair that hung down. And she was remarkable in many ways besides. She had read more widely and deeply than we had. But she carried her learning lightly. She was very funny. She had a big repertory of stories she could *tell*, not read, and of wonderful songs she could sing, like ballads and sea chanteys. And if some school occasion called for a new song, or a skit, it would appear overnight like magic in her hands . . . We all knew with no doubt whatsoever that she was a genius.

At the Walnut Hill School, Bishop wrote Anne Stevenson, she met for the first time "girls who were as clever, or cleverer than I was, and made friends, and began to cheer up a bit." Her years there, and then at Vassar, seem to have revived and strengthened her, but she emerged into young adulthood feeling that she had always been a guest in other people's houses.

Bishop's accounts of her childhood are marked by what one could think of as either a compulsive scrutiny of maternal, domestic scenes or as a loving attention to them, piecing together with inordinate curiosity episodes relating to her mother's family. And her habit of scanning such scenes for clues to *others'* domesticity and history left her preternaturally alive to the peculiarities of human arrangements, the signs and artifacts which allow us to assemble or dissemble intimacy. Though she was "independent" from eighteen on, her sense for these arrangements was a strength she wasn't able truly to exploit until she started to build a life in Key West in 1938. At that point her descriptive talents and her writing became part of an active attempt to create and re-create a life, to domesticate a world, as they were to be much more strongly when she settled later in Brazil. And of course what nourished this self-sufficiency were the absorbed, but somehow as yet no more than observed, domestic details of her childhood.

2 / Trial Balances

By the fall of 1934, Bishop was living in Greenwich Village at 16 Charles Street, in an apartment Mary McCarthy—they had become friends at Vassar—found for her. Jobs were hard to come by (it was mid-Depression) and she worked briefly, earning fifteen dollars a week, at the U.S.A. School of Writing, a shady and sad correspondence school for hopeful—and hopeless—writers. (She had a small income left her by her father but found a "real need for a little more money than I had.") "We were puritanically pink," Bishop writes. "Perhaps there seemed to be something virtuous in working for much less a year than our educations had been costing our families." That "we" suggests how much, despite her desperate shyness and the illnesses suffered throughout childhood, the Vassar years had given Bishop a spirited "modern" confidence. New York, in some ways, accelerated this feeling, and she was intensely aware of its power. As she had written in her notebook, New York and perhaps New York alone in this country offered "sudden intuitions into the *whole* of contemporaneity." With Margaret Miller, who was a painter, she was looking at modern painting and came to love particularly the work of Paul Klee. She was reading Wilenski's *The Meaning of Modern Sculpture* and despaired of finding terms half as precise and useful in contemporary literary criticism. She heard Gertrude Stein lecture in the New School that fall (and in fact knew Stein's work in college— was particularly interested in Stein's medical studies). And, of course, like many writers her age, she was an admirer (though never as openly as some an imitator) of Auden. His poems "colored our air and made us feel tough, ready, and in the know, too." One of the pieces she was working on in that first year, a masque called *The Proper Tears* (a fable about scientists and humanity), owes as much to Auden's *Paid on Both Sides* as it does to the seventeenth-century masque masters, Jonson and Fletcher, whose works she was studying assiduously at the New York Public Library. She had read Auden constantly in college and she would continue to read him:

His then leftist politics, his ominous landscape, his intimations of betrayed loves, war on its way, disasters and death, matched exactly the mood of our late-depression and post-depression youth. We admired his apparent toughness, his sexual courage . . . Even the most hermetic early poems gave us the feeling that here was someone who *knew*—about psychology, geology, birds, love, the evils of capitalism—what have you?

Bishop's confidence—a modernist spunk—was close to the surface when she came down to New York from Vassar. Yet she seemed, and was always to feel, both in and out of her generation. Her school and college friends called her Bishop or The Bishop, a bow to the independent and cheerfully authoritative air she must have projected. In 1936, when Moore, who had addressed her for two years as Miss Bishop, picks up a note of distress in her letters and asks to call her Elizabeth, she replies with what seems almost a stab of relief for the intimacy: "As first names go, I am really quite fond of my own and should be delighted to be called by it—because so few people do." Moore's life touched on some of Bishop's private and particular strengths which remained in abeyance, rooted in an imagination nourished by the nineteenth-century cast of her first six years. These were resources not immediately available to her, or which came coupled with reserves of guilt and confusion—linked to her sense that she had always been a guest in others' houses. In this year of her mother's death she does not write directly about her childhood experience in the journal which has been preserved. But she does, in many of the entries, take a melancholy view of herself:

My friendly circumstances, my "good fortune," surround me so well and safely, and only *I* am wrong, inadequate. It is a situation like one of those solid crystal balls with little silvery objects inside: thick, clear, appropriate glass—only the little object, me, is sadly flawed and shown off as inferior to the setting.

Emotional contradictions are everywhere in this her first New York journal: alongside the outgoing modernism and receptivity to the city are strong suggestions of guilt, reserve, withdrawal, and at times the sense that she was later to identify as homesickness. Contrary qualities which would one day come together as strengths in her writing were initially dispersed— and in her best work of this early period she made this dispersal of energies her subject.

Mary McCarthy once said of Bishop's writing, "I envy the mind hiding in her words, like an 'I' counting up to a hundred waiting to be found." The analogy is apt even down to the expectant concealed child. What one often hears "hiding" in Bishop's poems—especially the early ones she wrote in and about New York—is an instinctual self resisting a nervous seductive adult persona she associates with city life. The language of these early poems allows us to take them almost as Renaissance dialogues of soul and body. The prepositions in the title "From the Country to the City" (1937) are not just spatial, measuring a return from a weekend, but also suggest an epistle addressed from one realm to the other with the force of an interior drama. " 'Subside,' it begs and begs": this is the body's erotically tinged plea against the urban brain "throned in 'fantastic triumph' " (the latter a phrase borrowed from Aphra Behn's "Love Arm'd").

"The Man–Moth" and "Love Lies Sleeping," poems of the same period, involve similar messages and pleas from submerged figures resisting the encroachments of the febrile adulthood of the city: the single silent tear extracted from the man-moth bears witness to his plight and is a last extorted vestige of purity. The speaker of "Love Lies Sleeping" intercedes on behalf of city dwellers whose speechless representative is the dead staring protovisionary at the end of the poem. As that figure's head has fallen over the side of the bed, his vision inverted, so the man-moth sits in the underground train, always "facing the wrong way." A submerged self in these works is variously imagined and identified. But it is clear that in the poetry and prose Bishop wrote after she left college she was drawn to fables that gave body to a divided nature; alongside a hectic modernity one senses a shadowy space left for the absent or unrealized figures of a buried or inaccessible childhood. They may be elusive even in dreams. In "Sleeping Standing Up" (1938), the adult dreamer, freed to experience thoughts "recumbent in the day," can get only as close as the "armored cars of dreams" will permit. A curious image but one which suggests how rigidly separate she feels not only from the images of childhood but also from the modes of experiencing them:

—Through turret-slits we saw the crumbs or pebbles that lay
  below the riveted flanks
    on the green forest floor,
like those the clever children placed by day
    and followed to their door
  one night, at least; and in the ugly tanks

we tracked them all the night. Sometimes they disappeared,
  dissolving in the moss,
    sometimes we went too fast
and ground them underneath. How stupidly we steered
    until the night was past
  and never found out where the cottage was.

The dreaming adults succeed only in overrunning the traces of their earlier lives, not in finding the "cottage" the traces might lead to. When Bishop first used the Nova Scotia of her childhood as a setting for a short story, "The Baptism" (1937), it was with an eerie sense of a youthful life vanishing, withdrawing before her eyes. In "The Baptism" three young sisters, orphaned, face their first Nova Scotia winter on their own. The almost unspoken fact of the story is that the mother and father have only recently died. The parents' elided disappearance is taken for granted, as if it were perfectly natural for three young women to be living alone in a tiny remote village without some adult presence, some relative to oversee them.

Lucy, the youngest, becomes increasingly obsessed with a guilt whose sources she cannot identify and almost convinces her sisters that "she must have been guilty of the gravest misdemeanor as a young girl." One night she hears the voice of Christ above her bed and another evening has a vision of God burning, glowing, on the kitchen stove. "His feet are in hell." The growing ecstasy and alienation from her sisters ends in her decision—they are Presbyterians—to become a member of the Baptist church. She is only heartsick that for "total immersion" she must wait until the ice leaves the river. At the first thaw she is baptized, catches cold, develops fever, and dies.

Childhood images that Bishop was to look back on with affection in later works—the religious engravings in the family Bible, the singing of hymns around the piano—turn up here in a more dangerous context. Reading one of their father's old travel books, *Wonders of the World*, Lucy becomes overstimulated by a depiction of the Nativity: "the real, rock-vaulted Stable, the engraved rocks like big black thumbprints." Readers will anticipate the return of those images a good ten years later in "Over 2,000 Illustrations and a Complete Concordance." In that later poem Bishop remembers the engraving with yearning for simple belief in the domestic warmth it recalled. Lines of the engraving beckon magically to the eye, move apart "like ripples above sand, / dispersing storms, God's spreading fingerprint." But in 1936 and for the obsessive Lucy of "The

Baptism" the "big black thumbprint" seems to mock, if not besmirch, the scene. The engravings draw her away from her family, deeper into her mania, until finally, terrifyingly, the child disappears. The narration is reasonable, plain; nothing departs far from the ordinary but the obsessive child. (Bishop was trying to produce an effect something like Hans Christian Andersen's, she told Moore.)

Early deaths—several in Nova Scotia—are subjects to which Bishop was frequently drawn, as if scrutinizing the horizon for her own childhood. "The Farmer's Children," a story probably begun in the late 1930s but not published until 1948, deals with two boys who die of exposure, frozen to death in a barn; "Gwendolyn" (1953) recounts the death of a valued young playmate; and the poem "First Death in Nova Scotia" (1962) is about the laying out of a child, her dead Uncle Arthur. One of the books she borrowed from Moore, read and reread in 1935, was the diary of Margery Fleming, a Scottish girl, born in 1803, who wrote her journal as part of her tutelage in her sixth, seventh, and eighth years, and was dead before she was nine.

———

In these early years, it is clear, Bishop did not think of herself exclusively as a poet. The first work of hers that appeared outside school and college magazines was a short story, "Then Came the Poor" (1934), and the contributor's note said that she was writing a novel. Much of her writing energy in the thirties was absorbed by short stories. It was through narrative or through the fables of her early poems that she instinctively found some way to "place" her childhood, and it was a while before she learned to make description do the work that narrative first accomplished for her. At the time, then, that she was in a sense "going to school" to Marianne Moore, she had already struck out on a course independent of the older poet. Moore's influence was less a youthful passion to be outgrown—the case with most apprenticeships—and more a steady slow infusion assimilated into the bloodstream. Her notebook is filled with observations prompted by Moore's descriptive powers—and many of them find their way into her early poems, as with the watermelon pattern in "Love Lies Sleeping" and that description of the city seen by someone only half awake—the chemical "garden" that "trembles and stands again, / pale blue, blue-green, and brick."

But description as a principle of composition, description to serve her own particular purposes, she had not yet mastered. Moore's descriptions, as Bonnie Costello points out, were mostly mediated for her, a lens of print focusing her subject; she did much of her exploring through catalogues, journals, museum documents, exhibitions. Bishop, in her poems, was less the poised researcher, less the orchestrator of a varied ensemble of fact. For her, the descriptive style was to be most valuable when it grew out of mysterious and engaging encounters in her own daily life and travels. She would use observation as a kind of tentative anchorage, as a way of grasping for presence in the world. The "powerful and secret release" that description offered her, however much it owed to Moore, was to be of a different order from the older poet's.

The first poem to show Bishop's authentic transformation of Moore's style would be "Florida" (1939), which heralded the valuable domesticating discoveries of her life in Key West. In these early years, however, what she found immediately useful in Moore's work were subtler elements that linked Moore, curiously enough, to Gerard Manley Hopkins—qualities to which Bishop, with her musical training, was particularly sensitive. ("There are in her shaping of a poem," Moore wrote of Bishop in 1935, "curbs and spirits that could be known only to a musician.")

When Bishop was still in college she'd copied out a passage in T. S. Eliot's review of Moore's first book (noting, "This suggests a method of approach")—a comment on Moore's rhythm, and an example from "Those Various Scalpels":

Rhythm, of course, is a highly personal matter; it is not a verse-form. It is always the real pattern in the carpet, the scheme of organization of thought, feeling, and vocabulary, the way in which everything comes together. It is very uncommon. What is certain is that Miss

Moore's poems always read very well aloud. That quality is something which no system of scansion can define. It is not separable from the use of words, in Miss Moore's case the conscious and complete appreciation of every word, and in relation to every other word, as it goes by. I think that Those Various Scalpels is an excellent example for study. Here the rhythm depends partly upon the transformation-changes from one image to another, so that the second image is superposed before the first has quite faded, and upon the dexterity of change of vocabulary from one image to another. "Snow sown by tearing winds on the cordage of disabled ships:" has that Latin, epigrammatic succinctness, laconic austerity, which leaps out unexpectedly.

> your raised hand,
> an ambiguous signature:

is a distinct shift of manner; it is not an image, but the indication of a fulness of meaning which it is unnecessary to pursue.

Eliot's interest, and Bishop's too, was in the rapidity of transition—not the metrics of a piece but the real rhythm: "the releasing, checking, timing, and repeating of the movement of the mind." The phrase is Bishop's, from an article on Gerard Manley Hopkins written while she was at Vassar. As if to a magnet, her studies—musical and literary—seemed to draw her back to, reinforce and rationalize her early passion for Hopkins's verse. (His musical ideas, she told Moore, seemed to anticipate Schönberg's.) She had learned to admire a quality his writing shared with seventeenth-century prose, one for which the critic M. W. Croll helped her find words:

Their purpose was to portray, not a thought, but a mind thinking . . . The ardor of [an idea's] conception in the mind is a necessary part of its truth, and unless it can be conveyed to another mind in something of the form of its occurrence, either it has changed into some other idea or it has ceased to be an idea, to have any existence whatever except a verbal one.

Bishop was quick to make a connection to Hopkins, who, she says, "has chosen to stop his poems, set them to paper, at the point in their development where they are still incomplete, still close to the first kernel of truth or apprehension which gave rise to them." As unlikely as Hopkins may seem as a model for Bishop, her essay is as much a self-possessed declaration of her own poetic intentions as it is a lucid view of Hopkins's difficult practices. She was seduced not so much by his intensity as by a new rhythmic freedom and variety he gave to verse. Several features of his "sprung rhythm" especially appealed to her: There is leeway for any number of weak or unaccented syllables in a foot, so that the line kept its required number of accents but could expand or contract. "Reminiscent," Bishop said, "of the caprice of a perfectly trained acrobat: falling through the air to snatch his partner's ankles he can yet, within the fall, afford an extra turn and flourish, in safety, without spoiling the form of his flight." Weak syllables at the beginning of a line are scanned as part of the last foot of the line before, so that "the scansion is continuous, not line by line" or, in Hopkins's words, "All the stanza is one long strain, though written in lines asunder." Hopkins's odd rhymes ("England . . . mingle and") "usually 'come right' on being read aloud, and contribute in spite of, or because of, their awkwardness, to the general effect of intense, unpremeditated, unrevised emotion." Hopkins's devices

do break down the margins of poetry, blur the edges with a kind of vibration and keep the atmosphere fresh and astir. The lines cannot sag for an instant; by these difficult devices his poetry comes up from the pages like sudden storms. A single short stanza can be as full of, aflame with, motion as one of Van Gogh's cedar trees.

Most readers, especially young readers, respond to the obvious signs of Hopkins's energy—the smart alliterations, the gnarled syntax. But Bishop saw something subtler, something she could translate into the key of her own understated poetic voice. For, as Hopkins himself put it,

Sprung rhythm . . . is the nearest to the rhythm of prose, that is the native and natural rhythm of speech, the least forced, the most rhetorical and emphatic of all possible rhythms, combining, as it seems to me, opposite and, one wd. have thought, incompatible excellences, markedness of rhythm—that is rhythm's self—and naturalness of expression.

Bishop's ear was teased by the possibilities she heard in Hopkins for giving a poem "a fluid, detailed surface, made hesitant, lightened, slurred, weighed or feathered as Hopkins chooses"— by, for example, the light inner rhymes that deemphasize the end-rhyme scheme. When Bishop tells her story of the mammoth it is precisely Hopkins's "run-over" lines that allow her a rapid plausible tone, a flat declarative swiftness that can suddenly contract into muscular emphases, as when the romantic, moth-like creature loses something akin to his only weapon ("one tear, his only possession, like the bee's sting, slips"). In Moore's work, too, Bishop was alive to the plain, flat voice proceeding, her lines entirely arbitrary and with sudden ruffles of meaning that come with rhythmic effect. So, the short-syllabled last line of Moore's "The Steeple-Jack," which could when need be, because of its repeating quality at the ends of stanzas, suddenly become a rhythmic nugget like a refrain. At the end of the poem, beside the final "stands for hope," Bishop writes in her copy "NEVERMORE," a glance at Poe's rhythmic effect and what to her ear was a subtler scaling down—equally effective—in Moore.

―――

Bishop's stay in New York between Vassar and her first trip to Europe lasted almost a year—enough time for her friendship with Moore to take on the air of both a quirky family tie and a professional challenge. She responded to the intimacy— her glimpses of Moore's old-fashioned domestic ways—as much as to Moore's attentive editorial direction. She enjoyed playing her role of forward niece and was always trying to lure Moore out into the world: Come to the movies (*Son of Mongolia*, for example), come to Coney Island (Moore did), come to Spain (she couldn't), to a concert by Ralph Kirkpatrick—and, each spring, to the circus. (One year the lure was a Chinese family which ate and played cards while hanging by their hair.)

The other side of it was that almost from the start Moore encouraged the young poet's work, helped overcome her reticence about her verse. At first, fresh out of Vassar, Bishop replied to a request for poems (from T. C. Wilson, at the *Westminster Magazine*) saying that she hadn't any but a few light things which "I do just for fun . . . the only ones I have any success with." She may have counted among these the two "Valentines," skillful imitations of Donne and the Cavalier poets that had already appeared, in 1934, in the *Vassar Review*. But less than a year later, when she chose to reprint these along with a third "Valentine" and a sonnet about tears, imitating Hopkins, she was able to add the first poem in what was recognizably her own voice. It was "The Map," later set as the opening poem of her first book and eventually of her *Complete Poems*. The occasion was an anthology called *Trial Balances* that appeared in the fall of 1935, in which thirty-two young poets between the ages of twenty and twenty-five were introduced by more established poets. Louise Bogan presented Roethke, Stephen Vincent Benét introduced Muriel Rukeyser. Moore was asked to comment on Bishop and wrote a remarkably prophetic note in which she seems to be speaking out of a felt kinship of purpose, an instinctive grasp of Bishop's work that went beyond the poems *Trial Balances* collected. So Bishop is praised for her "methodically oblique, intent way of working," for being thoughtful but not, "like the vegetable-shredder which cuts into the life of a thing," a blunt purveyor of ideas. Moore predicts attitudes which Bishop held throughout her career, and almost seems to be writing an anticipatory defense against feminist critics as well.

Some feminine poets of the present day seem to have grown horns and to like to be frightful and dainty by turns; but distorted propriety suggests effeteness. One would rather disguise than travesty emotion; give away a nice thing than sell it; dismember a garment of rich aesthetic construction than degrade it to the utilitarian offices of the boneyard. One notices the deferences and vigilances in Miss Bishop's writing, and the debt to Donne and to Gerard Hopkins. We look at imitation askance; but like the shell which the hermit-crab selects for itself, it has value—the avowed humility, and the protection. Miss Bishop's ungrudged self-expenditure should also be noticed—automatic, apparently, as part of the nature.

The prescriptive ones and woulds and shoulds also anticipate some of the differences Bishop ("less driven into dens of innocence," as Randall Jarrell said) was to have with Moore. However "protected" Bishop's work might seem, it had a sharpness, a kind of exposure, that didn't always sit well with Marianne. Moore was very disquieted by the first "Valentine," with its baroque erotic play:

> Love with his gilded bow and crystal arrows
> Has slain us all,
> Has pierced the English sparrows
> Who languish for each other in the dust,
> While from their bosoms, puffed with hopeless lust,
> The red drops fall.

She did her best to "place" it:

One asks a great deal of an author—that he should not be haphazard but considered in his mechanics, that he should not induce you to be interested in what is restrictedly private but that there should be the self-portrait: that he should pierce you to the marrow without revolting you. Miss Bishop's sparrows ("Valentine I") are not revolting, merely disaffecting.

Moore seems disquieted that the raunchy English sparrows should be part of the "self-portrait," but finds a transparent way out of it. It was a naïve moment of embarrassment and candor that anticipates some later comic clashes about Bishop's more anarchic, more adventurous life.

Over the next few years Moore led or prodded Bishop toward a number of editors and journals. "She seems to have an instinct against precipitousness," the older poet wrote in October 1935, responding to an inquiry from Edward Aswell at Harper & Bros., "and I have not been able to persuade her to let me see more than a few pieces of her work." But "taking an interest in her progress does not amount to having assumed a gigantic burden." Bishop in fact had six poems to send Aswell or to show for the time since she left Vassar. Almost all this work later appeared in magazines to which Moore had recommended her. "The Man-Moth" (1936) and two stories, "The Baptism" (1937) and "The Sea and Its Shore" (1937), appeared in *Life and Letters Today*, a magazine founded by Moore's friend Bryher (Winifred Ellerman Macpherson). "Casabianca," "The Colder the Air," and "The Gentleman of Shalott" appeared in the April 1936 issue of *New Democracy*, to whose editor, the young James Laughlin, Moore had given Bishop's address. She urged Bishop to send things to Ezra Pound for *The New English Weekly* and later connected her with Morton Dauwen Zabel at *Poetry*. While Bishop was in Paris, Moore offered to type her poems for submission to magazines, an offer Bishop characterized as not only kind but "headlong." In those first years, Bishop seems not to have shown Moore any work in progress. "The Man-Moth" when it came out in the spring of 1936 took Moore by surprise. "It is difficult to sustain atmosphere such as you have there. But you do sustain it and one's feeling that the treatment is right is corroborated by one's sense of indigenousness, and of moderate key." She praised the vigilant construction and novel atmosphere and "a certain satisfactory doughtiness" in the *New Democracy* poems and "The Imaginary Iceberg," which had appeared in *Direction* the year before. In "The Gentleman of Shalott" she notes "the maintained unequipoise and isolating as it were of 'he can walk and run / and his hands can clasp one / another.' "

The *New Democracy* poems appeared while Bishop was still in Europe. When she returns in the summer of 1936, her friendship with Moore takes on a new tone and Moore's interventions become vital. Bishop appears to have suffered a crisis about her writing, though her report of it to Moore is characteristically understated. She is at West Falmouth on Cape Cod, with Margaret Miller and near her friend Louise Crane. Sailing. She has been reading St. Augustine's *Confessions*, Amiel's *Journal*, and *The Prelude*. "This heaped-up autobiography," she declares, "is having extreme results." She wants to try medicine or biochemistry, at which she was good in college. Having given writing a chance, she feels she's accomplished "nothing at all," and would rather do science than "become like one of my contemporaries." (This was no whim; Bishop actually applied to Cornell Medical College, and in 1963 she would tell Anne Stevenson that she seriously considered studying medicine for several years and still wished that she had.) Moore's reply is a careful one; she, with tactical calm, claims not to be "disturbed at all."

I feel you would not be able to give up writing, with the ability—for it that you have; but it does disturb me that you should have the *feeling* that it might be well to give it up. To have produced what you have—either verse or prose is enviable, and you certainly could not suppose that such method as goes with a precise and proportioning ear is contemporary or usual . . . I hope you will have reasons to be glad you allowed the *Southern Review* and Roger Roughton to have something.

It is now that Moore urges her to send some poems to Zabel at *Poetry* and insists—politely—on seeing her new work. "In fact I have rather a serious cause for complaint against you for stinginess in this matter." And this is the moment Moore stops calling her Miss Bishop and begins to address her as Elizabeth; the warmth and encouragement invited, by return mail, some poems which explain, more than Bishop's own flat statement, the kinds of lassitude and guilt she was feeling. They have "awful faults," Bishop wrote, "one being vague, another an extremely impolite, if true, display of your 'influence.' "

The poems she speaks of are "The Weed" and "Paris, 7

A.M.," which displace the surface gaiety of Bishop's New York poems with a more interior and disturbed vocabulary. "The Weed," as we have seen, vibrates between two equally removed states: the dreamer, "dead, and meditating," and her awakening into life as a growing weed pushes up through her heart and, severing it, releases a stream made up of racing images. The dreamer addresses the weed:

> "What are you doing there?" I asked.
> It lifted its head all dripping wet
> (with my own thoughts?)
> and answered then: "I grow," it said,
> "but to divide your heart again."

Bishop meant to capture in "The Weed" something of the allegorical simplicity of Herbert's "Love Unknown":

> . . . But at the length
> Out of the caldron getting, soon I fled
> Unto my house, where to repair the strength
> Which I had lost, I hasted to my bed.
> But when I thought to sleep out all these faults
> (I sigh to speak)
> I found that some had stuff'd the bed with thoughts,
> I would say *thorns*. Deare, could my heart not break,
> When with my pleasures ev'n my rest was gone?
> Full well I understood, who had been there:
> For I had giv'n the key to none, but one:
> It must be he. *Your heart was dull, I fear.*

Her own fable of "dullness" is even bleaker than Herbert's. Herbert's, as Joseph Summers points out, is an image of the dialogue between natural and spiritual man. In Bishop's poem the natural has more energy, but its purposes are suspect—to divide the heart—and its vitality resisted. What Bishop has responded to in Herbert's poem are the psychological possibilities: the translation of the dialogue into psychological terms as the mind seems to watch its own motions—to watch and resist its own motions. The poem presents a certain spiritual passivity. The drops that touch her face, like tears, are only *seen* to contain a small illuminated scene. They provide a way to arrest the stream of racing images released by the weed, but offer scenes she merely becomes aware of rather than interpreting or entering them. A similar dreamlike atmosphere pervades "Paris, 7 A.M.," which seems a translation of her New York poems into a grimmer key—without their exhilaration or sources of recovery. Here, as in "The Man-Moth" and "Love Lies Sleeping," the city submerges an instinctual life connected with childhood (the childish snow-forts of which the Paris architecture seen from above reminds her). But in this poem the submergence is effected by some more inexorable force of time and space. The clock faces of the opening lines—visited early in the morning—merge into the map of Paris, the Etoile with its dispersing circles ("Time is an Etoile; the hours diverge / so much that days are journeys round the suburbs"). And the sky, no longer the imagined "carrier-warrior-pigeon / escaping endless intersecting circles," is dead.

Moore's reaction was immediate and encouraging:

And the poems are so fine, and dart-proof in every way—especially "The Weed" and "Paris, 7 A.M."—that they shame my impulsive offer of helpfulness. This exteriorizing of the interior, and the aliveness all through, it seems to me are the essential sincerity that unsatisfactory surrealism struggles toward. Yet the sobriety and weight and impact of the past are also there. The great amount of care, the reach of imagination, and the pleasure conveyed, make it hard for me not to say a great deal; but I fear to make suggestions lest I hamper you. Specific comment is bound to be hapless. Still, I venture, in the way of soliloquy—not request—and should be *very* glad to have you keep everything just as you have it.

Moore's whisper of reservation in the midst of warmth and understanding was soon followed by the "suggestions" she wasn't sure she should make—not only about "The Weed" and

"Paris, 7 A.M.," but also about the sestina "A Miracle for Break-fast," which Bishop had sent Moore at the same time. And so began a period of four years in which Bishop's writing—prose as well as poetry—came under more detailed scrutiny from Moore than it would ever again. That the two remained friends was a tribute to the delicate balance they maintained between them. Bishop was more emotionally dependent upon Moore than she would later be, and more beholden to her for getting her poems into print. Yet her work was more divergent from Moore's than it would ever again be, its direction less certain. It required a lot of resistance, even stubbornness, on the younger woman's part if Moore's solicitude wasn't to become intrusive.

Some of their differences were subtle and substantive. While Moore recognized what Bishop was trying to do, she didn't always approve of it. Of some of the early stories she remarked that "tentativeness and interiorizing are your dangers as well as your strength." She wanted Bishop to change the opening of the poem "Paris, 7 A.M.," whose "interiorizing" she otherwise praised:

> I make a trip to each clock in the apartment:
> some hands point histrionically one way
> and some point others, from the ignorant faces.

"I tend to wish something less explicit than 'the apartment,' " Moore remarked, "something like this":

> I go from clock to clock,
> From room to room:
> Some hands point one way
> Some another, from the ignorant faces.

Bishop replied that she preferred not to replace "apart-ment": "To me that word suggests so strongly the structure of the houses, later referred to, and suggests a "cut-off" mode of existence so well—that I don't want to change it unless you feel it would mean a great improvement." Moore was satisfied by the explanation and made no further objections. Her misreading was natural, an oversight. But it suggests that Bishop's "interiorizing" was deeply ingrained, particularly responsive to muted signs of "cut-off" modes of existence. ("Apart" bears a similar stress in "The Weed," also a poem of that summer, where it completes a ghostly interior rhyme with "heart": "The rooted heart began to change / (not beat) and then it split apart.")

Their differences emerged again in their exchange about "A Miracle for Breakfast." Earlier that year Bishop had read and admired William Empson's *Seven Types of Ambiguity*, with its rediscovery and virtuoso reading of Sidney's haunting double sestina "Ye goatherd gods." She undertook her own sestina, "A Miracle for Breakfast," as "just a sort of stunt." It may have been suggested by an episode she recorded in her journal in the winter of 1935. The anecdote—or is it a dream?—is headed "A Little Miracle." She has only "one dry crumb" in the house for breakfast. Suddenly a woman buzzes and comes upstairs to give her a small box with three samples of something called "Wonder Bread," all fresh. "I breakfasted on manna." It was the kind of absurd surprise—and "Wonder Bread" was the kind of incongruous Americanism—that teased Bishop's imagination. Whether the incident was the germ for the poem or not, "A Miracle for Breakfast" addressed such common material as if responding to larger issues, the kind of sacramental question Wallace Stevens was asking in another poem of that year, "The American Sublime":

> The spirit and space,
> The empty spirit
> In vacant space.
> What wine does one drink?
> What bread does one eat?

In the exhaustive repetitions of her sestina Bishop turned over the question of just how far the physical could be "made to perform" a spiritual task. The word "miracle" ticks through the poem inescapably linked to the other revolving rhymes, words that set the natural scene and present the sacramental props: coffee, crumb, balcony, sun, river. Moore praised the "sudden change of scale" in lines that seem to fuse the disparate elements:

> A beautiful villa stood in the sun
> and from its doors came the smell of hot coffee.
> In front, a baroque white plaster balcony
> added by birds, who nest along the river,
> —I saw it with one eye close to the crumb—
>
> and galleries and marble chambers. My crumb
> my mansion, made for me by a miracle,
> through ages, by insects, birds, and the river
> working the stone. Every day, in the sun,
> at breakfast time I sit on my balcony
> with my feet up, and drink gallons of coffee.

But there were incongruities that Moore did not like: the expression "gallons of coffee," for example; and, among the end repeating words, "crumb" and "sun," too similar in sound "even as a phase of Chinese chromatics." Bishop understood her objections and eventually removed a "bitterly" that chimed oddly with "buttered" in the second stanza. But it is clear from her reply to Moore that there was a dimension to which the older poet, resisting clashing sounds, was not responding.

You are no comfort to me, at all, Miss Moore, the way you inevitably light on just those things I knew I shouldn't have let go—I must be unusually insensitive to be able to bear being brought face to face with my conscience this way over and over. I mean in A MIRACLE FOR BREAKFAST I knew I should not let the "bitterly" and "very hot" in the second stanza go. It is as yet unsolved. The boisterousness of "gallons of coffee" I wanted to overlook because I liked "gallons" being near "galleries." And the "crumb" and "sun" is of course its greatest fault. It seems to me that there are two ways possible for a sestina—one is to use unusual words as terminations, in which case they would have to be used differently as often as possible—as you say, "change of scale." That would make a very highly seasoned kind of poem. And the other way is to use as colorless words as possible—like Sydney [*sic*], so that it becomes less of a trick and more of a natural theme and variations. I guess I have tried to do both at once. It is probably just an excuse, but sometimes I think about certain things that without one particular fault they would be without the means of existence. I feel a little that way about "sun" and "crumb"!—but I know at the same time it is only justified about someone else's work.

Bishop sensed that the verbal "fault"—the jostling of "sun" and "crumb"—stood for a larger, energizing incongruity in her poem. The piece wavered not only between two notions of the sestina but between two views of her subject, one hard-edged and skeptical, the other susceptible to wonder and "changes of scale." Suggestions of ritual in the poem, of a "communion" breakfast administered by a man from a balcony, undercut themselves as if they were puppetry. (The man emerges exactly at seven. "A servant handed him the makings of a miracle." He stood, "his head, so to speak, in the clouds—along with the sun.") The expected "miracle" is entirely provisional, an invention of the waiting crowd, who imagine the "charitable crumb" will come to them as from "kings of old" and "like a miracle," and that the crumb "would be a loaf each, buttered, by a miracle." Colloquial expressions ("his head, so to speak, in the clouds"; "What under the sun / was he trying to do") take on new comic life as a measure of the distance between human pretensions (or appetites) and imperturbable nature.

There is a dimension of this mid-Depression poem which is deeply critical of the notion of "a chicken in every pot." Insofar as a miracle occurs, it is something to be witnessed and not something to be consumed. It occurs not in a moment but "through ages." The crumb becomes a "mansion" when its architecture is seen, eye close up, as evolving, "made for me by a miracle, / through ages, by insects, birds, and the river / working the stone." This section of the poem—the lines Moore singled out for praise—is the only one in which Bishop seems to trust to time, to "natural theme and variations," to sources of energy revealed in the physical world. These are also the only lines assigned to an "I" rather than the avid miracle-seeking "we." The rest of the poem belongs to a speaker impatient for revelation. Craving signs of it everywhere, she is skeptical of our powers to interpret, or even that the "miracles" are meant for us at all. "A window across the river caught the sun / as if the miracle were working, on the wrong balcony." "As if" sounds the dominant note in a poem that answers to a deeply divided nature. Bishop almost always took an ironic view of her allegorical yearnings; it was a side of her temperament that Moore's comments on the poem were not calculated to encourage. And Bishop herself, "loafing" like a modern Whitman on her balcony at the end of the poem, seems to enjoy the "boisterousness" of her gallons of coffee and to have left some of the transcendental severity behind. The revolutions of the sestina form have allowed her to reinterpret "miracles" not as apocalyptic but as something which may be as daily as breakfast. Revelations cannot be willed into being by withdrawn concentration on a single charged object. They come about more accidentally—for example, by envisioning the claims of a world slowly defined by agents smaller and larger than the human ("through ages, by insects, birds, and the river / working the stone.") However brittle its tone, "A Miracle for Breakfast" stands somewhat apart from other poems of this period, from "The Man-Moth," "Paris, 7 A.M.," and "The Weed." It is less withdrawn, makes the passage from inner to outer experience less of a shock. In one receptive moment it identifies Bishop's vision and energies with the discovery of biological and geological movement in the physical world.

———

It is not idle to think of Wallace Stevens in connection with "A Miracle for Breakfast"—the title is Stevensian, as are the issues it explores. Bishop had known his work since 1931. In 1936, the year Bishop wrote her sestina, Stevens published both *Ideas of Order* and *Owl's Clover* and was twice reviewed by Marianne Moore—"the most perfect and sudden illumination,"

Bishop said of the review that appeared in *Poetry*. "I had had a few 'ideas' about Stevens," she wrote to Moore, "but I had been wandering around them in the dark." Moore's comments on Stevens were enlivening partly because her terms were challenging—less sober, more eccentric than Bishop's. "Your remarks on 'bravura,' and 'the general marine volume of statement,' " Bishop wrote her, "have kept me in an almost hilarious state of good cheer."

Moore had chosen to emphasize Stevens's virtuosity in critical prose that is quite the equal of the "bravura" she was praising: "Upon the general marine volume of statement is set a parachute-spinnaker of verbiage which looms out like half a cantaloupe and gives the body of the theme the air of a fabled argosy advancing." There is a distinct moral and political dimension to Moore's essays, as there is to Stevens's *Owl's Clover*. She values Stevens's imaginative celebration of the physical world as an alternative to ideology, proletarian art, and an "age of concentric mobs."

That exact portrayal is intoxicating, that realism need not restrict itself to grossness, that music is "an accord of repetitions" is evident to one who examines *Ideas of Order*; and the altitude of performance makes the wild boars of philistinism who rush about interfering with experts, negligible.

Owl's Clover drew an even stronger defense of poetry from her:

In each clime the author visits, and under each disguise, the dilemma of tested hope confronts him. In *Owl's Clover*, "the search for a tranquil belief" and the protest against the actualities of experience become a protest against the death of world hope . . . "The widow of Madrid / Weeps in Segovia"; in Moscow, in all Europe, "Always everything / That is dead except what ought to be"; aeroplanes which counterfeit "the bee's drone" and have the powers of "the scorpion" are our "seraphim." Mr. Stevens' book is the sable requiem for all this. But requiem is not the word when anyone hates lust for power and ignorance of power as the author of this book does. So long as we are ashamed of the ironic feast, and of our marble victories—horses or men—which will break unless they are first broken by us, there is hope for the world.

The morality is in the method, a way of seeing and celebrating the world of things—what Stevens called the "verve of earth." He and Moore had an instinctive sympathy for one another's efforts at shaping a language of receptivity. She spoke of him as "a linguist creating several languages within a single language." Stevens used a similar figure in likening Moore's poems to "any playing of a well-known concerto by an unknown artist." He cites a section from Moore's "The Steeple-Jack" in which, in an apparently Northern landscape

> . . . the sea-
> side flowers and
>
> trees are favored by the fog so that you have
>   the tropics at first hand: the trumpet vine,
> fox-glove, giant snap-dragon, a salpiglossis that has
> spots and stripes; morning-glories, gourds,
>   or moon-vines trained on fishing-twine
> at the back door;

Stevens remarks

Moon-vines are moon-vines and tedious. But moon-vines trained on fishing-twine are something else and they are as perfectly as it is possible for anything to be what interests Miss Moore. They are an intermingling. The imagination grasps at such things and sates itself, instantaneously, in them.

Stevens noted that subject, for Moore, was often accidental; the delight lay in recapturing the flash of recognition at the moment of perception, the unexpected and revealing "intermingling" accomplished by the imagination. In her notebook of a few years before, we have seen Bishop puzzling over just these qualities: "immediate intense physical reactions, a sense of metaphor and decoration in everything—to express something not of them—something, I suppose, spiritual." Her terms were stiff and cautious, as if needing to justify the very materials of poetry to which she was attracted. The terms she would find in Stevens directed the imagination *outward* as a blooded appetite: it "grasps" and "sates itself, instantaneously." In Stevens and Moore the "sense of metaphor and decoration in everything" was not merely responsible for local effects; it was both the launching point of a poem and its purpose. Their work encouraged—if Bishop needed any encouragement—poems that answered to a place, an object, a moment in her travels. Alongside her early metaphysical inventions—"The Gentleman of Shalott," "The Man-Moth," "A Miracle for Breakfast"—there were to be poems in which she explored her imagination by responding to specifics of time and place: "Florida," "Cape Breton," "At the Fishhouses."

Years later, in one of those moments when strongly admired lines revisit a poet through conscious or unconscious channels, Bishop invested a fogbound Nova Scotian scene with the qualities Stevens praised in a similar scene of "The Steeple-Jack":

> the fog,
> shifting, salty, thin,
> comes closing in.
>
> Its cold, round crystals
> form and slide and settle
> in the white hens' feathers,
> in gray glazed cabbages,
> on the cabbage roses
> and lupins like apostles;
>
> the sweet peas cling
> to their wet white string

on the whitewashed fences;
bumblebees creep
inside the foxgloves,
and evening commences.

Moore's fog and foxgloves and flowers trained on strings are taken up in one of Bishop's scenes in which Nature quietly reclaims the world for itself, asserts its own economy; as the fog cuts off the human world, things settle and cling and creep inside, miming our need for comfort but utterly heedless of us. Everything that the imagination might feel about human frailty and receptiveness is conveyed through scene and "intermingling." The benevolent obliterating fog; the tenuous human props (wet white string and whitewashed fences). By the time she completed "The Moose" in the 1970s, Bishop had long since matured with the lessons of Moore and Stevens that began and were most important to her close to forty years before.

3 / Observations

Bishop was quite aware, as she remarked in one of her letters to Moore in 1937, that the older poet had "a very generous and protective apron." "And I am not sure," she added, "how much of it I should seize upon." Especially after the crisis in Bishop's self-confidence when she returned from Europe in 1936, Moore not only offered "corrections" for Bishop's poems but for a while took over the submission of her work to magazines. Bishop was grateful for the editorial help—the small grammatical and metrical suggestions for which Moore had been so famous at *The Dial*—and she was diplomatic at refusing what she did not need: "I'm afraid I am quite ungracious in that I accepted most of your suggestions but refused some—that seems almost worse than refusing all assistance." But Moore's efforts at "placing" Bishop's works were sometimes a source of embarrassment. Moore had sent Bishop's revised version of "Paris, 7 A.M." to Morton Dauwen Zabel at *Poetry*, and she urged Bishop to send him "The Weed" as well. When she learned that Bishop had already submitted the poem to Roger Roughton at *Contemporary Poetry and Prose*, she sent off a letter— apparently with Bishop's knowledge but too hastily to obtain her permission—asking Roughton to decide quickly; they could give the poem to Zabel if Roughton refused it. "I hope you may like it well enough to use it but in any case am pleased to think of seeing it in print, here or in England." Roughton, who had turned down an earlier version, rejected the revised poem as well. Moore retyped it, making two last-minute changes, and Bishop sent it off to *Poetry*. Then, out of impatience (Zabel hadn't yet printed "Paris, 7 A.M.") or perhaps mischief, Bishop withdrew the poem so that it could appear in the February 1937 issue of *Forum and Century*. As a result the two women went through a little ritual of scolding and apology. Bishop didn't like the poems by other writers published along with hers in *Forum*, "and even my own, there, although I am sorry for such conceit, too." After calling her "naughty," Moore let her off the hook by acknowledging that the poem would still not be in print if they had waited for Zabel; so why not send him something else to replace it? Bishop did, and in July 1937 Zabel published as a group (entitled "Two Mornings and Two Evenings") "Paris, 7 A.M.," "A Miracle for Breakfast," "From the Country to the City," and "Song" ("Summer is over upon the sea").

However trivial the incident, it did anticipate other little dramas of disobedience and dependency which kept a dynamic balance between the two women—exchanges which led Moore to remark, "You are not a novice in avoiding what you do not need." In January 1938, for example, Bishop sent off a short story, "In Prison," to *Partisan Review* without first asking for Moore's comments. She apologized for what was between them practically a breach of trust, but explained that *Partisan* wanted the story by February 1 and that she hoped to win a $100 contest. Moore's response to being bypassed was not unbarbed: "If it is returned with a printed slip, that will be why."

The friction went deeper than mere protocol. Bishop describes her story defensively as "one of these horrible 'fable' ideas that seem to obsess me." Whether or not she had time to submit the story to Moore, she had every reason to believe that Moore would not receive it with total approval. This was a period in which Bishop seemed to be more secure about her prose than she was about her verse—and to set more store by it as well. "If only I could see half as clearly *how* I want to write poems," she complained to Moore, and asked "quite frankly if you think there is any use—any real use—in my continuing with them." Moore, on the other hand, had grown more and more impatient with Bishop's short prose pieces. She had encouraged Bishop to send "The Baptism" to *Life and Letters Today*, but she was more equivocal and guarded about two stories she saw the following spring. "The Hanging of the Mouse," little more than a sketch in which Bishop imagined as a real hanging the accidental stringing up of her cat's artificial mouse, brought praise for its local effects ("At that hour in the morning the mouse's gray clothes were almost indistinguishable from the light"). But Moore's praise was tinged with concern: "Your faculty of projecting the imagination and maintaining an initial suggestion in absolute adjustment is a heavy responsibility for you . . ."

She was more explicit in her warnings about "The Labors of Hannibal," a story now lost and never published.

Your things have the insidiousness of creativeness, in that the after impression is stronger than the impression while reading, but you are menaced by the goodness of your mechanics. One should, of course, have the feeling this is ingeniously contrived but a thing should make one feel after reading it, that one's life has been altered or added to. When I set out to find faults with you, there are so many excellences in your mechanics that I seem to be commending you instead and I wish to say, above all, that I am sure good treatment is a handicap unless along with it, significant values come out with an essential baldness. I hope the unessential baldness of this attack will not make it seem that I am against minutiae.

Matters came to a head over "In Prison," which *Partisan Review* had been quick to accept. Moore probably read it for the first time in the March 1938 issue of the magazine. "Never have I seen . . . a more insidiously innocent and artless artifice of innuendo." What followed was Moore's longest critique of

Bishop's fiction, prickly in its praise and full of advice that would not be lost on the young writer at a particularly vulnerable moment in her career. It was a long time before Bishop published another story. At the time she did not interpret Moore's reaction as warning her away from prose, but, in fact, it added to the sweep of experience which, in the twenty-seventh and twenty-eighth years of her life, drew her decisively toward poetry.

Moore's comments had as much to do with the *use* of writing as with Bishop's short story. "Although [I] . . . am one of those who despise clamor about substance—to whom treatment really *is* substance—I can't help wishing you would sometime in some way risk some unprotected profundity of experience; or . . . some characteristic private defiance of the significantly detestable." "Unprotected" was a clear challenge to the protagonist of "In Prison," a man not guilty of any crime who chooses permanent confinement as a way of life. Moore praised

the potent retiringness, the close observation and interassociating of the circumstantial with the exotic; your mention of the Turkey carpets and the air bubble of potential freedom; the leaves and the inoffensive striping of the uniforms. All this should be ever present consolation to you I think, for any hard spots in progress; I am much hampered, in fact, in what I say, for fear of spoiling you.

Criticisms seem forced forward by two years of concerned scrutiny of Bishop's work.

Continuously fascinated as I am by the creativeness and uniqueness of these assemblings of yours—which are really poems—I feel a responsibility against anything that might threaten you; yet fear to admit such anxiety, lest I influence you away from an essential necessity or particular strength. The golden eggs can't be dealt with theoretically by presumptuous mass salvation formulas.

It is here that she tells Bishop, "I do feel that tentativeness and interiorizing are your dangers as well as your strength."

"In Prison" and "The Sea and Its Shore" (which had appeared a year before in *Life and Letters Today*) were not simply examples of "interiorizing" but Bishop's self-conscious studies of the habit of withdrawal for which Moore had been taxing her. The protagonist of each story lives virtually secluded, largely "inside his head," like the M. Teste of Valéry to whom Moore once called Bishop's attention. Edwin Boomer of "The Sea and Its Shore"—his initials are Bishop's and "Boomer" is the way her mother's family name, Bulmer, was pronounced— lives in a house "more like an idea of a house than a real one . . . It was a shelter, but not for living in, for thinking in. It was, to the ordinary house, what the ceremonial thinking cap is to the ordinary hat." The nameless hero of "In Prison" looks forward to his cell. He will not only go there in full possession of his faculties but, "in fact, it is not until I am securely installed there that I expect fully to realize them." What Bishop does in both tales is to ritualize her nomadic separatist existence and her cravings for withdrawal. The "hotel existence" the narrator of "In Prison" leads, the striped wallpaper of the hotel room that suggests a large silver bird cage, are only parodies, "a fantasy on my real hopes and ambitions." Boomer, in "The Sea and Its Shore," is in a sense part of a "priesthood"; his job is to keep the sands of public beaches clean, a human adjunct to "The moving waters at their priest-like task / Of pure ablution round earth's human shore."

Bishop told Moore that "In Prison" was her first conscious attempt at writing something according to a theory—something she had been thinking up out of a combination of Poe's theories and reading seventeenth-century prose. Both "In Prison" and "The Sea and Its Shore" move as if from a premise, with determined cogency. Dwelling places are the governing figures, retired chambers each with only one window to the world. In Boomer's chamber this makes for a kind of camera obscura that answers to a riddling description on one of the scraps he has gathered from the beach:

Much as a one-eyed room, hung all with night,
  Only that side, which adverse to the eye
Gives but one narrow passage to the light,
  Is spread with some white shining tapestry,
An hundred shapes that through the flit airs stray,
  Rush boldly in, crowding that narrow way;
And on that bright-faced wall obscurely dancing play.

The camera obscura is a classic illustration for the operation of the eye, the reception of images on the retina. It also represents a mode of description—one that emphasizes receptivity, the image conceived and recorded as part of a prior creation rather than being deliberately framed by the intervening and active artist. In "The Sea and Its Shore" Bishop combines that notion of seeing with her concern—as in "The Man-Moth," "The Weed," and "From the Country to the City"—for the buried, the inner life. The two concerns are familiar, but the combination is interestingly confused. Its contradictions— the desire to see the world by withdrawing from it—give these stories life. The confusion for Boomer—and for the narrator of "In Prison"—has to do with the degree to which one accepts the febrile adult world as intermediary or, more exactly, the degree to which one accepts its witness in print, the "insect armies of type." The protagonist of "In Prison" wants only one dull book to read, preferably the second volume and on some utterly unfamiliar subject, so that he can interpret it "not at all according to its intent. Because I share with Valéry's M. Teste the 'knowledge that our thoughts are reflected back to us, too much so, through expressions made by others.' "

One of the chief delights of Boomer in the other tale is to burn the papers he has impaled on his gathering stick, sometimes holding them aloft "like a torch, as if they were his paid bills," or flaming kebabs! He saves pertinent fragments and puzzles them out at home for clues about his life, as with the instructions to "the Exercitant" which urge him to seclude himself from friends and worldly cares in a house or room where "he comes to use his natural faculties more freely in diligently searching for that he so much desires." But by and large, print is a burden, even a threat he can liken to the Ancient Mariner's albatross. Sometimes it muddles his drunken vision so that letters appear to fly from the pages or so that "the whole world he saw, came before many years to seem printed, too." A sandpiper comes to look like a punctuation mark, and "on the narrow hems of the wings appeared marks that looked as if they might be letters, if only he could get close enough to read them."

The nightmare of the story is not simply a fear of being swamped, overwhelmed by a "sea" of phenomena, terrors to which Bishop had felt herself subject. Boomer is also victim to the failure of any ordering energy. Print behaves like chaotic matter, however temptingly at times matter seems reducible to print. The only real relief comes in the burning of the papers: "Large flakes of blackened paper, still sparkling red at the edges, flew into the sky. While his eyes could follow them he had never seen such clever, quivering maneuvers. Then there were left frail sheets of ashes, as white as the original paper, and soft to the touch, or a bundle of gray feathers like a guinea hen's." If, as the narrator has been saying, Boomer "lived the most literary life possible," then the story is a bitter enough account of the effort to touch the springs of an ordering imagination. In the extremity of retreat—Boomer's shanty, or the companionable prison of the other tale—Bishop explores alternatives to threats of engulfment. But Boomer's task is self-defeating and finds its painful yet satisfying relief in his destructive fires, and the relief of "In Prison" is all in the future.

Yet the narrative of "The Sea and Its Shore" is conducted with perverse merriment. A lot of its confusion can be attributed to Boomer's habitual drinking. As with the wicked cogency of "In Prison," the story casts an ironic light on the withdrawal both narrators so obviously crave. The stories are successful because they so urgently explore the impulses behind Bishop's writing in the preceding years, because they exorcise many of the faults Moore felt had knotted Bishop's writing, and because they raise the bleak possibility that Bishop might have reached a dead end in these prose retreats. One critic aptly calls them "fables about the insanity and bliss of one's calling" which "seem to have stopped once she found her poetic voice and, as it were, her own beach to comb." These are the last stories Bishop published for ten years. They seemed to free her not just for poetry but for an entirely new kind of poem.

———

In January 1937 Bishop wrote thanking Moore for her comments on "The Sea and Its Shore":

This morning I have been working on "The Sea & Its Shore"—or rather, making use of your and your mother's work—and I am suddenly afraid that at the end I have stolen something from "The Frigate Pelican." I say: "Large flakes of blackened paper, still sparkling red at the edges, flew into the sky. While his eyes could follow them, he had never seen such clever, quivering manoeuvres." It was not until I began seeing pelicans that my true source occurred to me. I know you speak of the flight like "charred paper," and use the word manoeuvres. I am afraid it is almost criminal. I haven't the book here and I wonder if you will tell me just how guilty I am and forgive what was really unconscious.

Bishop's notion of stealing is overly fastidious, especially since the word "manoeuvres" doesn't occur in "The Frigate Pelican" at all. (Bishop probably recalled it from the opening of "An Octopus.") The debt she is becoming aware of is more interesting and complicated, the borrowed detail symptomatic of more general strengths she owes to Moore. By this time Bishop is in Naples, Florida, having taken a slow train from Jacksonville "through swamps and turpentine camps and palm forests." The pelicans that she observes at fishing piers and at their nesting places upriver are indeed figures first colored for her by memories of a favorite Moore poem. But, almost to her surprise, the isolated literary detail takes its place in a real landscape which was to assume deepening importance for her in the next few years.

The poem "Florida," which would appear in print early in 1939, was one in which she truly and happily "stole" from "The

Frigate Pelican"—not just the birds, the way they flew, the charring, but the mangrove swamps and the rising moon. Here and elsewhere she would seem comfortable with descriptive details free of the symbolic matrix she devised for them in "The Sea and Its Shore." What happened was intimately involved with trips she took in 1937, a year totally consumed by travel. It was as if Bishop gave up her notions of fables—looking for fables to justify withdrawal—and trusted now almost entirely to description. Or rather, as if travel itself now provided the "narration" and descriptive details took the place of plot. "Florida" was part of a renewed activity in verse—she sent Moore ten poems in January 1938—and of a writing more intimately bound up with her travels. Bishop seemed enormously energized by her trip to Florida in 1937, so much so that she returned the next year and made Key West her winter home until well after World War II. Florida is her favorite state, she remarks, because it is so wild, or in its settled parts so dilapidated that it seems "about to become wild again." Her exchanges with Moore are more frequent—at least once a week when they are apart—and filled with details that would nourish her poems: names of shells, herons blue and white, pelicans coasting in on the tides, the scissor tails of the man-of-war birds, even alligator wrestling. She'd watched the famous Ross Allen creep up on a live alligator while delivering a talk: "It was quite a sight to see his large, solemn baby-face apparently floating bodiless on the surface of the water while from it came his imitations of the alligator's calls: the 'hello,' the love-call, the warning and the social call."

All this time, though she and Moore are sparring over Bishop's stories, they are also exchanging botanical and zoological lore about Key West—and not just lore but leaves, snakeskins, and other specimens. Bishop remembers being confounded as a child by a teacher's remark that some people preferred the description of a forest to the forest itself. "I never believed her," she writes to Moore, "but now I know that to send you a post-card is to get back something worth a thousand of them!" She and the painter Loren McIver went round one of the Key West flower shows with notebooks, thinking about what Moore might have jotted down. However random the exercise, Moore stimulated her to use details as a probe, to save them up, no matter how long, as they slowly revealed the indwelling strangeness of the landscape, its import for her. A photograph from Bishop elicited the following comment from Miss Moore: "The bayonet points of the palms above the confident little rooster have greatly the sense of the place." The underlying bellicose accent was something Bishop would recall in her own "Roosters," a poem from Key West in 1940.

Bishop's attitude toward Key West and the place of travel in her life was considerably affected by a six-month stay in Europe, June through November 1937, which separated her first visit to Florida and her settling down there. In mid-July, as Bishop and her friends Margaret Miller and Louise Crane were returning to Paris from a trip to Burgundy, the car in which they were traveling was forced off the road and overturned. Though all three were thrown clear of the car, part of Margaret Miller's right arm was sheared off and the arm had to be amputated to the elbow. The three women—and eventually Miller's mother, who arrived from America—stayed during the first months of Miller's recovery in an apartment on the Quai d'Orléans (on the Ile St. Louis), of which there is a gray wintry postcard view enclosed in the letter to Moore with Bishop's account of the accident. The young women were only twenty-six. Bishop describes how Miller, a painter, began to write with her other hand only two days after her operation, and how during a hospitalization for skin grafts she learned to draw with her left hand. "It is heart-breaking."

However plucky her letters, Bishop herself clearly felt under a great strain. She experienced severe recurrences of asthma and was hospitalized for ten days. Glancing at Moore's photo on her mirror proved one way of trying to get back to "normalcy." Once Mrs. Miller had arrived, Bishop and Louise Crane made a trip through southern France; after the trial to determine responsibility for the accident, and hoping that a warmer climate would counter Bishop's asthma, the two young

women left for Italy and ended their trip in Rome. Even Mrs.
Miller's presence seems to have added to Bishop's anxiety:
"Mother-love," she wrote to Frani Blough, "isn't it awful. I
long for an Arctic climate where no emotions of any sort can
possibly grow, always excepting disinterested 'friendship' of
course."

A year later Bishop published "Quai d'Orléans," a poem
which at the time must have been silently dedicated—as, many
years afterward, it was openly inscribed—to Margaret Miller.
It is colored by all the losses the accident entailed and recalled,
though none of them is specifically its subject: her friend's mu-
tilation; her own childhood losses; the loss of self-control and
surge of vulnerability she experienced when Miller's mother
appeared.

> Each barge on the river easily tows
>   a mighty wake,
> a giant oak-leaf of gray lights
>   on duller gray;
> and behind it real leaves are floating by,
>   down to the sea.
> Mercury-veins on the giant leaves,
>   the ripples, make
> for the sides of the quai, to extinguish themselves
>   against the walls
> as softly as falling-stars come to their ends
>   at a point in the sky.
> And throngs of small leaves, real leaves, trailing them,
>   go drifting by
> to disappear as modestly, down the sea's
>   dissolving halls.

At first this opening seems all Wordsworthian ease, the hushed
interlacing of what the mind half sees and half creates, the delicate mimicry of real leaves and giant leaf-like ripples which are
the wakes of the barges. Before the human presences are introduced, we witness a pageant of power and vulnerability twice

exchanged: the imagined "giant oak-leaf" of the ripples, geometric natural force harnessed to the human force of the barges, all this set against the "real leaves" more randomly "floating by." Then again the perfected dissolution of the "mighty wake" which "makes" for the wall and seems to will its own soft and ravishing extinction—that image set against the trailing disappearance of the "real leaves." The rhythm of the lines—both the way the images yield to one another and the way longer lines contract regularly to short—seems like an exhalation and contraction, a systole-diastole of power and powerlessness, as natural as breath. The current which writ large makes itself visible as giant leaves is also the agent that dissolves the real ones. Bishop insists on those "real leaves," almost as if their meaning were being slowly forced upon her and she were eventually hearing "real lives," a connection that finally comes to the surface at the end of the poem. What permeates the poem, mocking its swelling beauty, is attrition. The sea's "dissolving halls" are both agents of erosion and, from the sound of it, eroding themselves.

The two stilled observers are only mentioned in the last third of the poem, almost paralyzed by their separateness and by the separate losses each has read into the scene.

> We stand as still as stones to watch
>   the leaves and ripples
> while light and nervous water hold
>   their interview.
> "If what we see could forget us half as easily,"
>   I want to tell you,
> "as it does itself—but for life we'll not be rid
>   of the leaves' fossils."

What one friend wants to tell the other ought to be loosely paraphrasable as "If we could forget what we see as easily as it forgets itself." Yet that isn't at all what she means. The inverted syntax, as Patricia Robinson suggests, makes the scene itself almost an aggressor and the two women unwilling receivers of its message. Furthermore, the reversal insists that we see nothing that is not already colored by consciousness at the very moment of seeing—and will remain indissolubly so in memory. She seems to be recalling an image for consciousness from "The Weed": "As if a river should carry all / the scenes that it had once reflected / shut in its waters, and not floating / on momentary surfaces." For the two figures on the Quai d'Orléans, the consequences are graver, for seeing is inescapably tied to scarring. For them consciousness is life's petrifying residue.

What gives Bishop's "Quai d'Orléans" its power is the choked desire to comfort her friend, as well as the heightened receptiveness of the first two-thirds of the poem to a scene which, in the event, so excludes the two of them. This seems a new kind of poem for Bishop, without the predetermined fable of "The Weed," and one which allows a scene and a moment to make discoveries for her. The mood is familiar but the method looks forward to the Wordsworthian "readiness" of her great landscape poems of the next decade. This poem, divided and elegiac, marks one of those moments when Bishop becomes aware of what the involuntary can teach her.

———

Rome, where Bishop and Louise Crane spent the last few weeks of their stay in Europe, proved on the whole to be a disappointment, though Bishop was pleased to be able to tell Moore she'd seen the bronze pinecone (mentioned in Moore's "The Jerboa") in the Vatican collections. Of St. Peter's she remarked in her diary: "I never had so clear an idea before of the vast commerce, the *tides of gold* of the Church, and I never disliked it so much." Michelangelo's *Pietà* she found anticlimactic. On a rainy day the troops of priests marching across the Piazza San Pietro, each with his black umbrella, looked like ants. There is a grim surrealism about some of Bishop's diary entries: she suddenly recognizes the Keats House in the Piazza di Spagna without seeing the plaque: "It was almost as bad as having found the body, and then I saw the wreath hanging on the side of the house." Their whole stay must have been shadowed by the summer's automobile accident and its consequences. The details of the European trip lingered for ten years, to be recalled in "Over 2,000 Illustrations and a Complete Concordance," with its disenchanted view of travel.

There is palpable relief in the letters Bishop wrote when she was back in Key West in January 1938. For the moment she is staying in a boardinghouse, paying four dollars a week for her room, a little lonely and rereading Moore's letters for conversation. Her landlady's family—the Pindars—sing hymns all day. In a house nearby she can see a French horn, painted silver, and hung on it a pith helmet of the same color. The detail turns up, delightfully, in "Jerónimo's House," written in 1940, as do other features of Cuban houses it pleased her to report in other letters: bunches of tissue-paper flowers, blue sitting rooms, and "paper streamers up all the time to decorate the ceilings, like a children's party." The simile is omitted in the poem, but it suggests one of the elements—their childlike fantasy—that drew her to the Cubans and Negroes of the town. The Negroes have soft voices and tactful manners; they remind her of the tone of Herbert's "Take the gentle path . . ." Moore, who had never been there, imagines Key West as "a kind of ten commandments in vegetable-dye color printing," and Bishop, in mock indignation, says it is unfair for Moore to simply stay at home in Brooklyn and "hit the Key West lighthouse right on the head."

Within a few months Bishop and Louise Crane had bought the house at 624 White Street that for several years—until shortly after the end of World War II—she would consider home. The house was T-shaped, with two stories and a front portico supported by four slender pillars like stilts, and around it were fruit trees—bananas, avocados, mangoes, even a soursop. It was practically her first home since Vassar, and certainly the first she had ever owned. That stability, along with the village pieties and simplicities that recalled Nova Scotia, reoriented and energized her writing. For one thing it gave her a chance to explore the mysteries of survival in figures like the resourceful feckless Cuban Jerónimo or the primitive painter Gregorio Valdes, about whom she wrote a memorial piece just after his death in 1939.

Writing about them was a refraction, or perhaps a resummoning and exploration, of her own recuperative powers as a child.

What drew her to some of the humbler Key West figures was the air of frail improvisation—their houses, like their lives, paper-thin perishable "shelters from the hurricane." The cottages, Bishop wrote in a letter, all have "gorgeous" plants which "appear to have 'sapped the strength' of everything else in town." Wasps' nest and love nest, Jerónimo's clapboard house in the poem is minimal protection from the elements. Nothing in itself, it is lent a makeshift gaiety by the paper flowers, the leftover Christmas streamers, the brightly painted sparse chairs and tables, the radio with its flamencos. It is a house ready to be left:

> When I move
> I take these things,
>   not much more, from
> my shelter from
>   the hurricane.

Shortly after she wrote this poem, she read Moore's "A Glass-Ribbed Cage" (later "The Paper Nautilus") in the *Kenyon Review* and remarked, "The whole poem is like a rebuke to me, it suggests so many of the plans for the things I want to say about Key West and have scarcely hinted at in "José's House" [the original title of "Jerónimo's House"] for example. But I will try very hard, and won't write you again until I have something of the proper length and depth to send you." If Bishop hadn't linked the two poems, few readers would ever connect "Jerónimo's House" with Moore's elegant marine invention. Aside from two odd verbal coincidences—"perishable" and "wasps' nest"—there is no reason to think that Bishop had seen Moore's poem. (She knew Moore was writing about the nautilus as early as 1937, but seems to have read the poem for the first time in the *Kenyon Review*.) What matters is that she had a "plan" for what she felt prompted to write in Key West, that Moore's poem seemed to touch on it, and so closely that Bishop felt it a "rebuke."

Both poems present their subjects as, in Moore's phrase, "perishable souvenirs of hope"—figures otherwise as different as the Cuban house in Bishop's poem and the baroque mollusk in Moore's. Moore's poem takes place in no definite time or space, and has the secure ring of purposive choice. Having selected the particular vehicle for her explorations and discoveries—the paper nautilus—she engages in a kind of muscular inquiry and release that has the air both of laboratory detachment and of total identification. "The Paper Nautilus" locates and enacts a powerful source and expense of creative energy in the maternal provisions of the nautilus, the intricate constructions of her glass shell, the discharge of the ego in love:

> . . . the watchful
> maker of it guards it
> day and night; she scarcely
>
> eats until the eggs are hatched.
> Buried eight-fold in her eight
> arms, for she is in
> a sense a devil-
> fish, her glass ram'shorn-cradled freight
> is hid but is not crushed;
> as Hercules, bitten
>
> by a crab loyal to the hydra,
> was hindered to succeed,
> the intensively
> watched eggs coming from
> the shell free it when they are freed,—
> leaving its wasp-nest flaws
> of white on white, and close-
>
> laid Ionic chiton-folds
> like the lines in the mane of

a Parthenon horse,
round which the arms had
wound themselves as if they knew love
is the only fortress
strong enough to trust to.

The fierce polish of Moore's poem is something to which Bishop's "Jerónimo's House" does not pretend, but is part of the reason Bishop can refer to "The Paper Nautilus" as a "rebuke." Moore's poem is fully self-conscious about the discharge of watchful energy behind the apparent delicacy of the shell; she makes us aware of the restraint and expenditure of strength, the ferocity released in an act of creation, and so offers a new way to read the delicately incised markings that remain once the shell has served its biological purpose.

Bishop's poem doesn't move toward or invite statement the way Moore's does. If it identifies sources of creative energy in the impulse to protect, it doesn't do so with the maternal assurance of "The Paper Nautilus" but with something like childlike surprise at being sheltered. "Jerónimo's House" is more like a song, and Jerónimo is more like one of his own children. Bishop is much more tentative than Moore. She has chosen a "real" time and place, a "real" character through whom to conduct her poem; the effect is more of curiosity than assurance, as if she were performing an act which must be repeated often to make its significance clear. She has noticed in Cuban houses "the apparent remoteness of every object . . . from every other object." Things to Jerónimo are just there—the house is "endowed" and "adorned," the table furnished with "one fried fish," but there is nothing like the purposive provision of Moore's poem; he has hung the aluminum horn on the wall, but who has done the rest? Display to survive by—the radio's flamenco music, the gay streamers, the spattering scarlet sauce— is the order of the day. No marks, like the nautilus's frail engravings, are made; it is simply today's shelter from the hurricane, and its ornaments only temporary. The effect is that of Stevens's "The Man on the Dump" or a ramshackle version of the bravado of "The Emperor of Ice Cream." Bishop's poem is about dispossession as much as Moore's is about "imaginary possession."

Part of Bishop's effort in Key West was to identify the bedrock strength of survivors. She is interested in the qualities that allow certain unreflective figures to get past logic and cliché. Her letters delight in stories about her housekeeper Mrs. Almyda, along with the young black girl Cootchie and the mysterious Faustina, both of whom were subjects of poems. Of the prose pieces she wrote in Key West, there is the one about Gregorio Valdes and another, "Mercedes Hospital," about the flinty goodness of a woman, Miss Mamie, who almost single-handedly sustains the patients of a rundown infirmary. As Bishop finishes her tour of the hospital she slips ten dollars into Miss Mamie's hand for the Poor Box, and then thinks to herself that she should have put the money right into the box, that Miss Mamie will never do it. Finally she dismisses her doubts as irrelevant.

There is no reason for or against her robbing the Poor Box, no more than there are reasons for or against her staying at the Mercedes Hospital, or being kind or cruel to the patients. St. Simeon Stylites probably thought he knew exactly what he was doing at the top of his pillar and rejoiced in it. Miss Mamie hasn't any idea that what she is doing where she is needs explaining. She has managed to transfer the same feeling to her patients—giving them security from hopelessness. Simplicity of heart, never the vulgarity of putting two and two together.

I go out, and the palm branches move slowly like prehistoric caryatids. The Mercedes Hospital seems so remote and far away now, like the bed of a dried-up lake. Out of the corner of my eye I catch a glimpse of the salty glitter at its bottom, a slight mica-like residuum, the faintest trace of joyousness.

They test the written word, these dry nuances of saintliness ("never the vulgarity of putting two and two together"). It is partly for such tests that Bishop is drawn to Key West, as to the villages of her childhood and later to Brazil. For her one of the secrets of vitality is a language unblinking as childhood, open to and unembarrassed by anomaly.

Though she found in marginal Key West figures models of recuperative strength, her use of the human figure and interest in anecdote represented a false start in her Key West writing. It was the Florida landscape and its creatures which were to provide her characteristic way of locating herself in the world. Acts of observation would allow her to talk about dispossession. The semitropical landscape she had chosen as home was, as she had remarked in her letter to Moore, "dilapidated, and about to become wild again." It answered to and seemed to provide a way of testing the givens of her life: her being an outsider, uneasy, tempted to withdraw. As arresting as the scenic details of "Florida" is her careful entrance into that poem—observations in phrases, then sentences, changes in scale and point of view and only then, after some thirty lines, a stable present tense which fixes the observer in time and space ("Thirty or more buzzards are drifting down") rather than a generalizing present. The fittings of this landscape may recall Moore and "The Frigate Pelican," but Bishop's own place in the scene is much less assured than Moore's "directorship." It is the process, the *becoming*, identified with the scene that matters for Bishop. Her Florida is itself an organism, living and dying on a scale beyond human memory. It has its own geological and biological economy: oysters that cluster on mangrove roots; barnacles on the shells of dead and dying turtles; the eroded shore with its fading shells, themselves the product of time's delicate ornamentation. Nature has its own ecological theater, with cycles of predatory and decorative activity that completely exclude the observer. With the swamp and marsh as reflectors, energy passes through a self-sufficient closed circle of the four elements:

> Thirty or more buzzards are drifting down, down, down,
> over something they have spotted in the swamp,
> in circles like stirred-up flakes of sediment
> sinking through water.

Smoke from woods-fires filters fine blue solvents.
On stumps and dead trees the charring is like black velvet.
The mosquitoes
go hunting to the tune of their ferocious obbligatos.
After dark, the fireflies map the heavens in the marsh
until the moon rises.

Only after dark when the moon rises and color drains from the scene does the landscape "develop" for the speaker, ironically as if it were being turned back into a photographic negative: "the careless, corrupt state is all black specks / too far apart, and ugly whites; the poorest / post-card of itself." Bishop had learned from Moore about restraining her use of metaphors, using similes instead, and she has kept a metaphorical burden for the end, though it is certainly not an insistent one:

After dark, the pools seem to have slipped away.
The alligator, who has five distinct calls:
friendliness, love, mating, war, and a warning—
whimpers and speaks in the throat
of the Indian Princess.

In a world delicately created from its residues, what is human is dwarfed by the long scale of eroding nature with its fossils and predators, and by the flashy creations and fadings of each day. Or to put it another way, it is only by identifying the presence and powerful creations of decay that Bishop finds a place at the end of her poem for human response. The amphibian figure of the ending—the alligator which "whimpers and speaks in the throat / of the Indian Princess"—suggests nascent speech, primitive, distinct, and, because of her newfound receptivity, an integral part of the scene. There is an air of expectation at the close of "Florida" that comes not from anything the poem says, any narrative, but from the pleasure of having identified or located herself in the scene, however limited her place, however problematic the final image. The closing figure is androgynous as well as amphibian. It presupposes nonhuman energies ventriloquized by a human speaker, a tapping of strengths which are fundamental to as well as menacing in the self. Bishop's Key West poems in their attention to creatures and landscape brought her to acknowledge—to make use of R. P. Blackmur's phrase—"the presence of the barbaric, of other and partial creations within her own creation."

4 / Logarithms of Apology

The sense of promise in Bishop's Key West poems is distinctly at odds with the crises of confidence to which her letters of the period painfully return. "Florida" and two poems which were to follow in 1940, "Roosters" and "The Fish," were, as David Bromwich has suggested, her boldest testings to date of the powers of the self. Moore's intense version of the discharge of ego in love, "The Paper Nautilus," was, as we have seen, the poem that particularly recalled Bishop to her plans for "serious" poems in the Florida setting. She felt herself on the edge of new writing energies.

I have that continuous uncomfortable feeling of "things" in the head, like icebergs or rocks or awkwardly-shaped pieces of furniture—it's as if all the nouns were there but the verbs were lacking—if you know what I mean. And I can't help having the theory that if they are joggled around hard enough and long enough some kind of electricity will occur, just by friction, that will arrange everything.

It is ironic, or perhaps symptomatic, that Bishop, having found congenial promptings to write and a congenial home in Key West, should have suffered more about her work there than she ever had or would again. By 1940 she had written most of the poems that would make up her first book, *North & South*, and yet in the next six years she underwent a series of rejections that left her disappointed and demoralized. She stayed away from New York more and more, in part because she said she was afraid to face her friends until she had accomplished something.

The leap from magazine publication to a collection of her poems somehow seemed forbidding. As early as 1937 Bishop had had inquiries from James Laughlin about the possibility of publishing a book of her poems. She asked Moore if Random House wouldn't be better *"if* I ever had enough worth publishing, of which I have many of the blackest doubts." Moore urged her to consider Laughlin's offer: he has "real respect for the author." The older poet suggested that Bishop publish her poems along with some of her prose: her undergraduate essay on Hopkins, her story "The Baptism," a piece on Gertrude Stein and one on modern art she had heard about from Margaret Miller. They "support . . . and necessitate one another," are "of the greatest interest . . . for writing in general," Moore wrote.

Two years later, and without telling Moore beforehand, Bishop sent her "best poems" to Random House, was rejected, and took this as "an indirect blow at my laziness." She then tried Viking and Simon & Schuster—without success. Meanwhile, Laughlin had once again offered to do her poems, this time in the volume *Five Young American Poets*, which would include collections by both Randall Jarrell and John Berryman. She refused, this time because she suspected, perhaps unjustly, that she was being invited as a token woman and, as she told Moore, she didn't like being used for "Sex-Appeal." Laughlin went so far as to suggest that Bishop agree to his listing her name for the New Directions pamphlet series (it would be a "boon") and then withdraw if she wanted to. Moore herself took another line with Laughlin, arguing that Bishop shouldn't be making her first book appearance in the company of others: "Her idiosyncrasy is too special to be combined . . . She has worked patiently and privately for some time and has besides the talent of which you speak, a clarified understanding of forms and effects that I long to see accessible and attested."

In the summer of 1940 there was another flurry with publishers. Harcourt, Brace had written asking her for a volume of poems. Their response to the manuscript she sent was not a categorical refusal; indeed, they suggested that they would be interested sometime in the future when the manuscript was more substantial. But the whole series of skirmishes with publishers left Bishop full of doubts, grateful for Moore's support but feeling abjectly dependent. Matters were even more confusing because with the publication of "Cirque d'Hiver" in 1940 Bishop began her long association with *The New Yorker*. Moore had never been printed in the magazine, and shortly after Bishop's poem appeared, work of Moore's was rejected. Bishop was angry and embarrassed. On Moore's side it appeared to make no difference between them (though later, and until the early 1950s when she did finally appear in the magazine, it occasioned a few barbed comments). But this was another troubling ingredient in a period when Bishop already felt her relationship with Moore to be somewhat fraught.

In September 1940 Bishop left Key West for a visit to New York, stopping en route for several weeks with friends in North Carolina. The burden of apology and gratitude to Moore seemed especially strong as the time approached when they would meet again. Bishop wrote from the Carolina mountains: "There are so many things here that you would like that if I could only write about them properly I know it would give me more courage to write to you." After the Harcourt, Brace failure and an aborted attempt at a story and some "ballets," she was grateful for kind words Moore had said about her rhymes. But the refrain in these letters is full of shame: "It seems to me that I make such demands on your thought and time and almost never give anything in return. I scarcely know why I persist at all—it is really fantastic to place so much on the fact that I have written a half-dozen *phrases* that I can still bear to re-read without too much embarrassment." Or again, "I should just like to let myself go, Marianne, and give you masses and masses of Nature

Description—but I am so afraid that you may be displeased with me because of my recent laziness and miscalculations."

By mid-October Bishop was in Manhattan and involved in an episode that was part farce and part release of the energy that had been building up in her exchanges with Moore. She brought with her a poem which was probably part of the "serious" plans she had for writing about Key West; Moore's supportive letters had prompted her to get back to writing poems in North Carolina, and "Roosters" appears to be one of the pieces for which she hoped to win Moore's approval. The result was catastrophe, reined in only by whatever good sense and good manners the two women could muster in dealing with one another. The poem—as Bishop says, the most ambitious she had so far attempted—prompted both Moore and her mother to an "immediate flurry of criticism." Moore telephoned the day after Bishop mailed it to her and said that she and her mother had sat up late writing a revision. Their version reached Bishop in the next mail. Moore's note, mixing criticism with parental archness, was sealed with a silver star and warned: "Do not read at mealtime or on going to bed. D.D. [Dorothy Dix]." It began with decent praise:

Dearest Elizabeth, the Pope-ian sagacity, as I was just now saying to you, and your justice to "Peeter," and such a crucially enviable consummation as

> From strained throats
> A senseless order floats,

are like a din of churchbells in my ears, I am so excited (A little girl whom Mother had been teaching about the apostles said in one of her answers to a little written examination, "And don't forget Peeter.") "Flares begin to catch" is so precise and the rhyme with "patch," so perfect. I question as a desirable discord "v" and "s," and therefore suggest omitting "the many wives":

> The crown of red
> Set on your little head

is a notable condensation of overtones and the sound is ideal.

But accompanying these praises of Bishop's chromatics was a complete rewriting of the poem by Moore and her mother★ (almost what Louise Crane would call a "sizing version," Bishop said) which thoroughly ignored Bishop's form—triple-rhymed stanzas—and even changed the poem's title, naïvely, to "The Cock." Moore had never before gone so far with "corrections" of her young friend's work. Even the things she praised seemed to grow out of a misunderstanding of Bishop's intentions; the harmony of "strained throats" and "senseless order" which Moore admired was replaced in Bishop's final version by a harsher "deep from raw throats / a senseless order floats."

The ostensible irritant for Moore—which prompted a disagreement on the telephone—was Bishop's use of "water-closet" and perhaps "dropping-plastered," both of which were expelled from the condensation of the poem. Moore's reasoning is a classic of iron-willed delicacy:

Regarding the water-closet, Dylan Thomas, W. C. Williams, E. E. Cummings, and others, feel that they are avoiding a duty if they balk at anything like unprudishness, but I say to them, "I can't care about all things equally, I have a major effect to produce, and the heroisms of abstinence are as great as the heroisms of courage, and so are the rewards." I think it is to your credit, Elizabeth, that when I say you are not to say "water-closet," you go on saying it a little (like Donald in National Velvet), and it is calculated to make me wonder if I haven't mistaken a cosmetic patch for a touch of lamp-black, but I think not. The trouble is, people are not depersonalized enough to accept the picture rather than the thought. You saw with what gusto I acclaimed "the mermaid's pap" in Christopher S. but few of us, it seems to me, are fundamentally rude enough to enrich our work in such ways without cost. If I tell Mother there is a feather on her dress and she says, "On my back?" I am likely to say, "No. On your rump," alluding to Cowper's hare that "swung his rump

★Reprinted in an appendix to this volume, p. 265.

around." But in my work, I daren't risk saying, "My mother had a feather on her rump."

I hope Dorothy Dix's enclosure will not, as I said to you on the telephone, mean that I am never to hear from you or see you again.

Agitatedly, dearest Elizabeth,

Marianne

But it is quite obvious from the rewriting of the poem that there was more at stake than one or two vulgarities. Repeatedly, adjectives and phrases that are emphatically violent or crude are canceled: the rooster's "cruel feet" and "stupid eyes"; "torn-out, bloodied feathers." "A rooster gloats / over our beds" in Bishop's version is, in Moore's, discharged of some of its private, erotic burden and joined to a more neutral line before it: "a senseless order floats / across fastidious beds." Moore even turns the tin rooster that tops a church into a gold one. The rewriting insistently purges the poem of a Bishop that Moore clearly doesn't recognize.

There were some problems Bishop could address directly and forcefully. She wanted her "water-closet" and the other "sordidities"

because I want to emphasize the essential baseness of militarism. In the 1st part I was thinking of Key West, and also of those aerial views of dismal little towns in Finland & Norway, when the Germans took over, and their atmosphere of poverty. That's why, although I see what *you* mean, I want to keep "tin rooster" instead of "gold," and not to use "fastidious beds." And for the same reason I want to keep as the title the rather contemptuous word "Roosters" rather than the more classical "Cock"; and I want to repeat the "gun-metal" (I also had in mind the violet roosters Picasso did in connection with his "Guernica" picture).

Bishop always thought of "Roosters" as, at one level, her "war poem." She carefully dated it 1941 when collecting it in *North & South*. She told Moore that the "glass-headed pins" to which she compared the birds in their scattered crowings were meant to suggest the variously colored pins that point out projects on war maps. Because of intense strategic preparations in Key West she seemed acutely attuned to the approach of war. The poem, in fact, appeared, in a context uncharacteristically political for Bishop, as the lead poem in an issue of *The New Republic* edited by Edmund Wilson.

But there was another dimension of "Roosters" to which Moore was clearly not responding. It was more than an exposure of male bravado, though the opening twenty-six stanzas, over half the poem, are devoted to the combative criers of the morning who terrorize their "rustling wives" and, after wasteful clashes, end up on the ash-heap "with open, bloody eyes / while those metallic feathers oxidize." But "Roosters" is also a cousin of "Love Lies Sleeping," that poem of Bishop's about waking to the world and the less pleasant differentiated claims of the ego. It plays out, as many of Bishop's earlier pieces did, the violations of the morning, though in "Roosters" with more rage and even, as David Bromwich suggests, with self-reproach. "How could the night have come to grief?" has the unexplained private suggestiveness of many of Bishop's dawn poems. It was precisely this interiorizing element that Moore attempted to ignore in rewriting "Roosters." She tries to keep the poem at a uniform satiric distance from its subject. Responding to Bishop's

> and wake us here where are
> unwanted love, conceit and war?

Moore offers a more generalized "irrelevant love" for Bishop's "unwanted." But Bishop has already planted seeds of the notion that the roosters wake us, however unwillingly, to a problematic aspect of ourselves.

> each one an active
> displacement in perspective;
> each screaming, "This is where I live!"

> Each screaming
> "Get up! Stop dreaming!"
> Roosters, what are you projecting?

I know of no specific promptings for this poem, but there is no mistaking the moment when it takes its personal turn. After venting its resentments, it abruptly and unexpectedly acknowledges human complicity. As Bishop tells of St. Peter's betrayals of Christ and his eventual forgiveness, she seems to cast herself as a second "crier of the morning." Moore is quick to moralize the episode, writing: " 'Deny deny deny' / is not now as it was, the rooster's cry." Separating the past from the present and the emblem from the speaker, she blunts Bishop's sense of perpetual re-enactment, of the unavoidable mixture of self-assertion and a more benign consciousness: " 'Deny deny deny' / is not all the roosters cry."

"Holy sculpture / sets it all together: / one scene, past and future," Moore tells us. But Bishop is more tentative and exploratory: "Old holy sculpture / *could* set it all together / in one small scene . . ." (My italics.) What is incised in stone is not something past but the moment of betrayal as eternal suspended action:

> Christ stands amazed,
> Peter, two fingers raised
> to surprised lips, both as if dazed.

> But in between
> a little cock is seen
> carved on a dim column in the travertine,

> explained by *gallus canit;* [*crows*]
> *flet Petrus* underneath it. [*weeping*]
>   There is inescapable hope, the pivot;

yes, and there Peter's tears
run down our chanticleer's
sides and gem his spurs.

Tear-encrusted thick
as a medieval relic
he waits. Poor Peter, heart-sick,

still cannot guess
those cock-a-doodles yet might bless,
his dreadful rooster come to mean forgiveness . . .

What is rendered in the poem is sustained participation—even down to the sharp intake of breath at a "yes." Bishop experiences the power of the self as its conflated capacity for betrayal and remorse. Moore's version of the poem is less psychological, less human. The repetitions which Moore found obtrusive are really part of the poem's air of sustained interrogation, as if to let the experience sink in and to listen for answering rhythms inside: "Deep from protruding chests . . . deep from raw throats"; "A rooster gloats / over our beds . . . over our churches . . . over our little wooden northern houses"; "and one is flying . . . And one has fallen"; "a low light is floating . . . and gilding . . . gilding the tiny / floating swallow's belly . . ." The suspensions reflect an inner state—the protracted *delayed)* movement of consciousness—that is akin to Peter's, who "*still* cannot guess / those cock-a-doodles *yet* might bless, / his dreadful rooster come to mean forgiveness." (My italics.)

When Bishop returns to her morning scene in the last section of the poem, much of the opening bitterness of "Roosters" has been purged—or, more accurately, incorporated, accepted as natural to the rhythms of the day. "Love Lies Sleeping," four years before, held tight to its resentments; it resolved the clash of ego and world in that figure, head hanging perilously over the edge of the bed, for whom the image of the daytime city

> grows down into his open eyes
> inverted and distorted. No. I mean
> distorted and revealed,
> if he sees it at all.

"Roosters," by contrast and in not altogether pleasant ways, is a survivor's poem. It allows Bishop to identify her own problematic energies and feel them at home in the world. A fanciful conceit at the close connects the sun, through a biblical phrase Bishop loved, to Peter's presence at the trial of Christ:

> The sun climbs in,
> following "to see the end,"
> faithful as enemy, or friend.

The caprice of the ending, the insistence on the metaphor, is very unlike Bishop's usual practice. In one way Bishop's conceit naturalizes or neutralizes the notion of betrayal. But in the extravagance of its language, its montage of betrayer and sunrise, its wry equation of enemy and friend, it is alert to the bitter results of human presence in the world. What precedes has been a natural scene permeated by light and its blessings, a serene "preamble" to an uneasy resolution. The roosters are now almost inaudible, receding into the creaturely scene. But the energies that they have brought to the surface remain to trouble the end of the poem—disturbing questions about selfhood and its cost, now properly transferred from the beasts she resented to her own sense of herself.

"Roosters" is cousin to "The Fish," a poem Bishop had sent to Moore earlier that year. Both poems scrutinize creatures she imagines as bemedaled males—and the two pieces are probably more revealing about the questions of survival she was addressing in Key West than the character sketches she was also tempted to do (Jerónimo, Cootchie, Miss Mamie in "Mercedes Hospital"). Bishop refers to "The Fish" as a "trifle" and "if not like Robert Frost perhaps like Ernest Hemingway! I left the last line on so it wouldn't be." It moves with the childlike simplicity of a Hemingway narrative: bare subject and verb, alternating I's and he's, insistent stage directions (I caught, I thought, I looked, I stared and stared). But even this concise show of bravado—Bishop was later irritated with it as an overanthologized poem—has an air of mystery adhering. The fisher-poet is an insistent maker of similes:

> Here and there
> his brown skin hung in strips
> like ancient wallpaper,
> and its pattern of darker brown
> was like wallpaper:
> shapes like full-blown roses
> stained and lost through age.
> He was speckled with barnacles,
> fine rosettes of lime . . .

At first the comparisons are linked as in the concentration of someone just waking. She responds to the fish in tentative advancing similes that imply a whole cycle of domestic flourish and decay through which we half perceive a similar pattern in nature. (Full-blown roses, rosettes, and the confusion as to whether it is the wallpaper shapes or the full-blown roses that are "stained and lost through age.") There are moments of greater definition: "I thought of the coarse white flesh / packed in like feathers . . . and the pink swim-bladder / like a big peony." Then again images of problematic vision:

> I looked into his eyes
> which were far larger than mine
> but shallower, and yellowed,
> the irises backed and packed
> with tarnished tinfoil
> seen through the lenses
> of old scratched isinglass.

[86

The poem is filled with the strain of seeing—not just the unrelenting pressure of making similes to "capture" the fish, but the fact that the similes themselves involve flawed instruments of vision, stained wallpaper, scratched isinglass, tarnished tinfoil. This is why, on some readings, the poem has the air of summoning up a creature from the speaker's own inner depths—the surviving nonhuman resources of an earlier creation, glimpsed painfully through the depredations of time and the various frail instruments we devise, historically, to see them. [*plundering*] The "victory" that fills up the little rented boat is one that more than grammatically belongs to both sides. Like "Roosters," though without its bitterness and fear, this poem taps and identifies the nonhuman sources of human energies. What makes it different from Moore's animal poems is its interest in the difficulties of locating and accepting such energies.

"Roosters" and "The Fish" were Bishop's first efforts in a "type" Moore had made her own. Yet critics have felt sharp divergence between their respective bestiaries. (Bishop, in fact, did relatively few animal poems.) David Bromwich saw Bishop's as closer to D. H. Lawrence's creaturely poems, "protestant inquests concerning the power of the self." Jarrell, in 1945, spoke of the effect of Moore's poems as "visual and instantaneous rather than auditory and temporal, a state rather than a process. With some poets we are confused about where we began and where we ended, but are sure that we have been moved; with Miss Moore we know just where we are, but we stay there." In judgments quite categorical and more hostile than those of most of Miss Moore's critics, Jarrell accuses her of sending postcards to only the nicer animals—and asks why her animals never die. "In Miss Moore's poems even the animals' processes are habits, norms, and thus get the stability and finality of things. All her zoos are Egyptian." However one-sided the judgment, it reminds us by contrast of the element of *time* in Bishop's encounters. The end of "The Fish" is precisely a separation. "Roosters" closes with the advent of morning and the assimilation of the self's barbaric energies into a temporal order. Self-cognition is a perilous act in Bishop's writing—one to which Moore's observational poems pointed the way, but one she could not perform with Moore's sangfroid. Having embraced the observational method, she was faced in each poem with its cost. Imagining her poems as encounters in *time* allowed her to enter and experience the savage sources of survival, but to place them in a seemingly temporal and independent frame.

It is ironic that "Roosters," the occasion of a break with Moore, should be the closest Bishop had yet come to the type of poem Moore made famous. The rift was more startling than its comic origins suggest. Recalling the farrago years later, Bishop said that she never again sent Moore any of her poems for suggestions or approval. This was, as her letters show, not altogether true. She did continue to send Moore poems during the war years and occasionally thereafter, and had comments and suggestions from her on "Songs for a Colored Singer" and "Large Bad Picture" in 1943 and on "Anaphora" in 1944. But the "Roosters" incident, which took Bishop by surprise, dramatized her differences with the older poet more spectacularly than any of the irritations they had yet undergone. Each was quick to smooth over antagonisms through wit and politeness rather than air their disagreements at length. Moore would refer to herself disparagingly as Dorothy Dix or as Miss Rose Peebles, Bishop's "modern" but genteel teacher at Vassar. Bishop said Moore's criticisms made her feel like Klee's *The Man of Confusion*, and then proceeded to invite her to a Klee exhibition in Manhattan.

Moore's treatment of Bishop's new work was, after "Roosters," gingerly and restrained. She kept as much to matters of technique as she could and, if she disliked something, translated her disapproval into other terms. When, in 1942, Bishop sent her the story "The Farmer's Children" (which she did not publish until 1948), Moore replied ambiguously that it produced an overwhelming effect on her. "It is wonderful that I am not too swallowed by melancholy to be writing you a letter at all." Nevertheless Bishop's "way of selecting the unobvious though incontrovertible essential details makes me feel always: 'now this is the way to write. Why can't others write this way!' " Bishop's response was appropriately subdued. She was sorry the story had upset Moore: "I'm afraid I'll find your reasons quite unanswerable—for not liking it."

But there were other reasons, beyond the bruises of criticism, for the excessive delicacy and protectiveness between the two women. For Bishop, the wait for publication of the volume she had substantially completed in 1941 lasted almost five years, and as a result she found herself, more and more frequently, in a depressed, unproductive state. Moore wrote sustainingly: "When I said don't let writing be a threat I meant it is unjust to probity to reproach oneself for lagging. When often premature and dogged struggle spark one's ability to treat the material right at a mature and more favorable time." Moore herself published two books in this period, *What Are Years* (1941) and *Nevertheless* (1944), but she too, in ways different from Bishop, felt stalled in her career. The correspondence between her and Bishop sometimes reads as if between two countries under siege. By the 1940s one or the other of the Moores seemed, very nearly always, to be ill:

As for Mother, she has been battered by my witless misdemeanors, my goings about (as an imaginary favor) to such groups as the B[ryn Mawr] College one—omitting meals and dashing off; inaccurate notes late at night; and finally creeping home cowed and *guilty* with a fever the past week, so that I was a dead weight and had to be taken care of for two whole days. Handicapped as we are by the slightest thing wrong with either of us you can imagine how we feel about *you*, Elizabeth, entirely responsible for yourself.

Moore's terms are daunting, associating guilt and fever with independence. She is in awe of what she thinks of as the "struggle" of Bishop's travels. But "fortitude" is the word at 260 Cumberland Street and is linked to staying home: "Even just standing still and refusing to disappear is often one's greatest triumph of fortitude." An uncharacteristic note of complaint enters Moore's reports on their life in Brooklyn. Her mother is "always ironing; or segregating things so they will stay in order, and telling me 'nothing will more kindly cooperate with the will of the worker,' and this means less reading and no adventures."

Aside from these isolating psychological situations—Bishop's discouragements, Moore's bond with her mother—the two women's separation from the predominantly male literary scene seemed to be increasing. When the *Southern Review* marshaled its full complement of New Critics in an issue devoted entirely to Yeats, Bishop wondered "why I don't feel Yeats is as wonderful as all the people in the Southern Review number about him seem to think he is." Moore agreed:

I would be "much disappointed in you" if you *could* feel about Yeats as some of his acolytes seem to feel. An "effect," an exhaustively great sensibility (with insensibility?) and genius for word-sounds and sentences. But after all, what is this enviable apparatus for? if not to change our mortal psycho-structure. It makes me think of the Malay princes—the *horde* of eunuchs and entertainers and "bearers" of this and that; then suddenly the umbrella over the prince lowered, because a greater prince was passing. As you will suspect from my treachery to W. B. Yeats, I've been to a lecture on Java by Burton Holmes, and one on Malay . . .

Bishop was also growing impatient with Stevens, whose work she and Moore admired immensely in the 1930s. When "Montrachet-le-Jardin" first appeared in *Partisan Review*, Bishop termed it another example of "his old mother-of-pearl inlaid guitar—but phrases and verses are self-consciously beautiful." Moore approached it more charitably: "There are one or two characteristic and wholesome surprises in the poem somewhere I thought. But I too resist obliqueness just now, of any kind in anyone."

Against this overcrafting they set, with equal suspicion, the recent work of Auden and Eliot, in which Moore saw with some dismay (and with undiminished affection for both men) a turning away from the particular and a slackening of form. Beneath her reservations was the resolute feeling that each of the male poets had somehow abandoned the *materials* of poetry and sacrificed them for something more like prose. Bishop had similar doubts and continued to find Moore's work the unique model for accommodating prose content to poetic method. She felt her own work slipping away from specificity, everything leading to everything else. But Moore's "In Distrust of Merits," on the other hand, seemed to her a bastion against "the present terrible *generalizing* of every emotion." The two women were by now virtually alone in their commitment to the poetry of description. Eliot's meditative plainness in passages of the *Four Quartets* involved a refusal, a lack of engagement with the physical that to Moore might seem wrongheaded. Her own verse suggests that we discover our human natures by accepting and exploring prior creations—and not by projecting future immaterial ones.

Neither Moore nor Bishop would speak so baldly, systematically, or confidently about what it was they were doing. Their devotion to the concrete, to what natural detail mimes back about our natures, made them suspicious of generalities both inside and outside the poem. Nor could Bishop be anything but tentative about the discoveries she had made in "Roosters" and "The Fish." For the moment they did not constitute a settled direction in her work but rather an anticipation of poems she would write seven or eight years later. Still, when James Laughlin wrote asking for her three best poems to print in a Pelican anthology he was editing, Bishop immediately thought of "Roosters" and "The Fish" and, from her early work, "The Weed" and, as an alternate to "The Fish," "A Miracle for Breakfast." Moore tried gently to suggest alternatives to "Roosters": "I don't really oppose 'Roosters' but 'The Gentleman of Shalott' I would certainly not omit." Bishop eventually sent "The Imaginary Iceberg," another suggestion of Moore's, "The Weed," and, resolutely, "Roosters."

Her continued faith in that poem must have sharpened her sense of her differences from Moore. Moore would note in her review of *North & South* that "Miss Bishop does not avoid 'fearful pleasantries' and in 'The Fish,' as in the subject of the poem, one is not glad of the creature's every perquisite; but the poem dominates recollection." The remark recalls Bishop's refusal, in "Roosters," to sacrifice "a very important 'violence' of tone" for what Miss Moore must feel "just a bad case of the *Threes.*" (That last phrase refers to the triplet stanzas which bothered Moore almost as much as the tone.) It takes some patient disentangling to see the critical gap that yawns beneath phrases as polite as Moore's "Miss Bishop does not avoid" or "one is not glad of the creature's every perquisite." Moore counters dangerous natural instinct with her faith that "the poem dominates recollection." Her own "Fish" are preserved in the "black jade" of form and style so as to neutralize the unfathomable energy of the deep. To be fair to Moore, her poem lifts veil after decorative veil to expose the erosion and scarring that is part of natural process and human carelessness. But Moore enters her poem with such aplomb and virtuosity as to establish a countervailing power of mind:

THE FISH

wade
through black jade.
   Of the crow-blue mussel shells, one keeps
   adjusting the ash-heaps;
      opening and shutting itself like

an
injured fan.
   The barnacles which encrust the side
   of the wave, cannot hide
      there for the submerged shafts of the

sun,
split like spun
   glass, move themselves with spotlight swiftness

into the crevices—
   in and out, illuminating

the
turquoise sea
  of bodies . . .

The poem "dominates recollection" in ways that Bishop was discovering foreign to her own instinct and practice. In Moore's work she must have sensed a purity of possession with which she, the younger poet, never felt entirely comfortable. Bishop's descriptive poems are themselves critiques of descriptive powers. Since "Quai d'Orléans" she had become more aware that nothing was observed which had not been tinged by memory. The benisons of morning, the signs of fresh natural creation, are entwined with the residue of dreams and with bafflement about human motive and pain, as with the lover in "Roosters" who wonders in the innocence of the morning, "How could the night have come to grief?" The blessings of the physical world are never quite enough to "dominate recollection."

How far *are* our problematic energies naturalized—at home in the world? How much does the world tell us, in brute kinship, about selfhood? To what extent does it tease us with glimpses of unattainable ongoing harmony? These are questions that trouble the surface of "Roosters" and make it an unsettling poem. Rather than "dominate recollection" Bishop allows the presence of time (the arrival of morning) to lead her safely out of the poem and away from its earlier barbaric vision. The whole poem is conducted in present tenses, and always moving away from the simple reportorial present into its charged cousinly participles:

In the morning
a low light is floating
in the backyard, and gilding

from underneath
the broccoli, leaf by leaf;
how could the night have come to grief?

gilding the tiny
floating swallow's belly
and lines of pink cloud in the sky,

the day's preamble
like wandering lines in marble.
The cocks are now almost inaudible.

The sun climbs in,
following "to see the end,"
faithful as enemy, or friend.

The participles which open and close these lines (floating, gilding, gilding, floating) suggest a transfer of energy at once easy
and symmetrical. Light floats and gilds the vegetable, animal,
and mineral worlds; itself floating, it gilds the floating swallow.
Like the phrases in apposition ("the day's preamble / like wandering lines in marble") and like the gradual certainty of "leaf
by leaf," the participles are meant to sustain a movement, keep
it from ending. The triple-rhyme cantilena guarantees harmony—or appears to at first. But human betrayals puzzlingly
interrupt ("how could the night have come to grief?"), and
awaken a latent sense of self-deception. Are the "gildings" of
this poem, like those in Shakespeare's thirty-third sonnet,
merely cosmetic, as the image of the sun as faithful enemy dares
to suggest at the close? The voice Bishop chooses mimes both
blessing and doubt, memory only *partly* dominated by the
poem, the roosters only *almost* inaudible. Moore sees her beasts
as timeless studies. But in Bishop's work, time provides the
plot. On the edge of night and morning, of dream and waking,
her vision passes from clouded psyche to "objective" light.
Nothing is sustained for long, neither the glimpses of savagery
that link human and nonhuman survival, nor the memory-

tinged scrutiny of the physical world, nor an ongoing natural harmony impervious to human pain. A succession of moments allows her to explore and escape the full and final burden of her poems. Anomalous and irreconcilable insights rest side by side on the page. In "Roosters" the sun is "faithful as enemy, or friend." In "The Fish" victory belongs both to the wild survivor and his human counterpart.

It is to probe these contradictions that Bishop wrote another "dawn" poem, her most beautiful and most resolved. "Anaphora" (1944) revisits both "Love Lies Sleeping" and "Roosters." But it tackles these awakening moments with fewer warlike implications than either of them, or, indeed, than "The Fish." Conflict is absorbed into a celebration of one's daily "fall" into the waking world.

> Each day with so much ceremony
> begins, with birds, with bells,
> with whistles from a factory;
> such white-gold skies our eyes
> first open on, such brilliant walls
> that for a moment we wonder
> "Where is the music coming from, the energy?
> The day was meant for what ineffable creature
> we must have missed?" Oh promptly he
> appears and takes his earthly nature
>   instantly, instantly falls
>   victim of long intrigue,
>   assuming memory and mortal
>   mortal fatigue.
>
> More slowly falling into sight
> and showering into stippled faces,
> darkening, condensing all his light;
> in spite of all the dreaming
> squandered upon him with that look,
> suffers our uses and abuses,
> sinks through the drift of bodies,

sinks through the drift of classes
to evening to the beggar in the park
who, weary, without lamp or book
    prepares stupendous studies:
    the fiery event
    of every day in endless
    endless assent.

The poem is a kind of *ars poetica* for Bishop's future work. Its title identifies writing with the cleansing and tarnishing repetitions of each successive day. Observation is indissolubly linked to memory, "long intrigue," and "mortal / mortal fatigue." Unlike Moore, who takes electric, seemingly instantaneous possession of her subjects, Bishop treats the poem as a dialogue between a prior creation and the uses humans make of it. She trusts to gradual encounters, repeated submission to similar landscapes and scenes, slow tests of the ego which eventually mime back buried, once indistinct feelings. "Anaphora" opens with the pure promise of morning and manages to suggest as well the exhilaration of the blank page ("such white-gold skies our eyes / first open on, such brilliant walls"). It has its poet, too, a combination of what Stevens would name "the youth as virile poet" and the equally Stevensian beggar in the park—Apollo as Charlie Chaplin. Stevens's "Notes toward a Supreme Fiction," in which both the beggar and sun-god figure, had come out in 1942, and Bishop appears to have been encouraged by its faith in observing objects and scenes, its belief in process. One only approached truth; one never statically possessed it. "From this the poem springs," Stevens asserts in "Notes," "that we live in a place / That is not our own and, much more, not ourselves / And hard it is in spite of blazoned days." Bishop repeatedly places her poems at that harsh nexus of human and inhuman, though her interests are less philosophical, more psychological than Stevens's. She uses natural encounters and landscape to sift and clarify individual memory and pain.

Even the grammar of "Anaphora" passes uneasily from

inner to outer worlds. The subject of the poem is largely the transcendental creature, glorified version of ourselves, perfectly at home in the dawn of "Anaphora," who "instantly, instantly falls" and the sign of whose fall is human memory. Yet the second stanza for the briefest moment brings to the surface a mysterious and more alien energy:

> More slowly falling into sight
> and showering into stippled faces,
> darkening, condensing all his light;

There is no explicit subject to this fragment, nor even an implied one until the "his" of the third line. Meanwhile, we read "showering" as if it referred purely to light, and it throws the preceding line into startling relief. Of course it means that we witness the fate of the Apollonian creature, we see his fall. But it also refers to the fate of light, the pure medium, when it falls "into sight" inevitably clouded by human vision and concerns. Perhaps the double meaning is not worth worrying about, the differences too minimal. Yet "sight" has its nuances, and as "eyesight" or the "faculty of observation," it is a tarnishing agent for Bishop, not simply the power that helps us witness our Apollo's fall. "Suffers our uses and abuses" is equally shaded. Does it mean mainly that the fallen figure shares in human pain, as in "assuming memory and mortal / mortal fatigue"? How much does it admit of the feeling that we *inflict* "our uses and abuses" upon this purer creature? There are of course no "answers." The poem vibrates between personal history and guilt, on the one hand, and the purity and relentlessness of the natural world, on the other. Each, slowly, makes palpable the force and limits of the other in a patient and passionate accommodation of the ego to the world.

Anaphora, the rhetorical figure of repetition and renewal, is this writer's natural medium, as natural as wakening to the enablements and submitting to the disabilities of the day. It gives grammatical probity and ceremony to what is already evident in "Paris, 7 A.M.," "Love Lies Sleeping," and "Roosters." Its rhythms can suggest weary engagement ("mortal / mortal fatigue") and fiery rededication ("endless / endless assent"). And, of course, these phrases echo one another precisely, across the gap of the stanzas: their metrical dialogue interprets, then reinterprets the cycle which is the poem's subject. In the metrical anaphora of the close, "assent" replaces "fatigue," with a lovely Janus-like appreciation of the poem: "assent" as submission to the darkening uses and abuses of the day that is passing and as ardent anticipation of the fiery sun of the day to come. "Assent" becomes "ascent" and the poem's cycle begins afresh. "Anaphora" consists of twin sonnets, eccentrically formed and rhymed, which answer one another in unexpected ways, a kind of anaphora themselves. Each has a coda of short lines, like the sestet of a sonnet, in which the mood of the stanza changes, in the first from pure to clouded perception, in the second from tarnished to fervid imagination. Each sonnet corrects itself and is in turn corrected in ways that overlap their formal boundaries. The coda of the second sonnet revives and regenerates our interest in the opening.

The poem is, in fact, a nest of repetitions—alliteration, interior rhyme most prominently. Some assert a harmonious link between inner and outer worlds ("such white-gold skies our eyes"). Others—off-rhymes—remind us of the effort and failure to bring these worlds together ("ineffable creature . . . earthly nature"). The sounds of this poem, especially at the outset, are so noticeable as to become themselves part of the theme—the sinuous *effort* of the voice to accommodate what it encounters, to assert a tenuous authority from self to world. The voice—by turns confidently lyric, interrogative, tragic, then once again ardent—is governed by time, its vagaries and recurrences. Rather than be troubled by the assertiveness of "Roosters," "Anaphora" trusts to receptivity, allows discords to settle side by side. It takes up—but with refinement—the quarrel which began with "Roosters." Where Moore assumes peremptory possession of the things she describes, Bishop observes, then trusts to memory and change. She identifies not with Apollo but with the beggar in the park—the figure Stevens provided her, the poet who must daily reinvent godlike presence out of poverty and guilt and loss. Moore saw "Anaphora" in April 1944 and liked it immediately for its "unself-pity":

This has your best originality. It's not like anybody else's writing. It has such expanding allusiveness and romance and sombreness. The direct, emphatic attack, the naturalness, the enticement of "that for a moment we wonder / 'Where is the music coming from, the energy?' " Most of all perhaps the retarding in the last lines: "assuming memory and mortal / mortal fatigue."

In December of that year, Moore offered to write and recommend Bishop for a Houghton Mifflin poetry prize. Bishop's application was characteristically modest, even self-denigrating, saying that she wanted "to finish six or seven poems of what I hope may be a serious nature and more appropriate and intense form than these enclosed." Moore, beset by illnesses at home, got her letter off untypically late. She was full of praise for Bishop's scholarly resources and emphasized that beneath an apparently unliterary surface was a deep grasp of the cultural past. "In her writing, a feeling for strong personalities such as G. M. Hopkins, Franz Kafka, Dürer, Max Ernst, Eugène Atget, Purcell and other musicians, is assimilated beyond detection." Bishop's *North & South* won in a field of over eight hundred entrants. Bishop received a prize of one thousand dollars and the assurance that, after years of waiting and rejections, her book would finally be published.

In September 1946, Moore's review of *North & South* appeared in *The Nation*. The piece ("reckless," she said), the only one Moore was ever to do on a volume of Bishop's poems, was an implied farewell to their old master-apprentice relationship. It was as favorable as Moore's habitual understatement ever allowed her to be, full of private messages for Bishop (Moore kept singling out "Roosters" for praise), and yet still had about it an air of choked expression. It was not just that the balance of their relationship had altered. Moore's praise was not in any sense halfhearted, rather it was distracted, lacking her usual pungent flights, her wild summoning of comparisons to keep company with the poet's own.

It was called "A Modest Expert," applying to Bishop a favorite word of praise, one Moore had used tellingly of Wallace Stevens in reviewing *Ideas of Order* in 1936. With Bishop, Moore argues, the expertise is accurate and modest, a matter of "cautious self-inquiry." Bishop's "musicianly strategies" frequently invite, then avoid the closure of rhyme; she substitutes alliteration or the reiterated word to suggest the reaching after meaning. Moore actually singles out the difficult rhyming of "Roosters," so sustained and exploratory. Given the fact that her own "sizing version" of the poem had butchered Bishop's careful triplet scheme, the words of praise constitute a quiet admission of error and lay the issue finally to rest. Moore also acknowledges the younger poet's "fearful pleasantries" which sometimes marred Bishop's work for her. "Dignity has been sacrificed," Moore comments, "to exactness in the word 'neatly': 'The mangrove island with bright green leaves edged neatly with bird-droppings like illumination in silver.'" At a more resonant level the muted violence, the sombreness of many of Bishop's poems was now something Moore was tacitly acknowledging as a gap between them.

But the heart of her acknowledgment proved unexpectedly personal. Talking about "Roosters," she remarks that forgiveness seems essential to happiness, and then goes on to a comment of Reinhold Niebuhr's that "the cure for international incompatibilities is not diplomacy but contrition." Moore adds

Nor is it permissible to select the wrongs for which to be contrite; we are contrite; we won't be happy till we are sorry.

She wrote privately to Bishop: "As for 'you won't be happy until you are sorry,' it is my whole life. If I counted what I do and multiplied it, the inferno would be so congested, not a demon could find space to sit down." For her, in her extremity of feeling, a whole new dimension of Bishop's poetry had come into relief—not just in "Roosters" but in "The Unbeliever," a poem to which she had not earlier paid much attention.

Miss Bishop's speculation, also, concerning faith—religious faith—is a carefully plumbed depth in this small-large book of beautifully formulated aesthetic-moral mathematics. The unbeliever is not ridiculed; but is not anything that is adamant, self-ironized?

> ". . . Up here
> I tower through the sky
> for the marble wings on my tower-top fly."

With poetry as with homiletics, tentativeness can be more positive than positiveness; and in *North & South*, a much instructed persuasiveness is emphasized by uninsistence.

Years before, in 1938, Moore had feared that the chief dangers for Bishop might be "tentativeness and interiorizing." Now Moore, who had her own brand of tentativeness, was quietly willing to praise Bishop for her ironies, her explorations, her unfinished nature as a moralist—a poet whose *method* was her message. "Tentativeness" carried with it a private as well as a public burden of praise. Understated as it was, it must have assured Bishop that her independence finally pleased and satisfied the poet who had always meant so much to her.

One day we may know the full details of Moore's sufferings in the 1940s. Between her own illnesses and her mother's, she was growing more and more desperate. The Cecil Beaton photograph of the two of them makes them appear to be ravaged contemporaries, Marianne looking, if anything, older than her mother, more like a stricken sister than a daughter. Mrs. Moore stands forward, appealing, with a sad smile; Marianne looks early-American, expressionless, or all expression at rest, drawn patiently in. Moore writes of "the blackness of illness." When both Moores are sick simultaneously, Marianne speaks of nursing her mother as an allowable "egotism to overcome the degradation." She becomes abject in her relations with Bishop: "I am industriously sordid; with not one reading or event to make me less objectionable, Elizabeth; forgive it. And I'll surprise you some day by being fit to know." Or again: "We have not met for years, Elizabeth [they had met the year before, in February 1945; Moore's lapse suggests the degree of her distractedness], but let us doggedly see to it that we stay alive, and that adversity helps us to be a little less vulnerable . . . No news, no discoveries, but a world of gratitude that you and other friends do not hate, and cast me off. Please make up to us Elizabeth by prosperity of your own some of our defections and backsets and the 100% illiteracy of us." Or yet again: "I would like to, and am going to outgrow *torture*, Elizabeth, in any case transferring the sense of it if anyone so much as passes near me." Moore also converts her personal courage into an almost stifling fear for Bishop's health: "You are ill, dear Elizabeth, I fear you are. I know when trapped by illness or borne down by a weight of care one can't speak." Her guess proved right; it was a period when Bishop, in Key West, was suffering constant asthma attacks. "Dear brave Elizabeth," the next letter began. "It is a thing for tears Elizabeth." Or again: "In the letter I did not mention your health lest it seem like begging, but *what else matters?*" The "letter," curiously enough, is her recommendation of Bishop to Houghton Mifflin, and "begging," meant to be full of care, is also somewhat patronizing—as if Bishop's health affected the value of her book one way or the other. Or again in September 1945: "Don't conceal anything, Elizabeth, if you're struggling or in perplexity."

Moore's habitual air of concern was a little out of control in these years and may have caused Bishop some trouble in dealing with her. There were minor vexations, too: Bishop, for example, found it irritating that Moore used her phrase "the bell-boy with the buoy-ball" (in "Four Quartz Crystal Clocks") without her habitual note of acknowledgment. As her mother's death approached, Moore became increasingly desperate. In 1946 and 1947 her handwriting grew smaller and smaller, until finally, in the letter she wrote to announce her mother's death to Bishop, it suddenly exploded into oversize characters.

Mrs. Moore died on July 9, 1947, and was buried at Gettysburg, Pennsylvania, where she had been born. Moore went briefly to stay with friends in Maine. Bishop invited her to join her in Cape Breton, where she was spending part of the summer—but of course Moore did not. She was almost inconsolable, though she found in answering Bishop's letter the truly unselfish note: "How touching, Elizabeth, is consolation that is real. As I have said to you various times perhaps, it is those who need, who can understand need, and so often I think of you." That autumn she writes: "I'm trying to be peaceable about things, Elizabeth, and not aggrieved that life is just nothing like what life should be. I can't see how Mother should have been trustful and grateful *always*, no matter what the distress or the uncertain aspect; and I hesitating and backward." The following spring Bishop was able to report to Robert Lowell that she'd been to Moore's in Brooklyn for dinner and that things seemed to be going much better. Moore continued, discouraged, to work on her translation of La Fontaine—and showed Bishop quite a lot of it one day. "It sounds very much like her, of course," Bishop wrote Lowell. "I'm not sure how much like La Fontaine." Moore became the public figure of the controversy over Ford's Edsel automobile and a kind of mascot for the Brooklyn Dodgers. But in these years on her own she lost that centrality of authority that kept her from being merely eccentric.

In 1948 the *Quarterly Review of Literature* honored Moore's sixtieth birthday with a collection of poems and essays on her work. Bishop's contributions (three short essays and a poem) lived up to the opportunity to say once and for all what bound and separated the two women and to restore the emotional balance between them. Moore responded with spirited gratitude in a letter headed by one of her whirlwind salutations: "Words fail me, Elizabeth . . ." The prose and verse were "reckless" tributes. "Then the suicidal carnage of your treatise!"—meaning that Bishop had preferred her to Hopkins, Poe, and Shakespeare! "So many pretty and 'sweet' things in the course of your interpretation. The trouble and strain of such an effort, and the scientific subtitles! I am overwhelmed, it all seems a phantasy—like one of the interludes in *A Midsummer Night's Dream*. I keep wondering how it should be related to me." The "scientific subtitles" were in fact a way for Bishop to make short observations without the burden of sustained argument. Under the general heading "As We Like It," she writes of "Miss Moore and the Delight of Imitation," "Miss Moore and Edgar Allan Poe," and "Miss Moore and Zoography." The opening essay not only claims Moore as "The World's Greatest Living Observer," but asserts the legitimacy and seriousness of the descriptive poetry the two women were committed to. "The poems seem to say, 'These things exist to be loved and honored and we *must*.'"

Moore's cluttered but serene ability to enter into the life of *things* was always a matter of envy for Bishop, whose poems increasingly dealt with the crises of observer and observed. Her compliment to Moore is phrased as a wondering question: "Does it come simply from her gift of being able to give herself up so entirely to the object under contemplation, to feel in all sincerity how it is to be *it*? From whatever this pleasure may be derived, it is certainly one of the greatest the work of Miss Moore gives us." Running counter to this force was Moore's restraint in using metaphors, her preference for similes. It was a tactic she had learned from Poe, who argued that metaphors "dispose the mind to seek a moral in all that has been previously narrated" and who warned against such expressions lest they convey the "excess of the suggested meaning." "Miss Moore," Bishop points out, "does employ it [metaphor] carefully and it is one of the qualities that give her poetry its steady aura of both reserve and having possibly more meanings, in reserve. Another result is that the metaphor, when used, carries a long way, reverberating like her 'pulsation of lighthouse and noise of bell-buoys . . .'" It was this particular strategy which also allowed Bishop her own tough tentativeness; as if to demonstrate the power of simile over metaphor, the power of reserve, she had written at almost the same time that she was preparing her pieces on Moore a poem that more than adequately demonstrates both "reserve and having possibly more meanings, in reserve"—the lovely concatenation of similes called "The Bight."

The most arresting moment in these notes of Bishop's on Moore is atypically psychological, unguardedly shrewd. The subject is Moore's versification:

Sometimes I have thought that her individual verse forms, or "mannerisms" as they might be called, may have developed as much from a sense of modesty as from the demands of artistic expression; that actually she may be somewhat embarrassed by her own precocity and sensibilities and that her varied verse forms and rhyme schemes and syllabic logarithms are all a form of apology, are saying, "It really isn't as easy for me as I'm afraid you may think it is." The precocious child is often embarrassed by his own understanding and is capable of going to great lengths to act his part as a child properly; one feels that Miss Moore sometimes has to make things difficult for herself as a sort of *noblesse oblige*, or self-imposed taxation to keep everything "fair" in the world of poetry.

Moore, in her letter and in a phrase Bishop underlined and marked with an exclamation point, termed this "*alarmingly accurate*, Elizabeth, in what you say of the 'logarithms of apology' and the incredible effort of justifying the initial pattern." Bishop was acknowledging Moore's lightning understanding and defensive tactics of concealment, something very different from her own strategy of patient tentative encounter. Bishop's own writing was partly an effort to reintegrate her childhood guiltlessly into her work. Moore's precocious maneuvers, her "logarithms of apology," were ultimately too self-protective, too deliberately innocent for Bishop. As the years went on, it would become clearer that they were variously the Platonist and the Aristotelian of descriptive writing.

One of Bishop's best friends in New York found "Invitation to Miss Marianne Moore," the poem which accompanied these essays, "mean." Bishop, troubled, could only say that it wasn't meant to be. Certainly it enshrined more of Moore's eccentricities than her literary gifts. But, as Moore herself re-marked—and she was very pleased with the poem—"Lots of things, lots of things that mean more to me than to anyone else! But I did once tell K. and M. in some detail about our Renoir interview outside Room 315—you with your seal-enriched jacket and white gloves and pearl earrings and miniature note book full of queries that I would still like to have answered." The poem and essays brought their friendship full circle, back to the ardor and excitement of their first meeting. The notebook of which Moore speaks is still extant, carefully preserved by Bishop. It is there that her younger self copied out "The Jerboa" and then carefully counted the syllables and marked the rhymes. The names of the two women are written and crossed out at the bottom of the page. The subjects for a conversation are neatly listed and the questions remain forever to be answered:

Modern Bestiary	emphasis on *middle*
Hopkins	does she research *for* a poem
Crane? Stevens or	" " " & then the poem
H & H poetry	arrives
17th century	Book on Tattoo
connection with prose	The insulting expression "good for you!"
Herbert	The more " " "It's good for you!"
Crashaw	
how would she read its rhythms	Strange Animals I Have Known— Ditmars

Elizabeth Bishop

and Robert Lowell

1 / Prodigal Years

Elizabeth Bishop met Robert Lowell sometime during the
first few weeks of 1947; Randall Jarrell introduced them. Bishop's *North & South* had appeared in August 1946, Lowell's *Lord
Weary's Castle* in December. They met at a moment when
Bishop was ready to relish the excitement of a contemporary
to whom she might feel accountable. By now her friendship
with Marianne Moore had become a little distant—no longer
intimately tied to her work though still affectionate and familial,
as it would continue to be for the rest of their lives: wise,
eccentric aunt and amused, grateful, occasionally wayward
niece. Bishop was too shy—and too critical—to seek out friend-
ships with other writers. But the friendship with Lowell proved
to be complex and sustaining almost from the start. He quickly
became the challenging confidant to whom she would send her
work and the letter-journals of her life as she had to Moore in
the 1930s and early 1940s.

In an exchange almost thirty years later, Lowell and Bishop
looked back at the circumstances of their first meeting with by
then characteristic differences in temperament. "I see us still
when we first met," Lowell wrote in 1974,

both at Randall's and then for a couple of years later. I see you as rather tall, long brown-haired, shy but full of des. [*sic:* description?] and anecdote as now. I was brown haired and thirty I guess and I don't know what. I was largely invisible to myself, and nothing I knew how to look at. But the fact is we were swimming in our young age, with the water coming down on us, and we were gulping. I can't go on. It is better now only there's a steel cord stretch [*sic*] tense at about arms-length above us, and what we look forward to must be accompanied by our less grace and strength.

Bishop resisted his elegiac tone:

Never, never was I "tall"—as you wrote remembering me. I was always 5 ft 4 and ¼ inches—now shrunk to 5 ft 4 inches. The only time I've ever felt tall was in Brazil. And I never had "long brown hair" either! —It started turning gray when I was 23 or 24—and probably was already somewhat grizzled when I first met you. I tried putting it up for a very brief period, because I like long hair—but it never got even to my shoulders and is always so intractable that I gave that up within a month or so . . . What I remember about that meeting is your dishevelment, your lovely curly hair, and how we talked about a Picasso show then on in N.Y., and we agreed about the Antibes pictures of fishing, etc.—and how much I liked you, after having been almost too scared to go . . . You were also rather dirty, which I rather liked, too. And your stories about the cellar room you were living in and how the neighbors drank all night and when they got too rowdy one of them wd. say "Remember the boy," meaning you.

Bishop's irony, of course, gives way to affection. There was ardor on both sides of their friendship. Yet Bishop's particularizing, accurate character was always a challenge to Lowell's mythmaking, his way of noting things with a generosity or obliquity or malice just on the edge of fiction. Lowell wrote obsessively about other writers—friends, rivals, masters: Jarrell, Tate, Ransom, Berryman, Peter Taylor, Ford Madox Ford, Santayana, Pound, Eliot. As his friend Blair Clark points out, he "systematically apprenticed himself" to many of them. What he wrote about them was often a projection of his own ambitions and fears, a way of asking "how to think and live as a poet." But Bishop was a more resistant figure to him, a maverick, not quite like other poets he knew—"poor symbolic, abstract creatures," he called them. There was no question of "apprenticeship" on either side; but instead, over the years, the almost invisible give-and-take of two poets curious about each other and affected by each other's work. And all the confusing intricacies of Lowell's responses to women were involved, especially at the start.

Lowell and Bishop began writing to each other in 1947 and met more frequently in the next two years than they would for years to come. It was an unsettled time for both of them. Lowell and Jean Stafford were in the midst of a divorce; in 1947–48 he was living in Washington as Consultant in Poetry to the Library of Congress. Bishop was shuttling north and south, spending winters in Key West and summers in New England, unnerved by New York and avoiding it as much as possible. ("It is like a battered-up old alarm clock that insists on gaining five or six hours a day and has to be kept lying on its side.") The two poets could not have met at a better moment. Their friendship must in retrospect always have been colored by the immunity of those first two years. They were never lovers, but they had, then, something of the freedom of lovers with each other. Lowell had not yet suffered the first of his severe mental breakdowns, which occurred in the spring of 1949. In the fall of 1950, recovered, he left for Europe with a new wife, Elizabeth Hardwick. By the time they returned to the United States in 1953, Bishop was living in Brazil, where she would remain for fifteen years. After 1950, her friendship with Lowell was one of frequent letters and infrequent visits.

But in 1947 and 1948 they knew each other as young poets writing in the wake of successful first books and moody about what was to follow. The rudderless friendship they fell into served them well. The tone was conspiratorial and flirtatious, yet full of the glints of the literary needs they were to satisfy for each other. They were mischievous as children about the figures they most held in awe—Lowell about Jarrell and Tate, Bishop about Moore—and their curiosity about each other helped wean them away from their earlier literary attachments.

In 1947 and 1948 they improvised meetings as often as they could. Bishop stopped in Washington on her way to Key West in October 1947, when, at Lowell's invitation, she recorded poems for the Library of Congress and met William Carlos Williams, nervously holding a pink box of candy, about to take a taxi to his first visit to Ezra Pound at St. Elizabeths. Bishop stopped in Washington again on her return north in April 1948. They saw each other in New York in May when Lowell read with Marianne Moore, Louise Bogan, and Allen Tate at the New School. That August he visited Bishop for two weeks in Maine. They met again in November at a Bard College poetry conference and later in the month when T. S. Eliot lectured on Poe at the Library of Congress. Bishop thus played a part in what must have been one of the most exhilarating years in Lowell's career. At thirty, after a slower start than contemporaries such as Delmore Schwartz and Randall Jarrell, he was the formidable young winner of the Pulitzer Prize, a Guggenheim fellowship, and, of course, the Library consultantship. He was suddenly a visitor of Pound at St. Elizabeths, of Dr. Williams at Rutherford, a correspondent of Eliot and Santayana, a host to Frost at the Library.

All through the winter of 1947–48 Bishop and Lowell had played at what to do in the fall when Lowell's term at the Library expired. "Please come live in Paris," Bishop wrote him in February. Lowell wrote back that he couldn't leave the country because he was a convicted felon (he was jailed as a conscientious objector during the Second World War). But in July 1948 he wrote to say that Santayana, with whom he had recently struck up a correspondence, had offered him a trip to Rome; would Bishop come? Finally he settled on Yaddo, the writers' colony near Saratoga Springs where he had spent time before. He hoped to finish "The Mills of the Kavanaughs," the long poem to which he had been adding stanzas all winter. Bishop was studying freighter-trip booklets, but kept wondering if she should "tag along" to Yaddo. As late as January 1949 Lowell was still urging her to join him there: "It's my dream to maneuver you and the [Peter] Taylors here." By February Lowell was involved in the complicated and painful witch-hunting episode that scattered the few Yaddo residents, Lowell included. (Lowell, supported by other guests, accused Yaddo's executive director of harboring a Communist sympathizer and demanded at a meeting of the Yaddo board that she be fired. The incident—there were heated protests, petitions, and letters to the press when word of Lowell's accusations reached Boston and New York—ended in the board's dismissal of the charges.) Lowell was hospitalized in April for a mental collapse, and except for a few hasty notes, his correspondence with Bishop was temporarily broken.

————

What were Bishop and Lowell writing in 1947 and 1948? What was the nature of their exchanges before their lives took them to different continents? That Lowell was six years younger than Bishop hardly seemed to matter. He was much more at home than Bishop with the grit of the postwar poetry world: the predominantly masculine network of conferences, reviewing, and readings. He was willing to be a practical guide for her and would, for years to come, turn up grants that helped to keep the appreciative Bishop going while she was living in South America. He encouraged her to undertake reading engagements, which she was usually too nervous to accept. In 1949, when Marianne Moore turned down the poetry consultantship at the Library of Congress to finish her La Fontaine translation, Lowell was instrumental in securing the post for Bishop.

On her side, Bishop fell very easily into the role of amateur and outsider. Writing her first long letter to Lowell—she was in Cape Breton for the summer—to thank him for his discerning review of *North & South* in *The Sewanee Review*, she seemed to enjoy being by turns girlishly casual and then suddenly earnest: "Dear Robert (I've never been able to catch that name they call

you but Mr. Lowell doesn't sound right, either)." Some fellow
boarders have made off with her copy of his review, so she
relies on her memory. Then:

The clipping bureau sent me the first page from the July 20th Chicago
Sun "Book Week"—the one with the silly piece by . . .
    Heavens—it is an hour later—I was called out to see a calf being
born in the pasture beside the house. In five minutes after several falls
on its nose it was standing up shaking its head & tail & trying to
nurse. They took it away from its mother almost immediately &
carried it struggling in a wheelbarrow to the barn—we've just been
watching it trying to lie down. Once up it didn't know how to get
down again & finally fell in a heap . . .
    Well, as I was saying—by George Dillon.

    The transitions are pure Bishop—welcoming new claims
on her attention and relieved by spontaneity and distractions.
Later in life she was to be less skittish and more assured about
the habit, one James Merrill described: "Why talk *letters* with
one's gifted colleagues? They too would want, surely, to put
aside work in favor of a new baby to examine, a dinner to shop
for and cook, sambas, vignettes . . ." But, early in her career,
like her character the Gentleman of Shalott for whom "half is
enough," it was a matter largely of stress, a low level of tol-
erance for the literary world, a high level of dependence upon
those who could mediate it for her.
    Lowell took a place that Marianne Moore had filled; Bishop
instinctively chose those two writers whom, whatever the truth
of the matter, she imagined as industrious, as figures who completed the artist's life for her in ways of which she felt herself
incapable. It wasn't simply a need for directorial or practical
counsel, at which both Moore and Lowell were adept, but a
matter of something more intricate and ingrained and vital to
her work. Knowing Lowell allowed her to play out—as she had
with Moore—little private dramas of disobedience which
seemed to nourish the discomfited poems she was writing: "The

Bight," "The Prodigal," "Over 2,000 Illustrations and a Complete Concordance." There were, in fact, two Lowells for her—one the disciplined productive poet against whom she could test and explore her anarchic side and the other who actually provided her with suggestive models of how to do the testing and exploring. In a New Year's letter in 1948 she teases and defers to Lowell: "I shall try to profit by your stern example." Or again, thanking him after a visit to Washington, she remarks that Lowell had "jerked" her up "to the proper table-level of poetry." The following January, expressing her fears about the Library of Congress appointment, she writes: "I've always felt that I've written poetry more by *not* writing it than writing it, and now this Library business makes me really feel like the 'poet by default.' "

Bishop liked to represent herself as wayward to other poets, especially to men. "When I think about it," she wrote years later to James Merrill, "it seems to me I've *rarely* written anything of any value at the desk or in the room where I was supposed to be doing it—it's always in someone else's house, or in a bar, or standing up in the kitchen in the middle of the night." It was in her early letters to Lowell that her self-consciousness about her writing habits, the sparsity of her published work, her slowness of composition became an enriching subject of curiosity to her. There, after all, was Lowell at the Library—arranging readings and recordings, visiting Pound and Williams, receiving Frost, writing biographies of the English poets, adding stanza after stanza to "The Mills of the Kavanaughs," or announcing with perfect aplomb in May of 1948 that he would have to put the long poem aside until September, as if the Muse were on regular call. Testing herself against his apparent self-discipline, Bishop began to sense the buried links between her writing peculiarities and what she felt as the isolation and anarchic drift of her life. She began to feel her very waywardness as a matter for nourishing poetic investigation—an instinct, still shadowed, about an imagined weakness that was yet to be unmasked as a strength.

Bishop had been asked to read at Wellesley—it would be a first reading for her—and wrote to ask Lowell's advice. In the course of her letter a miniature psychic drama is played out.

I take your remarks about writing a lot *now* very much to heart & I'd like to look forward to a long stretch of nothing but work. I've been sick most of the last month—asthma—it doesn't completely incapacitate one but is a nuisance. Well—I was asked to speak at Wellesley, too, on March 22—and at the time I accepted. Now I am wondering if it is really worth it to go all the way back North at that time of year . . .

Then, after a few other reasons, it comes down to:

This is in confidence—I'm sort of scared. But I remember the little you told me about your speaking experiences in Washington cheered me up tremendously and I suppose I should or must begin sometime . . . Seldon [*sic*] Rodman has written and wants me to come to Haiti— I would board, it seems, with Margaret Sanger! He has a jeep and knows all the little villages where the painters and poets live and I know it would be beautiful, but—you can imagine why I hesitate. I suppose it is too good an opportunity to pass up and . . . I seem to be talking to you like Dorothy Dix but that is because *you* apparently are able to do the right thing for *yourself* and your work and don't seem tempted by the distractions of travelling—that rarely offers much at all in respect to work. I guess I have liked to travel as much as I have because I have always felt isolated and have known so few of my "contemporaries" and nothing of "intellectual" life in New York or anywhere. Actually it may be all to the good.

Anyone, with hindsight, would say that in this passage Bishop glides toward her own true north, that it was "all to the good." Some years later these questions of travel were to supply Bishop with a new life and material for a whole book of poems. But it was the openness and confusion that mattered in 1948 and Lowell's presence forcing it forward.

A paragraph later in the same letter she starts describing Key West:

The water looks like blue gas—the harbor is always a mess here, junky little boats all piled up, some hung with sponges and always a few half sunk or splintered up from the most recent hurricane—it reminds me a little of my desk.

A few months later that nugget of description had passed into the opening of one of Bishop's best poems, "The Bight":

At low tide like this how sheer the water is.
White, crumbling ribs of marl protrude and glare
and the boats are dry, the pilings dry as matches.
Absorbing, rather than being absorbed,
the water in the bight doesn't wet anything,
the color of the gas flame turned as low as possible.

The letter's detail about the littered desk is wonderfully concealed, changed, and charged by a pun in the final version of the poem:

Some of the little white boats are still piled up
against each other, or lie on their sides, stove in,
and not yet salvaged, if they ever will be, from the last
      bad storm,
like torn-open, unanswered letters.
The bight is littered with old correspondences.

Of all the correspondences in this ramshackle scene, only the poem's bracketed subtitle—[*On my birthday*]—insists on the deeper anxieties "The Bight" draws upon. The poem crystallizes out of a letter to Lowell about her writing, her apparently aimless life, her sense of being a "poet by default," though unlike her letter to Lowell it faces these feelings with a certain gaiety. Or to put it another way, the letter to Lowell is part of a dialogue which engaged her in her poetry. His example was among the provocations to a series of remarkable descriptive poems in which Bishop explored her isolation and its compulsive link—only lightly touched upon in her letter—to travel. "The Bight," "Over 2,000 Illustrations and a Complete Concordance," "At the Fishhouses," "Cape Breton," and "The Prodigal," all poems of the period 1947–50, are early and important attempts to naturalize her homelessness. These landscape poems, which sometimes seemed to her inseparable from a wasted and wandering life, mimed back feelings otherwise unavailable.

Bishop had written to Lowell that she was worried lest she "have only two poetic spigots, marked *H & C*." With an odd mixture of envy and irritation she remarked of Jarrell, "Of course he has all the material in this world." She needn't have had misgivings about what seemed the limitations of a primarily descriptive style. Even before *North & South* appeared, she had turned a poetic corner. She had found a way to make description serve the purposes narrative served for others. Terming herself a "minor female Wordsworth" was her self-mocking recognition of the links between her landscapes and autobiographical writing. But the terrain she was describing—North and South, Nova Scotia and Florida—drew to the surface unexamined feelings about her parentage and the irregularity of her life.

In August 1946, and again in the summers of 1947 and 1948, Bishop had visited Nova Scotia and Cape Breton. She stayed in Great Village, where her mother came from and where she herself had spent her virtually parentless childhood in her maternal grandparents' home. These visits to Nova Scotia—her first in many years—would reverberate over the rest of her writing life. She wrote to Marianne Moore that she had forgotten how beautiful it was there. We can judge the intensity of her feelings from the persistent recall of details that first turn up in letters of the 1940s and from their delayed slow absorption into her work. She saved these recollections for years, some of them not coming to the surface until her very last book, *Geography III* (1976): Great Village with its elms, the big farm collies, the Bay of Fundy with its salt marshes and long lavender-pink tides. In 1946 she came back to the United States on a bus: "We hailed it with a flashlight and a lantern as it went by the farm late at night. Early the next morning, just as it was getting light, the driver had to stop suddenly for a big cow moose who was wandering down the road." It was more than twenty-five years before she completed work on the poem that returns to that moment, "The Moose." By then she was able to make of the incident her most mysterious reweaving of the hitherto disparate elements of her Nova Scotian life: its losses, its domestic warmth, and its primitive nonhuman splendor.

There were family stories, too: reawakened memories, things her aunts told her. She tried in 1948 to write a story called "Homesickness," recalling an incident which happened to her mother that Bishop recounts in a letter to Anne Stevenson:

My mother went off to teach school at 16 (the way most of the enterprising young people did) and her first school was in lower Cape Breton somewhere—and the pupils spoke nothing much but Gaelic so she had a hard time of it at that school, or maybe one nearer home— she was so homesick she was taken the family dog to cheer her up.

Bishop was still working on the story fifteen years later and was never able to finish it. My point is that the Nova Scotia trips of the late 1940s made deep impressions upon her, seeded her future work, and yet there were only certain ways she was able to write about them at the time.

The letters she sent from a trip to Cape Breton in 1948 are bright with human detail, as was the story she tried to write about her mother's stay there as a young woman. But the poem that emerged from the trip, "Cape Breton," is of a landscape nearly abandoned, its busy domesticity almost concealed, the glimpses one gets of social rituals deliberately tantalizing and mysterious to the observer. The emotional center for her is the uncanny scrutiny of the landscape, her sense of something being withheld:

Whatever the landscape had of meaning appears to have been
    abandoned,
unless the road is holding it back, in the interior,
where we cannot see,
where deep lakes are reputed to be,
and disused trails and mountains of rock
and miles of burnt forests standing in gray scratches
like the admirable scriptures made on stones by stones—
and those regions now have little to say for themselves
except in thousands of light song-sparrow songs floating upward
freely, dispassionately, through the mist, and meshing
in brown-wet, fine, torn fish-nets.

Everything seen and heard in these lines is in fact unseen and unheard, imagined from the merest hints of what is "reputed to be." Bishop gives us an odd troped version of what separates us from natural experience—odd because her tropes, a simile and a metaphor, dramatize what is hidden in terms of humanizing activity, creations, a primitive alphabet, song. Her terms suggest some smoldering sought-out meaning—revelation, "admirable scripture"—and they refer us with those daring repetitions of words Bishop is fond of (the kind of thing we are warned away from in elementary grammar), repetitions that for a moment tease us into some sense of plain identity between human speech and things: "the admirable scriptures made on stones by stones"; "light song-sparrow songs floating upward."

It is this kind of description—disturbed, patient, expectant scrutiny of abandoned Northern scenes—that Bishop was writing in the late 1940s. As for narratives, the painful *stories* about her own childhood, these were yet to be written. She would attempt them only in the 1950s after she had safely and happily taken up a life in Brazil that in part recalled the restorative warmth, intimacy, and scale of her Nova Scotia village. Descriptive poems like "At the Fishhouses," "Cape Breton," and parts of "Over 2,000 Illustrations and a Complete Concordance" were for her at the time more potent than narrative, and preceded it. Submission to the Northern landscape—its ancient

emptiness, the dwarfed intimacies of its human communities—
was like relearning a forgotten harmonic scale. At its best the
experience subsumed inescapable human pain into deep per-
spectives like those at the end of "At the Fishhouses." There,
having immersed herself in details of the isolated powerful
scene, eroded and silvered over by the sea, Bishop envisions
intense transformations of the four elements, as if herself absorbed in their cycle. Behind her are the "bluish" firs, imagined
vestiges of Christianity, "a million Christmas trees . . . waiting
for Christmas"; before her the sea "icily free above the stones":

> If you should dip your hand in,
> your wrist would ache immediately,
> your bones would begin to ache and your hand would burn
> as if the water were a transmutation of fire
> that feeds on stones and burns with a dark gray flame.
> If you tasted it, it would first taste bitter,
> then briny, then surely burn your tongue.
> It is like what we imagine knowledge to be:
> dark, salt, clear, moving, utterly free,
> drawn from the cold hard mouth
> of the world, derived from the rocky breasts
> forever, flowing and drawn, and since
> our knowledge is historical, flowing, and flown.

Lowell, when he read the poem in *The New Yorker*, recognized immediately the "great splendor" of the descriptive
part, but questioned "a little the word BREAST [sic] in the last
four or five lines—a little too much in its context perhaps; but
I'm probably wrong." What he picked up, of course, was the
flicker of human drama, of a vestigial implacable female presence behind the scene—as in *The Prelude* when the young
Wordsworth's landscape is suddenly and unintentionally shadowed by feelings which have to do with his dead parents. That,
no doubt, is why Bishop's poem has often been felt as Wordsworthian in its evasions and circlings. Originally "At the Fishhouses" began with more details about Bishop's grandfather,

but her revisions suggest the degree to which she chose not to overstress the poem's human and personal center. Her eye, as Howard Moss suggests, is a *dramatic* eye; yet she often experiences traditional dramatic problems—character, comic or tragic action—by fitting out a stage for them, a stage upon which the protagonists will not necessarily appear. By the end of "At the Fishhouses" Bishop's own place as protagonist is apparent; her sense of being an outsider is powerfully banished at the cost of identifying herself with severe, if universal, natural laws. These Nova Scotia and Cape Breton poems anticipate the stories of her childhood, a subject which up to this point she had only approached obliquely in surrealist versions—in "The Baptism" and in "The Farmer's Children."

But what was missing in her Northern landscape poems of this time, and what only became fully available to her in the stories of 1953 written after she'd settled in Brazil, was the remembered recuperative power of village life. In 1947 and 1948 domestic stability seemed locked in the past. Its landscapes were remote from the adult life she was leading—the congenial untidiness of Key West, reflected in "The Bight," the sense of waste she describes to Lowell. Bishop's letters to him from Key West are full of gay truancy. She mocks herself as a kind of female Hemingway who plays pool and goes to cockfights:

The only intellectual life here, I gather, is taking place below stairs at the Casa Marina (that's the $40 a day hotel—where Seldon [sic] stayed, and where the tennis stars are). The little Polish tennis assistant, who seemed to be Seldon's amie of the moment, came to see me, bringing me his poems, and riding on a huge boy's bicycle all headlights and horns & flags, etc. She said it belonged to the head dishwasher there (who also has a *horse*) and that he is avidly reading Seldon's poems and wants to get hold of mine—all the dishwashers do. (When Seldon came to my party he brought along the tennis champs and the elevator boy and the newspaper concession girl—all modern poetry addicts, I gathered.) Maybe I should move out to the Casa Marina as a scullery maid. The Polish girl of course writes poetry, too—I think she said one every night.

The poets multiply like the false Henry IVs in battle at Shrewsbury. All this is recounted in the same letter in which Bishop speaks of herself as a "poet by default." In the letters she may treat her situation wryly, comically. But this life, refracted in poems such as "Over 2,000 Illustrations and a Complete Concordance" and "The Prodigal," is felt distinctly as a dereliction.

It was in the alert haunted squalor of "The Prodigal" that Bishop acknowledged a great deal that she owed to Lowell, both to his poems and to their shared darker moods. There was a little time-telling refrain, an audit of their respective ages, that they tapped back and forth just after Lowell's two-week visit to her in Maine in 1948. To Lowell's "Thirty-One / Nothing Done," Bishop responded, "Thirty-seven and far from heaven." Characteristically, in his self-mockery Lowell leaves room for the effects of work and ambition. Bishop had a more settled pessimism and was more reticent about expressing it—constitutionally so, but also because in their encounters she was unnerved when Lowell exaggerated his loneliness. She wrote to a friend earlier that summer:

It seems to me that Cal isn't nearly as much alone as most of the artists I know—that all artists have to go through long stretches of it, at least. Maybe I'm just saying that because this is certainly one for me; I am beginning to feel like Admiral Byrd.

And she wrote to Lowell himself:

I think you said a while ago that I'd "laugh you to scorn" on some conversation you . . . had had about how to protect oneself against solitude and ennui—but indeed I wouldn't. That's just the kind of "suffering" I'm most at home with & helpless about, I'm afraid . . . Sometime I wish we could have a more sensible conversation about this suffering business, anyway. I imagine we actually agree fairly well—it is just that I guess I think it is so inevitable & unavoidable there's no use talking about it, & that in itself it has no value, anyway—as I think Jarrell says at the end of "90 North," or somewhere. ["Pain comes from the darkness / And we call it wisdom. It is pain."]

She finds ways to deflect the subject—sometimes with a shrug ("I've really got it bad & think I'll write you a note before I go out & eat some mackerel"). Or, in the same letter, with an almost pointless anecdote—pointless except to assert a grim balance:

I like this story from the N.Y. Times—a composition by a child in the 3rd grade: "I told my little brother that when you die you cannot breathe and he did not say a word. He just kept on playing."

She then tells Lowell she thinks Eliot is one of the few living writers who can portray suffering convincingly—"& then I don't even like him when he gets that oh-so resigned tone." She is indignant about the end of Auden's poem "Musée des Beaux Arts": even if it is describing a painting, "I think it's just plain inaccurate . . . —the ploughmen and the people on the boat will rush to see the falling boy any minute, they always do, though maybe not to help . . . Oh well—I want to see what you'll think of my 'Prodigal Son.' "

In the midst of her resistance to Lowell's talk of his isolation, she has in fact been writing a poem about her own, a way of acknowledging a temperamental affinity too precarious to indulge. She was attracted to Lowell's grimmer imaginings if only she could absorb them at her own pace. "The Prodigal Son" was finally ready three years later and published as "The Prodigal," a title that was a shade more personal. "First I think it's too much like a Lowell then I think it isn't at all, then it seems to be again . . ." It was a poem she first mentioned in May 1948, one that she worked hard on that summer, and one to which she was at least partly prodded by a series of exchanges with Lowell that year.

He had sent her at New Year's a small private-press selection of poems by Tristan Corbière, with *en face* translations by Walter McElroy. (The book had attracted both Lowell and Jarrell and encouraged the latter to produce some Corbière versions of his own. Jarrell, in a review, praised Corbière's language, a sort of living contradiction made up of "puns, mocking half-dead metaphors, parodied clichés, antitheses and paradoxes, idioms exploited on every level," praised his "wonderful toughness and irony and intelligence.") Bishop's reaction was characteristically wary. "Le Poète contumace," she said, was a marvelous poem. But some of the others were "unbearable"— "too much reality, as Eliot would say." "I can see in them the kind of thing one should try to/could do, but half-consciously shie [*sic*] away from." She had the same embarrassed interest in one of Lowell's own poems, "Thanksgiving's Over," a spin-off of Corbière, which he sent her the following month. She liked it very much but calls it "the most unbearable, greyest New York atmosphere . . . one wants to read it without really looking at it directly—that damned celluloid bird." His meter distracted her from a poem she was writing; his words "seem to be jostling each other's shoulders."

Lowell had been reading Corbière's "Le Poète contumace" after finishing his own "Mother Marie Therese," and he wrote to Bishop: "I felt with a shock all the things he could say that I couldn't. So this came—not much like Corbière, but starting there." Lowell picked up the macabre side of Corbière's poem but, as he himself recognized, none of its gaiety or rapid changes of tone, however much he envied them. The idea of the *poète maudit* always appealed to Lowell as a way of identifying his own generation, and Corbière's poem is very much a Baudelairean night piece, the desperate amused wooing of a dead Lilith—or is she the Muse? But "Thanksgiving's Over" is much more locked into hallucination and private nightmare than Corbière's poem was. Its protagonist, Michael, dreams one Thanksgiving night of his insane wife, dead that year. Most of the poem is devoted to her imagined monologue, the wife scourging a guilt-ridden husband in a phantasmagoria of religious mania and sexual recrimination that issues in her leap from their Third Avenue window and eventual death in a sanatorium.

However "averted" (her own word for it) Bishop's eyes were from such poems, certain Lowell images drew her: the "celluloid and bargain cockatoo" on the wife's window pull; or the wife's vigil-candle described as a caged bird, like the wife herself ("Bars / shielded her vigil-candle, while it burned / Pin-beaded, indigo; / A bluebird in a tumbler"). One discouraging day, in Maine, Bishop writes Lowell, "There is a small lobster-pond with four posts at the corners that reminds me strongly of your sunken bedstead-grave." She is thinking of something toward the end of the then unfinished "Mills of the Kava-naughs": "as your disheartened shadow tries / The buried bedstead, where your body lies."

It was not simply that Bishop had some of Lowell's images in her head but that in this telling year he had given her a way of talking about her own instability and had implicitly challenged her to do so. When Bishop calls herself a "poet by default," she is alluding to the English title—not the best translation—of "Le Poète contumace" in the Corbière selection Lowell had given her, and to the train of imagery attached to it:

> —*Manque de savoir-vivre extrême—il survivait—*
> *Et—manque de savoir-mourir—il écrivait . . .*

> For want of knowing how to live, he kept alive—
> For want of knowing how to die, he wrote . . .

The English version of these two lines is by Randall Jarrell, and whatever suspicions Bishop had of the Corbière mode she focused upon Jarrell:

Jarrell's poetry seems to be getting more and more diffuse . . . I'm afraid Corbière has been a bad influence on him, bringing out more and more of his rather maudlin, morbid streak— Maybe it's a combination of Corbière and trying to write NOT like Cal.

"The Prodigal" was the poem in which, I think, Bishop sorted things out for herself, a kind of meditation on these literary currents and on a mood she somewhat shared with the two male poets. But, most important, it reflects on the tension she must have been feeling between her Key West life and the newly awakened memories of Nova Scotia.

[126

The brown enormous odor he lived by
was too close, with its breathing and thick hair,
for him to judge. The floor was rotten; the sty
was plastered halfway up with glass-smooth dung.
Light-lashed, self-righteous, above moving snouts,
the pigs' eyes followed him, a cheerful stare—
even to the sow that always ate her young—
till, sickening, he leaned to scratch her head.
But sometimes mornings after drinking bouts
(he hid the pints behind a two-by-four),
the sunrise glazed the barnyard mud with red;
the burning puddles seemed to reassure.
And then he thought he almost might endure
his exile yet another year or more.

But evenings the first star came to warn.
The farmer whom he worked for came at dark
to shut the cows and horses in the barn
beneath their overhanging clouds of hay,
with pitchforks, faint forked lightnings, catching light,
safe and companionable as in the Ark.
The pigs stuck out their little feet and snored.
The lantern—like the sun, going away—
laid on the mud a pacing aureole.
Carrying a bucket along a slimy board,
he felt the bats' uncertain staggering flight,
his shuddering insights, beyond his control,
touching him. But it took him a long time
finally to make his mind up to go home.

Some of the details, Bishop realized later, came from Lowell. In "The pigs stuck out their little feet and snored," she was half remembering the spiders thrown into the fire in Lowell's "Mr. Edwards and the Spider": "There's no long struggle, no desire / To get up on its feet and fly— / It stretches out its feet / And dies." A small reminiscence on Bishop's part, but revealing. Her poem is touched throughout by Lowell's taste for allegory, but she turns Lowell's spiders, indifferently submissive to apocalypse, into a more homely version of unthinking brute survival. The frightening part of Bishop's poem is its air of sanity—two nicely rhymed sonnets—its ease and attractiveness only just keeping down panic and fear. She is so alive to the attractions of the world that represents her undoing—those light-lashed eyes of the pigs, the glass-smooth dung, the glazed mud. Here are no lightning tests of the will but instead a pleasant eroding daily damnation, no less infernal than Lowell's recall of Edwards's hellfire, but seductively hard to identify in those pints hidden behind a two-by-four and in the flicker of forked lightning on the pitchforks. The prodigal lives as with averted gaze, defined only by the pigs' eyes following him or by feeling the bats' "uncertain staggering flight."

Bishop's is the sort of fluid landscape Lowell admired in Corbière, one that darted almost unnoticeably from outer to inner weather and back. So, in Bishop's opening line, "lived by" is both a stage direction and a creed, as if the "brown enormous odor" were the prodigal's very breath. "Light-lashed," with faint erotic suggestions of wakening, as Anthony Hecht once pointed out to me, sustains the impression of action tellingly internalized. Knowledge comes in glints, the barnyard floor the uncertain screen on which life is literally projected. Its glazed mud and burning puddles are taken as signs of a reassuring sunrise. The prodigal knows the lantern by the "pacing aureole" it "laid on the mud." The teasing colors of salvation are merely plastered on by comparison with the solid world of the cows and horses secure in their barn, an Ark, a little heavenly landscape of its own with "overhanging clouds of hay." Time is elusive for the prodigal: he thought he *almost* might endure; it took him a long time *finally* to make his mind up. Everything is extended, except, of course, the horrible decisiveness of the sow that *always* ate her young or the paternal dependability of the farmer, a Noah who religiously locks away his brood each night.

Yet it is hard to know what it might mean for the prodigal "finally to make his mind up to go home." *Home* is the one

line ending without a true rhyme. The only images of domesticity are directed to the animal world: the violent mother (the
sow that always ate her young) and the loving grandfatherly
farmer who seals his animals comfortably in their Ark. One is
a child's nightmare; the other, a child's fantasy of security,
threats reduced to the faint forked lightnings caught by the
pitchforks. Like another great poem of this period, "Over 2,000
Illustrations and a Complete Concordance," "The Prodigal" is
suspended between revived childhood memory and what adult
life offers as if randomly, aimlessly. The two worlds seem definitively locked off from each other in imagination. It is not
odd that poems about exile and instability should include such
potentially restorative images. What is odd is that they presented
themselves to Bishop in such an unavailable form, a child's
miniature or tableau sealed off from adult suffering. The worlds
of parodied family intimacy and of the prodigal lie side by side,
but separate, as if waiting for a spark to pass.

At the close of "Over 2,000 Illustrations," the weary adult
traveler turns away from her real travels ("Everything only
connected by 'and' and 'and' ") to biblical illustrations recalled
from childhood.

> Everything only connected by "and" and "and."
> Open the book. (The gilt rubs off the edges
> of the pages and pollinates the fingertips.)
> Open the heavy book. Why couldn't we have seen
> this old Nativity while we were at it?
> —the dark ajar, the rocks breaking with light,
> an undisturbed, unbreathing flame,
> colorless, sparkless, freely fed on straw,
> and, lulled within, a family with pets,
> —and looked and looked our infant sight away.

The passage is true to a whole penumbra of desire. You
can hear the disappointed traveler who remained indifferent
while she was "at it" to any signs of Immanence the old Bible
had prepared her to find in the desert, a traveler beset by in-

coherence and the final terror at the yawning grave of a prophet. You can also hear the young girl whose "vision" was equivocal from the start, domesticity being more real for her in the illustrated Nativity of the family Bible than in her own parentless childhood.

> The eye drops, weighted, through the lines
> the burin made, the lines that move apart
> like ripples above sand,
> dispersing storms, God's spreading fingerprint . . .

tool used for engraving

We know from something Bishop wrote some years later—and to which we shall return—how directly those lines were prompted by reawakened memories of Nova Scotia: "As a child, I used to look at my grandfather's Bible under a powerful reading-glass. The letters assembled beneath the lens were suddenly . . . as big as life and as alive, and rainbow-edged. It seemed to illuminate as it magnified; it could also be used as a burning-glass." Such feelings were obviously close to the surface back in 1948—the religious awe that links "God's spreading fingerprint" of her poem to the remembered rainbow edge of letters under the glass as the Bible page comes alive, magnified, illuminated. A grandfather-god presides. Yet, in the formal arrangement of Bishop's poem, such memories are strictly cordoned off from adult life, unavailing, displaced as a childlike fantasy.

In the eccentric phrasing of the closing lines, she thinks of the old Nativity, "the dark ajar," as if a door through which the excluded child witnesses "the rocks breaking with light." With images reminiscent of the impassioned close of "At the Fishhouses," among that earlier poem's fires that "feed on stones," she sets her childlike tableau, as protected as Brünnhilde, "lulled within, a family with pets." All this is witnessed with a swoon of desire, an infant's undistinguishing desire and envy, an implied dimming of sight, and, if "infant" keeps its Latin root (Bishop had originally written "silent"), speechlessness.

———

"I am very sick of sounding so quiet," Bishop wrote Lowell at the time she sent him this poem. Whether this complaint of hers was genuine or not, the poem itself was a way of focusing her attraction to him and to his "black-tongued piratical vigor." Certainly he helped release and shape the discontent she expressed in key poems of these years. But in 1947 and 1948 her responses to him were more wholehearted and charged than any single connection might suggest. His poems disturbed and challenged her. She talked about them as if they were things to be *undergone*, as with the "sense of horror and panic" in his Werfel imitation, "The Fat Man in the Mirror." "The Mills of the Kavanaughs" was "one of the most harrowing things I've ever read." But Lowell drew from her an ardor that she identified with her youthful experience of books. Reading his "dream poem" ("Falling Asleep over the Aeneid") was like reading Macaulay when she was little, or some plays of Dryden: "it has so much richness and almost gaiety in spite of its subject." Bishop wrote Lowell that she found his poetry "so strongly influential that if I start reading it when I'm working on something of my own I'm lost." Putting it that way confirms her resistance as much as his influence. It would be useless to try and separate—as Bishop herself could not—what she valued in Lowell from the reactions to his work which made her more herself. She would write years later to Anne Stevenson, apropos the work of Webern, Klee, and Schwitters (she owned a Schwitters in Brazil): "I don't care much for grand, all-out efforts— but on the other hand, I sometimes *do* . . . I admire Robert Lowell's poetry very much and much of Lord Weary's Castle couldn't be more all-out." And with similar ambivalence, again to Anne Stevenson:

Most of my poems I can still abide were written before I met Robert Lowell or had read his first book. However, since then he has influenced me a great deal, in many ways. He is one of the very few people I can talk to about writing freely & naturally, and he is wonderfully quick, intuitive, modest, and generous about it. With the exception of Marianne, however, almost all my friends up until Cal (Lowell), and since, have not been writers.

In the same letter she remarks that she admires Emily Dickinson for "having dared to do it, all alone." ("I still hate the oh-the-pain-of-it-all poems, but I admire many others, and mostly phrases more than whole poems.") Dickinson's "doing it all alone" was "a bit like" Bishop's own beloved Hopkins. "I have a poem about them comparing them to two self-caged birds, but it's unfinished."

Whether Bishop was tempted by or feared being a "self-caged bird" herself, her friendship with Lowell definitively guaranteed that she would never be one. She had often felt trapped by the fact that her poems were largely brief and few, and indignant about the condescension she experienced as a "female poet." She may also have felt somewhat restive about the constant public association with Moore—not just the "maidenly" image, but Moore's increasingly eccentric public behavior. (Though Bishop could remark a little harshly to Lowell, in 1948, that Marianne appeared to be "entering upon the prophetic stage," she and Moore were never estranged and would continue their loving exchanges until the end.) Then, too—a problem she shared with others of her generation—writing lyrics as she did must have seemed, at least as reflected in the public eye, a shrunken literary gesture. Lowell, on the other hand, acted as if this problem didn't exist. His lyrics—"all-out," as Bishop said—seemed like splintered epics. When Bishop came to know him he was writing narrative fables of decay. The constantly swelling "Mills of the Kavanaughs" amazed and intimidated her. More important than any of Lowell's images or rhythms she was likely to assimilate, Lowell also put her in touch with strong ambitions she couldn't or wouldn't have identified with in herself. He was really a talismanic figure who made it seem one could be an ambitious poet without writing something as massive as Pound's *Cantos* or Williams's *Paterson*.

Bishop's first taste of this must have been Lowell's review of *North & South* in *The Sewanee Review*. Few first books have been so immediately praised and understood as Bishop's was. Randall Jarrell's review in *Partisan Review*, which preceded Lowell's, was particularly discriminating about her tone: "Instead of crying, with justice, 'This is a world in which you can't get along,' Miss Bishop's poems show that it is barely but perfectly possible—has been, that is, for her." Lowell, on the other hand, addresses the book from the cool high slopes of Parnassus, his sweeping authoritative praise couched in a prose itself greedy for comparisons and judgments: the first of Bishop's "Songs for a Colored Singer" is "of the same quality as MacNeice's 'Bagpipe Music' and Auden's wonderful 'Refugee Blues' "; "Roosters" and "The Fish" are "large and perfect and, outside of Marianne Moore, the best poems that I know of written by a woman in this century." (How did Bishop respond to that?!) Lowell even rated the poems in descending order. But Bishop found the heart of the review immediately and thanked him for the insight: "It's the first review I've had that attempted to find any general drift or consistency in the individual poems and I was beginning to feel there probably wasn't any at all. It is the only review that goes at things in what *I* think is the right way." Lowell read the poems with a vigorous allegorical temper which intrigued her as much as her apparent down-to-earthness mystified him. When he first read "At the Fishhouses," he wrote her, "I'm a fisherman myself, but all my fish become symbols, alas."

Lowell's review of *North & South* has almost the air of a psychological profile, an unnerving perception of patterns the writer herself might be only dimly aware of. He not only described her published book but seemed uncannily to be describing her divided state of mind in the years after *North & South* appeared. It also seemed an assurance that the poems were indeed part of a larger work. Ardent symbolist that he was at the time, Lowell was not to be deterred by surface.

On the surface, her poems are observations—surpassingly accurate, witty, and well arranged, but nothing more . . . One is reminded of Kafka and certain abstract paintings, and is left rather at sea about the actual subjects of the poems. I think that at least nine-tenths of them fall into a single symbolic pattern. Characterizing it is an elusive business.

There are two opposing factors. The first is something in motion, weary but persisting, almost always failing and on the point of dis-integrating, and yet, for the most part, stoically maintained. This is morality, memory, the weed that grows to divide, and the dawn that advances, illuminates, and calls to work, the monument "that wants to be a monument," the waves rolling in on the shore, breaking, and being replaced, the echo of the hermit's voice saying, "Love must be put in action"; it is the stolid little mechanical horse that carries a dancer, and all those things of memory that "cannot forget us half so easily as they can forget themselves." The second factor is a terminus: rest, sleep, fulfillment, or death. This is the imaginary iceberg, the moon which the Man-moth thinks is a small clean hole through which he must thrust his head; it is sleeping on the top of a mast, and the peaceful ceiling: "But oh, that we could sleep up there."

The motion-process is usually accepted as necessary and, there-fore, good; yet it is dreary and exhausting. But the formula is mys-terious and gently varies with its objects. The terminus is sometimes pathetically or humorously desired as a letting-go or annihilation; sometimes it is fulfillment and the complete harmonious exercise of one's faculties. The rainbow of spiritual peace seen as the author de-cides to let a fish go, is both like and unlike the moon which the Man-moth mistakes for an opening.

This is an astonishing piece of criticism because it is so inward with Bishop's poems and because it so accurately de-scribes the nature of the divided human who is so often their protagonist. Lowell suggests clearly the terms in which Bishop was experiencing her conflicts—and this at a time when, though they had met, he didn't know her well or know very much about her. At that moment, in 1947, Lowell's insight was ex-tremely valuable for Bishop, and reinforced her need to *use* her waywardness as a poetic strategy.

2 / The Summer of 1948

The privileged nature of the early years of the friendship between Bishop and Lowell had almost as much to do with the moment of their encounter as it did with their considerable gifts. Those first years stood as prologue to the more settled attachments of their lives—Lowell's marriage to Elizabeth Hardwick, Bishop's long stay in Brazil with Lota de Macedo Soares. Distance kept their friendship fresh, gave it a certain immunity, allowed it an imaginative space outside the abrasions of an intimate daily life. Bishop was the one close friend who was at some remove from the series of breakdowns that began for Lowell in 1949 and were to return with alarming frequency in the fifties. (She was in Key West when Lowell was first hospitalized and probably saw him only once before he and Elizabeth Hardwick left for Europe in September 1950; by the time they were back, and during the most concentrated period of attacks, she had settled in Brazil.)

For Lowell, 1948 was the telling year in their relationship; in retrospect it must have seemed to him a period slightly outside time. Though Lowell's life was already shadowed by the pressures that brought on his first breakdown, his friendship with Bishop was relatively free of them. It gave him—at least momentarily—the illusion of a fresh start without the taint of his knotted personal history of the preceding few years. It at least *seemed* to be a relationship in which emotional and literary needs were taking shape simultaneously, pleasurably, naturally.

Lowell's intense efforts of the forties had begun to take their toll. To find his poetic vein in *Land of Unlikeness* and *Lord Weary's Castle*, to focus the anger and irritations of his early years, he had narrowed his work both emotionally and stylistically, passed quite deliberately through the needle's eye of his denunciatory mode. As his ambitions clarified—the epic Miltonic ambitions and the religious and political convictions that supported them—the strain too must have become more intense. A lot of his potential for life and variety—the liveliness one hears in his letters, the range of subjects he attempted in his earliest verse—had been choked off by the necessary and severe definition of his powers in the 1940s. No wonder he looked at Bishop's verse with a certain curiosity and relief.

Lowell often grew by assimilating the work of other writers—appropriating stories and styles of his friends or befriending those he learned from. It was precisely Bishop's *difference* that made him seek her out as a poetic ally. But she was a more resistant figure than the male poets he admired. He had sent *North & South* to George Santayana and then wrote Bishop that he and she and Trumbull Stickney were the only modern poets Santayana liked at all. Santayana's comment was in fact more complicated and didn't entirely satisfy Lowell:

I liked *North & South* especially for its delicacy. If it were not for the Darling Woman who is looking for a husband that shall be monogamous, I should have thought that Elizabeth Bishop had little sense of reality: but I see that she sees the reality of psychic atmosphere or sentiment in their overtones, and prefers for the most part to express that. It is very nice, but a little elusive.

"Of course, he's all wrong about your sense of reality," Lowell wrote in forwarding the comment to Bishop. "I guess he'd like your new poems best."

Santayana missed what Lowell most prized and puzzled

over in Bishop's work. In his review of *North & South* Lowell had praised the "splendor and minuteness" of Bishop's descriptions, but he was intrigued not so much with the descriptive gift in itself as by its direction, the "sense of reality"—what Santayana called the "reality of psychic atmosphere"—that Lowell could only define by contrasting her with other poets. For example, her connection to Moore was obvious. "Both poets use an elaborate descriptive technique, love exotic objects, are moral, genteel, witty, and withdrawn." Yet Bishop was "softer, dreamier, more human, and more personal . . . less idiosyncratic, and less magnificent." Lowell felt her to be "present in her poems; they happen to her, she speaks, and often centers them on herself."

In her "bare objective language" she reminded him of William Carlos Williams. Yet Williams's brand of realism brought Lowell and Bishop to one of their first disagreements. Bishop objected to Williams's extensive use in *Paterson* of angry reproving letters from a young woman poet who felt Williams had enticed her and then ignored her and her work. To Bishop, using the letters seemed "mean"; she refused to believe Richard Eberhart, who said in his review that they were made up. "They're much too overpowering emotionally for the rest of it," she wrote Lowell, "so that the whole poem suffers." *Paterson* had wonderful sections, but "I think Williams has always a streak of insensitivity . . .

and then maybe I've felt a little too much the way the woman did at certain more hysterical moments—people who haven't experienced absolute loneliness for long stretches of time can never sympathise with it at all.

Lowell could see that Bishop's letter sounded a note of authentic feeling and that the appropriation of realistic details could never be, for her, its own justification. In his reply he tried to meet Bishop on her own ground. Yes, the letters were terrifyingly and typically real. To read them straight through on their own would be "too monotonous, pathological." Yet in the poem they are "placed and not pathological, the agony is absorbed." He felt their purpose in the poem was in fact to show the narrator damned for his own insensitivity ("She's mad, but he, like Aeneas, can't handle her and shows up badly"). "*Paterson* has been like water to me," he adds, "and my judgment may be subjective."

The exchange over William Carlos Williams is clearly related to other aspects of their friendship: Bishop's finding "The Mills of the Kavanaughs" harrowing (she chose to praise the descriptive passages), her unwillingness to exploit her own loneliness in her verse—though clearly it was her association with Lowell that would press her to explore it, not long afterward, in "The Bight" and "The Prodigal." However affected she was by her friendship with Lowell, however much poems like "The Bight" and "The Prodigal" grew out of it, she saw a clear line between exploring loneliness and exploiting it and felt that Williams and Lowell did not always observe the distinction.

What Lowell valued in Bishop's work as her sense of reality had to do also with the reticence of her personal style, and with his taking this sense of reality—her writing poems more objective and more outgoing than his own—as a form of health. Lowell always felt both release and a challenge in the ease of Bishop's presence and expressed it with varying degrees of surprise and self-criticism: "You always make me feel that I have a rather obvious breezy, impersonal liking for the great and obvious—in contrast with your adult personal feeling for the odd and genuine." Or again, "You and Peter Taylor always make me feel something of a fake—so I love you both dearly." Or, simply: "You're so warm and friendly to me; it's such a joy seeing you." The authenticity of Bishop's manner (personal as well as in her writing) intrigued and challenged him. "She has gotten a world, not just a way of writing," he would say later, comparing her descriptive language in its abundance with that of the Russian novelists: "In [her] 'Man-Moth' a whole new world is gotten out and you don't know what will come after any one line. It's exploring." In 1948 there was a healthy confusion in his mind as to what was assimilable in a life, a style, at once resembling and yet so divergent from his own.

What was to crystallize these feelings was the two-week vacation Lowell spent, in August 1948, in Stonington, Maine, where Bishop had already settled for the summer. Lowell kept referring what he knew and felt about Bishop back to that brief holiday. For more than fifteen years, he turned the experience over in drafts of poems that mix curiosity and affection. The time in Stonington echoed—somewhat to Bishop's surprise—in their encounters as well, until in 1957, after the troubled visit Bishop paid to Lowell and Elizabeth Hardwick, again in Maine, some of the knots were at last untied. It was then that Lowell, finally accepting the choices each of them had made—or provoked by the ghost of what might have been—wrote Bishop, telling her that in 1948, nine years before, he had wanted, or thought he wanted, to marry her.

———

Bishop was spending the summer of 1948 in Maine, first at Wiscasset, which proved too much a showplace, "a museum town, and sound, sound asleep," and then, more congenial to her taste, at Stonington, a fishing town. Lowell knew the territory both from his youth and from the last years of his marriage to Jean Stafford ("In Maine your friends pour in like lava—hot from their cities"). He associated Stonington with a daydream of fishing for a living and with a yellow house he almost bought—Jean Stafford called it Fatso. He spent the second and third weeks of August in the boardinghouse where Bishop had settled. They were, in Lowell's words, "a crowd of three," since he had arranged a visit for Carley Dawson, an "older woman" with whom he had taken up in Washington and to whom he had introduced Bishop on her last trip through. Whether the affair was reaching its natural conclusion or whether Bishop's presence prompted a change in Lowell's behavior, Mrs. Dawson made a stormy departure just before the two weeks were up, "removed" from town by Bishop's friend Tommy Wanning. "It's all in *Adolphe*—a bit warmed up and romanticized but not much," Lowell wrote Bishop from Boston a few days after his departure, speaking of one of the more muddled love affairs in his life. Lowell met Mrs. Dawson during his term at the Library of Congress and in the wake of his romance with Gertrude Buckman (the one Jean Stafford wrote so bitterly about in "An Influx of Poets"). Carley Dawson had been the mistress of St.-John Perse—not an unattractive detail for Lowell—and Lowell's feelings about her were obviously intense and confused enough for him to have talked of marriage while he was still disentangling himself from the Buckman affair. The attachment had its regressive elements—probably welcome to Lowell at that troubled and lonely moment. Mrs. Dawson paints him as moody, ardent, a kind of captive toy wild pet (and smelling like a badger when she first met him, she told Bishop), eager to be sheltered and fed but coming and going as he pleased. (He was officially staying at the Cosmos Club.) By the time they got to Maine, Lowell had clearly built up some healthy resentments, and Bishop's presence seems to have been the catalyst to release them. Some years later, he remembered Mrs. Dawson only ironically, in lines that would be sifted out of a poem to be called "The Two Weeks' Vacation—For Elizabeth Bishop."

My old flame Mrs. D. (haunted us
"like a passion") with English voice
Mary Chess freshness
and her Madame du Barry
Black and burnt gold eyebrows.
In her air-blu "ski-suit"
Blouse, trousers, cape, and even gloves to match
She survived a whole day of
Deep-sea hand-lining
For cod, skate and skulpin
She made us bait her hooks.
Each morning Mrs. D. was there
To meet us with another crashing ensemble.
Mrs. D.

Irritation at her respectability is mixed with a certain swagger and cockiness—"All this for me!" he added in a later version of the description of Mrs. D.'s "ensembles":

> And on the next to last night
> I came down the corridor, in pajamas,
> No doubt arousing false hopes
> And said . . . Well, who cares, my old flame left;
> And I never heard from her ever after.

But whatever led up to Carley Dawson's departure is no more than a prologue to what really engaged Lowell (and eventually came to be material for better and less bitter verse)—the last day of his vacation, which he spent alone with Bishop.

Bishop remembers that they went fishing with her lobster-man landlord. Then they swam, or rather stood, "numb to the waist in the freezing cold water, but continuing to talk. If I were to think of any saint in his connection then it is St. Sebastian—he stood in a rocky basin of the freezing water sloshing it over his handsome youthful body and I could almost see the arrows sticking out of him." It was evidently that day that Bishop recounted the whole story of her childhood, her mother's insanity, her isolated life. Lowell's unvoiced response was one he turned over and over again in his mind for many years. "I assumed that it would be just a matter of time," he wrote her in 1957, "before I proposed and I half believed you would accept." Lowell's account in that letter of their day together in Stonington nine years before—I quote it at length later on—has something of the high romance of Yeats's story of falling in love over a shared tale of childhood misery ("It seemed that our two natures blent . . . / into the yolk and white of the one shell"). But Lowell was telling it in 1957 from the vantage point of his marriage to Elizabeth Hardwick (he was, that year, a new father) and from his knowledge of Bishop's attachment to Lota de Macedo Soares. It was an effort—movingly, after nine years—to seal off the romance, to keep it from blurring his relationship with Bishop, and to understand finally what he had been reaching out for in Stonington in 1948. Theirs had been a temperate passion, he writes her from Castine in 1957: "Our friendship really wasn't a courting, was really disinterested (bad phrase), really led to no encroachments."

That word—encroachment—turns up more ambiguously in a soliloquy Lowell drafted for Bishop, a kind of absolution he imagined her feeling on leaving Castine in 1957, a companion piece to his "confessional" letter. Bishop speaks:

> My uncertain fingers floated to my lip,
> I kissed them to you, and our fellowship
> Tore free from its encroachment like a star . . .

The lines, which Lowell later rejected, suggest more knotted feelings than Lowell's letter does. They remind us that memory sifts out complications, transposes intensities. Lowell himself speaks of being callous as well as timid back in 1948. Bishop's reactions that first summer—what little we know of them— were not unclouded. For one thing she was baffled at hearing from *other* people—never from Lowell himself—that he was in love with her, wanted to marry her. For another thing, it wasn't only his behavior with Mrs. Dawson that was alarming and out of control, and Bishop's responses to him are, at least in part, cautious. She found just before the Maine visit and perhaps at Mrs. Dawson's prompting that one of Lowell's letters "sounded a little excitable." After the Stonington episode, she wrote to Mrs. Dawson that she'd given up, for the moment, the idea of going to Yaddo because "I realize that if I want to remain friends with Cal at all I'd better not see him for some time." And even allowing for the fact that Bishop was writing to the woman Lowell had injured, it is odd that she chose to write frequently to her at this point. As if this were someone whose experience she could take as a warning and against whose opinions about Lowell she could clarify her own—and as if the very act of writing Mrs. Dawson might strengthen her confused feelings, help her resist the obvious attraction.

Bishop's letters mix discomfiture with annoyance, but also betray something of the flirtation the whole episode had encouraged between her and Lowell. He had, on their day alone together, apologized to Bishop for involving her. But, as she explained to Mrs. Dawson,

We were both somewhat embarrassed, & I suppose wanted to avoid discussion, for different reasons—I was afraid I might get mad & say things that were none of my business & might spoil the somewhat precarious balance of our friendship, such as it is. I like to talk about poetry to him, & he is one of the very few other poets I know. —At present I have commissioned him to find me a rich husband in Washington—I think a nice comfy Oriental would do—one with lots of diamonds & absolutely no interest in the arts.

In the meantime, she received what must have been a long bill of complaint from Mrs. Dawson about her own affair with Lowell, and a note from Lowell—another apology, but teasing as well, with a list of proposed suitors (Theodore Roethke and Joseph Alsop among them) and plans to draw up a questionnaire to screen them.

Bishop's reply to Mrs. Dawson is suspicious in its tone and not so eager to play along with the notion that she had "commissioned" Lowell's list of suitors:

My one feeling just now about our better intellectuals is—*stay away.* It may be some comfort to you to know that I had a letter from C [Lowell] in the same mail & he has already begun to be "mean" to me, try to get "rises," etc.—it began even before he left, of course. He just can't help himself, I guess. I had thought that maybe I was "good for him"—maybe I am, but I think sooner or later I couldn't take any more of that ego-maniacy, or whatever it is—it's too bad, I do want to remain friends but I think it is going to require great care & fortitude & a rhinoceros-skin into the bargain. [*In margin:* And one can't remain completely objective always, you know.] One of his recent letters concluded, "Be a good girl & come to Yaddo." And that is all the poor dear knows about how to get along with people!

And later in the letter:

Tommy [Wanning] had C's number pretty well—I said something about how he seemed so confused & unhappy, & T. said "And how he loves it!"

It is not easy—or even necessary—to disentangle the complex feelings that built up over the Stonington visit and its aftermath. Bishop was not about to reveal to Mrs. Dawson any attraction she felt for the younger Lowell. Nor perhaps was she willing to acknowledge much of it to herself. She was taking some of Mrs. Dawson's experience as a warning. And besides, she was angry and embarrassed at what must have been something of a scandal in a small town. Rumors about it had already reached some of Lowell's friends ("Sordid Bohemian parties in Stonington with odd Bohemians drinking absinthe," he reported back to Bishop) and Bishop was doubly annoyed that he passed the gossip back to her. Lowell had been at a high pitch for much of his stay and very drunk the night of the final blowup. "It has all been very tough & I'd like to know what a good psychiatrist would make of it," Bishop wrote to Mrs. Dawson.

On the other hand, if Lowell's account of their day alone can be trusted, a great deal of the strain, before and after, must have come from their interest in one another. The flurry of teasing letters when he left Maine, the mutual joking about Bishop's "suitors," probably owed as much to Lowell's timidity about "proposing" as it did to his callousness or to roguishness. Bishop years later said that she *might* have married him, would even have wanted a child by him, but for the history of insanity in their families, and John Malcolm Brinnin remembers the look of dismay when he told Bishop—at Yaddo in the summer of 1949—that Lowell and Elizabeth Hardwick were to be married. The correspondence between Bishop and Lowell was intense until about February 1949, and then, of course, the Yaddo episode and Lowell's first breakdown shattered the mood. At its best there was an attractive ardor about the connection; Lowell, for example, sent her a German grammar as a gift and Bishop replied that it made her feel like the heroine of a George Eliot novel. As late as December 1948 Bishop wrote to Carley Dawson—once again one must take into consideration whom she was addressing—

As far as Cal goes, Carley—you know we confine our conversation to books & literary gossip; it is almost never personal & I like it best that way. He has never said anything about you since that one day in Stonington & I think that is probably right. And I imagine I'd understand that side of him as little as you do.

Lowell's own account of his delays in "proposing" to Bishop supports this, but also suggests how charged their meetings must have been. They were together two or three times that fall—without, as Lowell would put it, "encroachment." In early November there was a poetry weekend at Bard College. Lowell came down from Yaddo and roomed with Richard Eberhart; Bishop came up from New York with Loren MacIver and Lloyd Frankenberg and they stayed with friends nearby. On the first evening (Bishop reported a few days later to Carley Dawson) Dr. Williams read—"talked, rather, in a completely scatterbrained way." Next day Louise Bogan gave a talk and then

all the POETS were dragged up front around a table and you know *made points* and dragged in dynamos and for some reason the rhythm of milking a cow seemed to figure quite a lot, too—amounting in all to no more than each one's elucidating his own style but all very well received & everyone kept saying it was the best thing that ever happened at Bard. Those present were Richard Wilbur, Eberhart, Cal, Lloyd, Jean Garrigue, Williams and Miss B., me, & a wild man from California in a bright red shirt and yellow braces named Rexroth who did his best to start a fight with everyone and considered us all effete and snobbish easterners. He never quite succeeded and finally had to prove his mettle or his reality or something by taking three of the prettiest undergraduates off for an evening in the cemetery.

When the poets, unexpectedly, were asked to "read," Bishop begged off and had Lowell do it for her ("The Fish").

Lowell would remember, writing Bishop in 1957, going home drunk to the Bard poets' dormitory on the Saturday night of that weekend, holding Bishop's hand. Bishop remembered it more ironically. She and Elizabeth Hardwick had helped Lowell back to his room, taken off his shoes, loosened his tie, opened his shirt . . . At which point, in the version Bishop offered years later, Hardwick said, "Why, he's an Adonis"—and, Bishop went on wryly, "from then on I knew it was all over."

True or false, the story is faithful to the rhythm of their meetings that year: drinking, the evasion of intimacy, and, from late in the year on, Lowell's growing involvement with Elizabeth Hardwick. At the end of November—two weeks after Bard—both Bishop and Lowell went to hear T. S. Eliot lecture on Poe at the Library of Congress. Bishop had been "on the wagon for a long time." Only two nights before the lecture she had been "the only sober person present" at a "pretty wild and noisy" evening in New York with Lowell, Lloyd Frankenberg and Loren MacIver, and the Tates. She saw Lowell for a quiet lunch the next day, probably the last time she saw him alone before his breakdown. "He must get very dull at Yaddo and obviously has such a wonderful time making up for it when he gets away and is very overexcited, drinks too much, etc. —but there is something so childlike about his enjoying himself that I can't seem to mind, although I wished he'd looked a little better at the Washington affair."

In Washington it was Bishop's turn to be overexcited and start drinking. She'd come down from New York with her friend Pauline Hemingway, and they went to Eliot's lecture on Friday evening—the auditorium jammed, and Eliot looking "white & hot & exhausted." He managed to be quite funny at times, Bishop thought, but she was "a little disappointed" in what he said about Poe. "I spotted all the POETS in the reserved section—an impressive array," she wrote Carley Dawson (who was in San Francisco); most of them were "quite tight." At a party afterward she saw Lowell, though only briefly. Carley had offered the use of her apartment, and Bishop and Pauline Hemingway spent the night there. Then on Saturday, after Pauline had left for New York and shortly before she was to have met Lowell and Auden for lunch, Bishop's "troubles" began. She started drinking, alone in the apartment, and by the end of the day had polished off all the open bottles in the Dawson liquor cabinet. She became quite sick that night, called AA on Sunday, and got herself taken to a convalescent hospital, where she stayed five days. She was helpless to give an explanation. "I didn't even have so very much to drink (fortunately there wasn't much there)," she wrote Mrs. Dawson a few days later. "I'm so overcome with remorse before I even get drunk . . . and it's much more the mental aftermath than the physical." This sort of thing had happened before but was happening less frequently. Still, she'd felt it coming on a week or so earlier, after the Bard weekend and a Gotham Book Mart party—the famous one for the Sitwells and all the poets. "I think I had just been doing too much, seeing too many people, etc. —I get along better on boredom & adversity than on gaiety &, relatively speaking, success." Two weeks after the Washington episode she was still not feeling herself and decided not to visit Lowell at Yaddo, saying she "should probably avoid all intellectual excitement for a while."

Who knows how much of the stimulation was owing to Lowell and how much to the eddies and currents of the public poetry world in which he was so energetically involved and to which Bishop was so unaccustomed? Neither Bishop nor Lowell was very stable. For differing reasons, crests of euphoria and drinking kept the two of them from any sustained intimacy at a time when each might have been free to enjoy it. Whatever their conscious intentions, the encounters of 1948 served as a warning that, well matched as friends, they were destined to lead very different lives and needed different kinds of people as lovers and to take care of them. Lowell, at this point, probably didn't know that Bishop's sexual preferences were for women, nor would this necessarily have stopped her from becoming more deeply involved with him. But a lot of the evidence suggests that even as early as the Stonington episode and the blowup with Mrs. Dawson, Lowell's feelings toward women had reached a complicated point that in some ways anticipated his breakdown of the following year. Mrs. Dawson said that Lowell resented being sexually attracted to her, and certainly one element in Lowell's mania of 1949 was an obsession with sexual purity. It may have been precisely the *lack* of real sexual tension between him and Bishop that gave their relationship its special and lasting immunity. Peter Taylor remembers that in Bloomington, at the height of Lowell's religious mania, he gave Taylor for safekeeping a rosary and Bishop's photograph.

Whatever precipitated their mutual attraction, the summer of 1948—with all its vicissitudes—confirmed it. Conscious of and resistant to Lowell's melancholy, less obsessive than he about loneliness, Bishop nonetheless responded sympathetically and immediately to their conversations about it. And it was soon after Lowell's visit that she sent him, from Stonington, a draft of "The Prodigal," that poem of hers most openly indebted to his work.

3 / Prose

In November 1951 Bishop set out on a trip that would change the course of her life. She had won the first Lucy Martin Donnelly Fellowship from Bryn Mawr and sailed from New York on a Norwegian freighter (nine passengers) bound for the Straits of Magellan. Bishop had read a great deal about South America, and especially admired E. Lucas Bridges's *Uttermost Part of the Earth*, a book which, "although it is factual and not a fact of the imagination, should be classed with *Robinson Crusoe* for a suspense of strangeness and ingenuity and courage and loneliness." She envisioned herself as "a sleeping mouse dreaming of nibbling away to measure the circumference of a vast dream cheese." Loneliness, measurement, and dream—these were inseparable promptings which made her interest in travel seem, as her metaphor suggests, more like an appetite, a wary curiosity which guesses at, yearns for the interior from a tour of its circumference.

In Rio de Janeiro, Bishop stopped over to visit Brazilian friends. There, she had a violent allergic reaction to the fruit of the cashew and had to give up her dream trip to the Straits of Magellan. After she recovered, finding herself "enthralled by the Brazilian geography and landscape, by the paradoxical, affectionate, spontaneous Brazilian people, and the complications of a world at once feudal, 19th century, and contemporary," she decided to stay on and started building a country home (near Petrópolis, a mountain resort about forty miles from Rio) with Lota de Macedo Soares, an old friend whom she had first met in New York in 1942. For some fifteen years, with occasional visits to New York, Bishop shared with Lota their house in the mountains and an apartment in Rio de Janeiro. What began by accident, almost as a whim, soon became, thanks to Lota, a deep attachment. It was Lota who mediated Brazil for her, whose understanding and whose way of life made Bishop almost instantly a part of the world that so attracted her. Elizabeth Hardwick, who saw them often while she and Lowell were in Brazil in 1962, describes Lota as

witty indeed, civilized—and yet different from the women I had known. She had wonderful, glistening, dark eyes and wore glistening dark-rimmed glasses. You felt, or I felt, in her the legacy or curse of the Spanish-Portuguese women of the upper classes. Some of the privileges and many of the restraining expectations were there, and they were not altogether in balance because she was not smug and not naturally tropical and indolent. She spoke French and had lived in France, I think. Her English was fluent, fractured, and utterly compelling.

However talkative and sophisticated, Lota was also, in Hardwick's eyes,

somehow melancholy too, the Iberian strain. I think there was great shyness also, and the rather unbalancing combination of the proper and the misfit . . . It did not appear that Lota got on well with most of her family, her sister or sisters. Brazil pioneered in the face-lift and that gives you some idea of the occupation of the well-to-do Brazilian woman.

L. was very intense indeed, emotional, also a bit insecure as we say, and loyal, devoted and smart and lesbian and Brazilian and shy, masterful in some ways, but helpless also. She adored Elizabeth and

in the most attractive way, in this case somewhat fearfully, posses-
sively, and yet modestly and without any tendency to oppress.

The two were a *combinazione* very striking. Lota would drive a
car with great zest and speed and Elizabeth couldn't or didn't drive.
Lota was helpless in the kitchen and about the household, which
Elizabeth indeed was not. Lota was watchful in the matter of Elizabeth's drinking and the sober period had lasted many years and did
not last out the summer, when at the end there was a brief, I think,
regression or defiance or just plain inclination.

But on the whole Bishop thrived in what she herself felt was
"an atmosphere of uncritical affection."

She would write to Lowell in the second year of her stay:
"I am extremely happy, for the first time in my life." The
change was especially striking after her "dismal" year in Washington as Consultant in Poetry at the Library of Congress and
after an equally depressing stay at Yaddo in the fall and winter
of 1950–51. As she put it to Lowell, "I certainly didn't really
want to wander around the world in a drunken daze for the rest
of my life—so it's all fine and dandy."

Alcohol and asthma continued to rob Bishop of rest and
her work time, as they had for years. We know more about
her afflictions in the late 1940s and the 1950s because Bishop
had begun to report them in detail in her letters to a New York
doctor, Anny Baumann, who served Bishop all her later life
not just as a physician but as conscience and even psychiatric
adviser. The connection was important enough for Baumann
to become the dedicatee of her next book, *A Cold Spring*. Bishop
explains to Dr. Baumann that she has had asthma from childhood on but that in the 1940s she has had it almost every day
and night, has never been able to lie down in bed. Her letters
record a constant struggle to find an effective drug, especially
in Brazil—mostly falling back on adrenaline and cortisone and
packages of monosodium sulfate sent with some difficulty from
a New York pharmacy. Her alcoholism was equally troubling:
the usual—but no less painful for its familiarity—roller coaster
of depression, drinking bouts, guilty recovery, and resolutions

to stop drinking. Her father, grandfather, and three uncles had to give up alcohol—and Bishop is acutely conscious in 1951 that she has reached the age at which her father died. Her drinking seems to have dwindled in Brazil—to one or two evenings a month—thanks to Lota's influence and a life that seemed less exhausting, less upsetting than in her habitats to the north, Key West and New York.

Lota's family had been prominent in Brazilian society and in diplomatic circles for generations, and through her Bishop met most of the country's writers, artists, and intellectuals, though her version for Lowell was that she knew about ten people, two of them " 'literary'—and I go to Rio once in three or four months." Nor did she feel out of touch with American literary life. "I was always too shy to have much 'intercommunication' in New York, anyway, and I was miserably lonely there most of the time . . ."

Brazil placed Bishop at an enabling distance from America. She had all the "news" she needed through correspondence and periodicals. (They subscribed to *Partisan Review, The Hudson Review* and *Kenyon Review, Botteghe Oscure, Poetry*, the airmail *New York Times Book Review*, and so on.) But more important, she began to write letters, fiction, and poems which were to allow her to be both "in the world" and (to use the title of her story) "in the village." She led a life, in its intimacies and domesticities, curiously reminiscent of her happiest years—the early ones in Nova Scotia. In its strangeness there was an odd streak of familiarity: "What I'm really up to," she was to say much later, "is recreating a sort of deluxe Nova Scotia all over again in Brazil. And now I'm my own grandmother." She found herself trying to write a poem about salt codfish, "having come from the land where it's prepared to the lands where it's a weekly institution."

By the middle of 1952 it was clear that Bishop planned to stay in Brazil. On a brief trip to the United States, she packed up all her books, which were to be in the studio that Lota was having built especially for her. Though she and Lota kept an apartment in Rio "on that famous carte postale beach," Bishop always preferred the house in Petrópolis, where the country was "magnificent and wild." It wasn't just the setting which drew her, but also the fact that for years the house wasn't finished, that there was a Crusoe-like element of improvisation and planning in their lives. The house, "ultra-modern," was on the side of a black granite mountain "with a waterfall at one end, clouds coming into the living room in the middle of the conversation, etc." At first they had to use oil lamps; the floors weren't yet laid, just cement "covered with dogs' footprints." But there were all the Key West flowers she knew, plus orchids, Northern apples, and pears.

By the time Elizabeth Hardwick visited in 1962, the house was

filled with beautiful old furniture of polished Brazilian woods; a large old painted mermaid ship's prow stood in the hall and all about there were brilliant little treasures collected by Elizabeth—crèches made by nuns, necklaces of feathers made by Indians, shells, boxes, paintings. And they had their Manuelzinhos (or one such) and a few not very handy half-breeds padding around barefoot. It was a setting, not elaborate, but personal, charming and done with careful, anxious expressiveness.

Bishop's studio, up behind the house and overlooking the waterfall, was built of gray-blue rock with mica in it—one large whitewashed room with a fireplace and a herringbone brick floor, a place where she could gather all her books and papers together after years of dispersal.

Sometimes life there reminded her of her daydream of being a lighthouse keeper "absolutely alone, with no one to interrupt my reading or just sitting—and although such dreams are usually dismissed at 16 or so they always haunt one a bit, I suppose—I now see a wonderful cold rocky shore in the Falklands, or a house in Nova Scotia on the bay, *exactly* like my grandmother's—idiotic as it is, and unbearable as the reality would be."

Once after three days alone in the Petrópolis house—alone

except for the cat being dewormed and the toucan, which had a sore foot, Bishop wrote:

The most terrific storm in my experience here raged all those days. (A family of seven were wiped out in a landslide in Petrópolis—the road was impassable, etc.—although I knew none of this until later.) And I read Coleridge, and read him, & read him—just couldn't stop—until he and the waterfall *roaring* under the windows, and ten times its usual size, were indistinguishable to my ears. By the time he'd had "flying irregular gout," got himself drenched once more, was in debt, hating his wife, etc.—I couldn't believe that I really existed, or not what you'd call *life*, compared to that —dry, no symptoms of any sort, fairly solvent, on good terms with all my friends (as far as I know).

Not that Brazil, at other moments, did not interfere with such absorption. There were the natural accidents, revolutions, even the steady procession of other people's babies through the house. Nearby—two minutes away—lived a Polish zoo man whose collection included a black jaguar, a camel, beautiful birds—and, a gift to her, the toucan. This of course provided material for many letters to Moore. The bird was called Uncle Sam. It was black with "electric blue eyes, a blue and yellow marked beak, blue feet, and red feathers here & there—a bunch under his tail like a sunset when he goes to sleep." Toucans sleep tails up over their backs and heads under their wings, "like large inverted commas." The blue skin glimpsed underneath when it bathed was "just the color of blueberries—or as if he had blue jeans on under the feathers." One night during the rainy season she forgets to put the cover on his cage. "It started pouring and when I rushed out he was standing stretched straight up with his beak in the air and his eyes shut, the water pouring down him—like Brancusi's 'Bird in Flight' —I didn't know he could make himself so long."

The joy in shaping such day-to-day encounters for her American correspondents—not only, but especially, Lowell and Moore—is apparent in her letters. More so than ever, they are

[154

full of poems in the making—sometimes, as with the toucan, entering into drafts but not finished. Through her letters Bishop made Brazil a place where she could lead congenially double lives. In one sense the letters were the shuttle between her art and her life, a new loom. Coleridge and the toucan, North and South—she could take the present in its confused and exotic and absorbing randomness and also, in correspondence, bring into play the distanced eye of friends. More important, her new home allowed her to heal the deepest breaches in her life—to strike a balance between village and city and to give voice to both the child and the adult, once sundered, in her experience. It is rare that the imaginative possibilities of a life find so real a base. But, as Auden said of Henry James—a passage Bishop was fond of quoting: "It is sometimes necessary for sons to leave the family hearth; it may well be necessary at least for intellectuals to leave their country as it is for children to leave their homes, not to get away from them, but to re-create them."

Not long after she settled in Brazil, and partly as a way of exercising her Portuguese, Bishop began translating what was to appear in 1957 as *The Diary of "Helena Morley."* Her original and more accurate title for it was *My Life as a Girl (Minha vida de menina)*; it was a well-known Brazilian book first published in 1942, the diary of a young girl between the ages of twelve and fifteen reared in the remote mining town of Diamantina, in the interior state of Minas Gerais, in the 1890s. "There's a huge family of aunts and uncles and ex-slaves, ruled by a grandmother, all very poor and religious and superstitious, and the girl really wrote extremely well. She is funny and hardheaded and the anecdotes are very full of detail about the life, food, clothes, priests, etc." What engaged Bishop's interest was the authenticity and mystery of youthful energies revealed in the child's *own* words: "This was a real, day-by-day diary, kept by a real girl, and anything resembling it that I could think of had been observed or made up, and written down, by adults."

Bishop's attention to childhood during these first years in Brazil, though it may have had its source in the losses and displacements she herself had experienced, went boldly beyond them. *"Helena Morley"* struck a vein she was to explore in fiction written at the same time that she was engaged in the translation. What gave her fiction its haunting and unfamiliar force was Bishop's reawakened sense of the recuperative powers of childhood, the secrets of survival—her own and those of the young "Helena Morley."

——

Robert Lowell, back in America after three years in Europe, wrote playfully and grumpily about Bishop's absence: "Like a rheumatic old aunt, I would gladly spoil all your fun just to have you back." In fact, the separation—and the correspondence it entailed—proved fruitful for both of them. Neither was able to write much poetry at the time. Both of them turned, under quite different pressures, to autobiographical prose; and each profited from the competitive scrutiny of their exchanges. Lowell had written her from Amsterdam of himself and Hardwick and Bishop: "You know we are a unique class, the only three American writers of our generation who don't have to work. Usury has made us; I can hear Karl Marx muttering out a review to prove that our biases are identical." Despite the proprietary tone and the glibness of the statement, Lowell was suggesting something important about his own work and Bishop's in the 1950s. Leisure allowed each of them to consolidate and assimilate the landscapes of their pasts. Even in Europe, Lowell was tempted in that direction. Choosing Amsterdam for his second winter in Europe—he and Hardwick had spent their first winter abroad in Italy—Lowell explained that the Dutch city had been "a baroque, worldly, presbyterian, canal-and-brick, glorious Boston." By the summer of 1955 he had decided, not without trepidation, to return to the Boston he had left so angrily twenty years before. He and Hardwick bought a house at 239 Marlborough Street, not far from where his parents once lived, but the thought of going back to Boston "sometimes makes me feel like a flayed man, who stands quivering and shivering in his flesh, while holding out a hand for his old sheet of skin." It was in the 1950s that both his parents died and that he began to suffer regular and severe psychotic episodes. The pressures were partly relieved or faced down in the move to Boston, in attempts at autobiographical prose, and eventually in the poems which would appear as *Life Studies* in 1959.

For Bishop, on the other hand, it was only in the protection of and prompted by a life both exotic and domestic that she began to write directly about the losses of her own childhood years: two remarkable stories, "In the Village," which tells of her mother's insanity and early disappearance from her life, and "Gwendolyn," the story of the death of a young playmate. Both were published in *The New Yorker* in 1953. She wrote "In the Village" in a single stretch, straight off the typewriter—the first time she'd ever done such a thing. She had made notes for various bits of the story but no more, and then was given too much cortisone for her asthma—occasionally, still, it was very bad—and couldn't sleep. "I sat up all night in the tropical heat," she told Elizabeth Spires years later. "The story came from a combination of cortisone, I think, and the gin and tonic I drank in the middle of the night. I wrote it in two nights."

She told Lowell—encouraging him to write *his* autobiography—that writing the two stories had given her a great deal of satisfaction: "that desire to get things straight and tell the truth—it's almost impossible not to tell the truth in poetry, I think, but in prose it keeps eluding me in the funniest way." Lowell, too, found prose a recalcitrant medium: "a hell of a job," he wrote her, "it starts naked, ends as fake velvet." The point for each of them was not simply a deflection into prose. They were exploring the *limits* of prose as a vehicle for autobiography—just the reverse of what these efforts appeared to be. They were sharpening and altering their notions of what it meant to tell the truth in verse.

"In the Village" is the less oblique of Bishop's two autobiographical stories. But both of them bear out her remarks about the indirection of prose, as does the order in which they were written. "Gwendolyn," written first, recounts events which occurred two years or so after the crucial last breakdown and disappearance of Bishop's mother. Indeed, "Gwendolyn" elides those painful memories, with no explicit acknowledgment that it is odd for a young girl to be living with her aunts and grandparents. It recalls the mode of "The Baptism," that other story in which the suspension of family ties and the isolation of children are taken for granted. Such foreshortened views of childhood—were these the necessary preludes to the writing of "In the Village," whose action underlies and precedes the earlier stories and more openly embraces the links between personal present and past? Lowell advised her to put the three "girls' stories" together as a "grown-up novel." They would indeed have made an arresting collection—not just for what they reveal about Bishop's early years, but for what they reveal of the strategies she needed in approaching the center of her youthful experience. "Gwendolyn" and "In the Village" are an especially striking diptych. Bishop tells both stories through the eyes of the young girl she was. The adult can be seen trying to recapture the waywardness and unpredictability of childhood vision, to which her translation of *"Helena Morley"* had helped attune her. Morley, "funny and hardheaded," had the toughness Bishop associated, often guiltily, with her own powers to survive a blasted childhood.

Both stories try to sort out loss, guilt, and strength—to find a style for survival and memory. "Gwendolyn" is the more schematic of the two; it insists, perhaps too rigorously, on causation and explanation. It recounts the death of a playmate, pampered and delicate in ways the narrator feels she herself as a child was not. The fact that Gwendolyn was diabetic only heightens her young friend's sense of her as a foil, the perfect little girl, all sugar and spice, carefully tended and dressed by doting parents. ("Patriquin," the surname of the "real" Gwendolyn, becomes "Appletree" in the story, a stylized reminder that the fictional Gwendolyn is "pink and white, exactly like a blossoming apple tree.") The figure of the doomed child is a magnet for a number of conflicting feelings. Her early death is one of Bishop's inexplicable childhood losses, like that of her own mother, or her cousin Arthur, near her own age, about whom she would write in "First Death in Nova Scotia" (1962). At the same time, she feels envy and even some revulsion for

Gwendolyn as "beautiful heroine," a role that "grew and grew until finally it had grown far beyond the slight but convincing talents she had for acting it." Both she and her grandmother feel distaste for the saccharine demonstrativeness of Gwendolyn's parents, who almost "eat her up" and "kiss her to death." She finally comes to identify Gwendolyn with a doll of her Aunt Mary's, preciously hidden away in pink paper, and only once, when the young narrator has bronchitis, brought out for her to play with. The doll has lace drawers like Gwendolyn's, a contrast to her own ragged dolls. At the end of the story she and her cousin Billy do something "really bad" by ferreting out the doll, wreathing it in flowers, and then realizing "with wild joy" that the nameless doll should be called Gwendolyn and that they were performing her funeral.

The act serves as a kind of atonement, but is even more resonant because, along with envy, the child has at another level experienced a cautious identification with Gwendolyn. The shock of Gwendolyn's death is crystallized by a hallucination in which she sees the child's closed coffin standing outside the church and then imagines the dead girl "shut invisibly inside it forever, there, completely alone." She screams involuntarily; then she remembers howling with just such inexplicable pain a few years before when she discovered some prized marbles, especially a favorite pink one, encrusted with dirt. The horror of finding them soiled, buried in their strawberry basket, prompts a reaction like the one she was to have to Gwendolyn in her coffin, one of those sensations visited upon us without warning. Disorder, the loss of purity—these are particularly painful to the young girl. The specter of Gwendolyn in her coffin is very different from the children's graves with their toylike lambs which she admired in the village cemetery. The death of Gwendolyn confirms the burial of any sense of purity or immunity or pampering she might have associated with her own childhood, and the doll Gwendolyn's funeral, which closes the story, is inextricably bound to her own sense of being "bad," unworthy. The figure of Gwendolyn draws to it, then, a cluster of irreconcilable feelings: inexplicable loss of childhood figures, envy, identification with the death of the young. Through Gwendolyn's death the bristling contradictions can be both experienced and kept at a safe symbolic distance. The fiction has performed its function neatly. Too neatly, perhaps. Over and over Bishop consigns these children who die young—Gwendolyn, her cousin Arthur, Lucy in "The Baptism"—not to extinction so much as to a tortured perpetual innocence, "forever, alone" like the doll-like whitened figure of Cousin Arthur:

> But how could Arthur go,
> clutching his tiny lily,
> with his eyes shut up so tight
> and the roads deep in snow?

The image of youth "buried alive" was one she would counter in her next story, "In the Village." She seems now more at home with the lessons of *"Helena Morley,"* "the book that has kept her childhood for us, as fresh as paint." What shines through "In the Village" is the child's puzzled and persistent attentiveness to the outside world, a mystery to which her adult counterpart returns again and again. The story sets the two sides of Bishop's girlhood—one numb and threatened, the other receptive and full of natural promise—next to each other without comment or connection. Unlike "Gwendolyn," the story refuses explanation, resists the innate desire of fiction to suggest a scheme of causes and effects. Most of "In the Village" is told as by the child, and objects hold intense interest for her precisely because of what remains unspoken and unexplained—what must be pieced out and, shadowlike, apprehended about her parentage and the early disappearance of her mother. In a shop window, for example, she notices "something new: shoes, single shoes, summer shoes, each sitting on top of its own box with its mate beneath it, inside, in the dark. Surprisingly, some of them appear to be exactly the colors and texture of pink and blue blackboard chalks, but I can't stop to examine them now." The speed with which a perilous detail— the absent mate—is only grazed, then the eye diverted by surface for its own sake, is typical of the way this story negotiates troubled waters. Bishop is concerned here with the unresolved, the undetermined nature of childhood perception as a clue to survival; questions of guilt and innocence of the sort that obsessed her in "Gwendolyn" become largely irrelevant.

"In the Village" bears out Bishop's remarks about the difficulty of "telling the truth" in prose. However childlike the prose, these memories of her mother's disappearance require complicated narrative strategies and evasions, now the present tense, now the past, now the third person, now the first. The strategies themselves, her way of receiving her story, eventually become its subject. We are—she is—to be confused at a climactic moment. In the very first scene, in understated pasts, we have been shown the mother as she is being fitted for a dress—a purple dress, because, after two years, she is thinking, hesitantly, of coming out of mourning. She has been home and away, hospitalized several times, and her daughter, at this point referred to as "the child," unused to having her at home, watches from the doorway.

> The dress was all wrong. She screamed.
> The child vanishes.

In two sentences separated as paragraphs, and with a quiet shift to the present tense, the "child" vanishes literally from the doorway, and figuratively from the story, to be replaced by a narrative "I" who takes responsibility for putting together the pieces of her life and trying to survive the scream. Sometimes the "I" sees her story in a removed past, but, especially at a crucial juncture—the moment when the *mother* vanishes, never to be seen again, ever, in her life by her daughter—it is all vividly present.

There has been a fire one night in a neighbor's barn. The young girl is aware of confusion in her own house, "she," the mother, calling for the grandmother, etc.; but all the child is ever to know of it is what, even at the moment of the writing, she presents through the whispered overheard scramblings of the adults to shield her:

> But now I am caught in a skein of voices, my aunts' and my grandmother's, saying the same things over and over, sometimes loudly, sometimes in whispers:
> "Hurry. For heaven's sake, *shut the door!*"
> "Sh!"
> "Oh, we can't go on like this, we . . ."
> "It's too dangerous. Remember that . . ."
> "Sh! Don't let her . . ."
> A door slams.
> A door opens. The voices begin again.
> I am struggling to free myself.
> Wait. Wait. No one is going to scream.

The sense of menace from overheard incomplete conversations of her childhood is one about which Bishop had written in letters to Lowell. Here it is so vividly relived that the present tense seems not only to be that of intensely remembered childhood but, at certain instants, the present tense of the moment of writing. "Now I am caught in a skein of voices . . . I am struggling to free myself . . . Wait. Wait. No one is going to scream." She had chosen to elide a similar climactic moment in "Gwendolyn": "If I care to, I can bring back the exact sensation of that moment today, but then, it is also one of those that from time to time are terrifyingly thrust upon us." In "Gwendolyn" the statement seems too rationally realized; in "In the Village" volition plays no part. The child is caught in a skein of voices; so is this particular adult writer at the moment of writing, and the story refuses to tell the two of them apart. What ordinary narrative devices will satisfy the needs of such moments? Bishop once wrote in her journal:

> I think when one is extremely unhappy—almost hysterically unhappy, that is—one's time sense breaks down. All that long stretch in Key West, for example, several years ago—it wasn't just a matter of not

being able to accept the present, that present, although it began that way, possibly. But the past and the present seemed confused, or contradicting each other violently and constantly, and the past wouldn't "lie doon." (I've felt the same thing when I tried to paint—but this was really taught me by getting drunk, when the same thing happens, for perhaps the same reasons, for a few hours.)

In trying to paint, Bishop experienced a confusion of present and past—a reminder, perhaps, that observation served a psychological as well as a scientific purpose. The observant child of "In the Village," so enthralled by details of Nate the blacksmith's shop and the intimate pastoral of her village even when she is suffering the violence and shame of loss, becomes a model for the adult telling her story. The story appears to do away with the usual censorship of fiction, the shaping to "explain," sculpting the story to reveal cause and effect. (Not that it doesn't have its own concisions, evidences of writerly choices.) Bishop attends much more to the "skein of voices" than to the logic of cause and result. Scenes and sounds from the blacksmith shop at the back of the garden are woven with choric frequency through moments of crisis. The clang of the anvil precedes the mother's scream.

> *Clang.*
> The pure note: pure and angelic.
> The dress was all wrong. She screamed.
> The child vanishes.
> Later they sit, the mother and the three sisters, in the shade on the back porch, sipping sour, diluted ruby: raspberry vinegar. The dressmaker refuses to join them and leaves, holding the dress to her heart. The child is visiting the blacksmith.
> In the blacksmith's shop things hang up in the shadows and shadows hang up in the things, and there are black and glistening piles of dust in each corner. A tub of night-black water stands by the forge. The horseshoes sail through the dark like bloody little moons and follow each other like bloody little moons to drown in the black water, hissing, protesting.

Outside, along the matted eaves, painstakingly, sweetly, wasps go over and over a honeysuckle vine.

A tense writer would have lingered over those bloody moons, drowning, hissing, protesting. Coming as they do after the scene of the mother's scream, some details do in part refract the young girl's anger and helplessness. But that is not the point for Bishop. Feeling is deflected, refigured as the child becomes absorbed in the outside world, here Nate's blacksmith shop. The scream is never totally banished from this story, but it is repositioned by Bishop's insistence on the present tense. It is not simply a question of reproducing the past with some immediacy, as in the sudden overpowering recall of a moment, in Proust. With Bishop it is also the "surround" that she tries to recapitulate, the things we failed to notice in our concentration on pain—the equivalent of the backdrop of a conversation, audible to us only when we play it back on a recording. Writing, she attends not to a single obsessive tone but to the "skein of voices." The past is changed as it is reframed in the present, and the use of observation and present-tense description is to let the known tune be heard not only in a new key but as one instrument in a richer orchestra. Explanation becomes irrelevant as the present refigures the past.

The entrance into a narrative present coincides with the description of the blacksmith shop. James Merrill reminds me that this is an early exposure to a kind of art—the dangerous fire that is to throw them into panic later in the story is in Nate's shop perilously mastered, turned into a game which still bears traces of violence ("hissing, protesting"). By the end of the story, pain and receptivity to the outside world have practically merged.

Clang.
Clang.
Nate is shaping a horseshoe.

Oh, beautiful pure sound!

It turns everything else to silence.

But still, once in a while, the river gives an unexpected gurgle. "*Slp,*" it says, out of glassy-ridged brown knots sliding along the surface.

Clang.

And everything except the river holds its breath.

Now there is no scream. Once there was one and it settled slowly down to earth one hot summer afternoon; or did it float up, into that dark, too dark, blue sky? But surely it has gone away, forever.

It sounds like a bell buoy out at sea.

It is the elements speaking: earth, air, fire, water.

All those other things—clothes, crumbling postcards, broken china; things damaged and lost, sickened or destroyed; even the frail almost-lost scream—are they too frail for us to hear their voices long, too mortal?

Nate!

Oh, beautiful sound, strike again!

Voices are evanescent, and this writer's task seems to be almost a musical one, accommodating them to one another—the triumphant clang of the anvil, the almost-lost scream. At moments it is finally hard to tell them apart: the "it" that sounds like a bell buoy at sea might be, according to the grammar of the piece, either Nate's forging or the mother's cry of pain. The "it" that speaks with the four elements' tongues may also be, syntactically, either. "In the Village" employs a pictorial and musical art for traditionally narrative purposes. It positions and repositions the scream in a flow of language and landscapes which eventually almost absorb it. With the questions and intensives of the final lines one can almost hear the writer's effort and wished-for relief: "But surely it has gone away, forever"; "are they too frail for us to hear their voices long, too mortal?"

"In the Village" stands as a prologue to the descriptive poetry Bishop would write in Brazil. It was not simply that the two village worlds—Brazil and Nova Scotia—often fused in her imagination. Memories were to be dealt with—perhaps the rigidity of "Gwendolyn" taught her this lesson—not by elegy or by looking for narrative cause and effect in the past but by enlarging the frame, the "surround," in which the past is summoned back to a refiguring present. Writing fiction that served to define the limits of fiction, Bishop found the means to re-energize her poetry.

_____

After reading "In the Village," Lowell wrote to Bishop calling it "a great ruminating Dutch landscape full of goneness." It was January 1, 1954, and Lowell was entering one of the worst years of his life. Charlotte Lowell died that February in Rapallo, and her son, after bringing her body back to America, suffered another severe breakdown. "When Mother died," he writes in "Near the Unbalanced Aquarium," "I began to feel tireless, madly sanguine, menaced, and menacing." To Bishop he wrote: "These things come on with a gruesome, vulgar, blasting surge of 'enthusiasm.' One becomes a kind of man-aping balloon in a parade—then you subside and eat bitter coffee-grounds of dullness, guilt, etc." His marriage to Elizabeth Hardwick, already under stress in Europe, almost did not survive this latest crisis. They separated for a period and Lowell was hospitalized at the Payne Whitney Psychiatric Clinic in Manhattan. It is there that one of the strangest episodes in his writing life began: he undertook a series of prose sketches, autobiography, which kept him busy for almost four years. He hoped they would "supply me with my swaddling clothes, with a sort of immense bandage for my hurt nerves." The impulse is entwined with his resolve to move back to Boston, and with his decision in 1955 to return to the Episcopalian Church. "On the surface," he wrote Bishop, "I feel eccentric, antiquarian, a superstitious, skeptical fussy old woman, but down under I feel something that makes sober sense and lets my eyes open." There was a useful wildness and abandon about his willingness to think of himself as a spinster or an infant in need of swaddling. In one of the autobiographical pieces, "Antebellum Boston," he even imagines a happy life with his mother in the years *before* his birth, before he existed.

When I was three or four years old I first began to think about the time before I was born. Until then, Mother had been everything; at three or four, she began abruptly and gratingly to change into a human being. I wanted to recapture the mother I remembered and so I began to fabricate. In my memory she was a lady preserved in silhouettes, outlines, and photographs . . . I was a little doll in a white sailor suit with blue anchors on the pockets, a doll who smiled impartially upon his mother and father and in his approbation thus made them husband and wife. But when I was at last three years old all that began to change. I could no longer see Mother as that rarely present, transfigured, Sunday-best version of my nurse. I saw her as my mother, as a rod, or a scolding, rusty hinge—as a human being. More and more I began to try to imagine Mother when she was happier, when she had been merely her father's favorite daughter, when she was engaged and unmarried. Perhaps I had been happiest then, too, because I hadn't existed and lived only as an imagined future.

I found that all I had to do was to hold my breath when Mother talked about her girlhood and then it all came vividly to me. The large houses, the staff of servants, the immense house parties, the future— and I was there, living it all. One day I held my breath longer and longer and more perfectly than ever before. I found myself breathing with ponderous, earthy effort. I found I was ill with croup . . .

A piece such as this is of clinical as well as literary interest. It allowed Lowell to inhabit his dead mother's life innocent of taboos and to deny time, growth, and ruin. It also allowed him to explore a train of disconcerting images. "Near the Unbalanced Aquarium" has him imagining the neo-Gothic clinic building as "a wedding-cake; no, not a wedding-cake but the tall bride standing with her sacrificial silver knife beside the wedding cake; no, not the bride of flesh and blood, but a narrow, late Gothic bride, all arches, groin, and stone lace-work . . ." It was only a step from there to another draft version: "a hard, enamelled wedding cake, and beside it, holding the blunt silver knife of the ritual, stood the tall, white stone bride . . . my mother in the brief, sacrificial frost of her wedding dress on a day in 1915, now forever less a lived day than the surface of its photograph on my father's bureau." The sexual disgust, the rage at his father, the identification of his mother with the clinic in which he found himself, the primitive vision of her "sacrifice"—all these are glanced upon by the freewheeling, freely associating prose. The chains of images are designed to explore or search for causes of his behavior and predicament—or at least that is what they started out to be. A year later, he wrote to Bishop that he had over one hundred pages of autobiographical drafts: "It's quite clumsy inaccurate and magical, but may work out possibly. I like being off the high stilts of meter, and feel there's no limit to the prosiness and detail I can go into."

Many of the drafts survive in the collection of Lowell's papers at Harvard—written and rewritten versions, several of which were later marked to indicate details Lowell used in the family poems of *Life Studies* (1959). For the greater part of a decade after the publication of *The Mills of the Kavanaughs* in 1951 Lowell had been blocked in writing verse, publishing only a few poems. The autobiographical prose was not only therapy, and not just a way of rehabilitating himself to live in Boston, but also the excavation of material he would later find useful for verse. Poems such as "My Last Afternoon with Uncle Devereux Winslow," "Terminal Days at Beverly Farms," and "Sailing Home from Rapallo" are here in embryo. The drafts have been carefully gone over with suggestions in Elizabeth Hardwick's hand. Only one prose piece, "91 Revere Street," was published in Lowell's lifetime—dry, acerb, literate satire of his parents' genteel, inhibited household. He wrote Bishop that it seemed "thin and arty" by comparison with her "glorious" stories. It was indeed more brittle and visibly crafted than "In the Village" and less exploratory and wild than his other pieces of autobiographical prose.

What is arresting in these stories is not so much their own integrity and finish as their power to eliminate certain kinds of writing from Lowell's repertoire. "91 Revere Street" was a brilliant performance, but not one to be fruitfully repeated. Other pieces—memories of childhood guilt and naughtiness, affectionate sketches of his Grandfather Winslow, his mother's father—are obsessively Freudian. They flail about as if to search out the childhood secrets which lie behind his adult sufferings. They propose and reject explanation after explanation. The poems which emerge from many of these sketches have, as a result, been sifted over a number of years; they represent a pared-down and severe notion of how to talk about one's past.

"My Last Afternoon with Uncle Devereux Winslow," the opening poem of the autobiographical series in *Life Studies* and the poem in which the young Lowell first identifies with a dying elder, began as a rambling memory of an energetic and mischievous young Lowell who spent most of his time among women. One impulse behind the poem seems to have been the resemblance between his doctor at Payne Whitney and Uncle Devereux, victim at twenty-nine of Hodgkin's disease—apparently the child's first brush with death. But the different drafts all include stories of childhood punishment. In one his grandfather's summer house, described in detail that persists in Lowell's versifying of the material, is backdrop to the young boy's raid on a hornets' nest. He is stung thirty-two times, faints, and comes to in the familiar world of the poem "Uncle Devereux." "I knew," the narrator concludes, "that for once I had really lived." In another version he removes all the cartridges from his grandfather's pistol and rattles them in a cocktail shaker until they explode. He is sent to bed for three days. In his grandfather's garden is a piece of fountain statuary described in Lowell's later poem as "a pastel-pale Huckleberry Finn" who "fished with a broom straw in a basin / hollowed out of a millstone." But in the prose sketch the figure is more heavily drawn: "About the neck my Grandfather had hung a little card on green ribbon. The card said in my Grandfather's slanting green ink letters, 'I am a callow youth. My name is Verdant Greene.' This was for me." Lowell is tempted in these early stabs at autobiography to tell stories and moralize them—not so much for the benefit of others as to slake his thirst for explanations of pain that is ultimately inexplicable.

Lowell learned from his prose pieces how, eventually, to dispense with narrative. "Uncle Devereux" was originally framed by a family celebration, his grandfather's proud dedication of a new root house in the garden. Bits of the "story" remain, but cut loose from narrative moorings. The young boy sits mixing black earth and lime, a haunting image in the poem as it reflects on the energies of life and death and the fact that "Uncle Devereux would blend to the one color." The dedication of the root house becomes irrelevant.

Young Lowell, in the prose piece, is dressed up for the occasion: "I had been wearing my creased pearl gray flannel shorts for all of three minutes . . . I was acting up. I was trying to be perfect and Olympian. I was the model boy in the plate glass window of Rogers Peet's Men's Store below the State House on Tremont St. in Boston." In "My Last Afternoon with Uncle Devereux Winslow," a whole section of the poem is devoted to the boy's costume, but not because he is dressed for a particular occasion. It is a "scene" in itself, timeless, a brooding emblem, rather than being part of a larger "story."

> I was five and a half.
> My formal pearl gray shorts
> had been worn for three minutes.
> My perfection was the Olympian
> poise of my models in the imperishable autumn
> display windows
> of Rogers Peet's boys' store below the State House
> in Boston. Distorting drops of water
> pinpricked my face in the basin's mirror.
> I was a stuffed toucan
> with a bibulous, multicolored beak.

The poem has a condensed vigor pointed toward psychological insights. It leaves open a possibility not entertained in its prose forebear: that the models in the store windows are those chosen for him by others rather than his own notions of perfection. The boy becomes one among a series of ancestral icons—images that populate this poem. The figure of the stuffed toucan is an added confirmation. In fact, the technique of the poem, however solidly it draws upon the details of Lowell's prose, is radically different from the earlier sketches. The impulse is carried not so much by forward movement, by narrative verbs, as by the constant addition of adjectives—the "imperishable autumn" is only one such addition; the poem is filled with them. The effect is of a hieratic world of suspended images—the posters, furniture, etc.—each with its own reference locked inside it, but somehow muffling the living world, and the story is told through icons rather than as ongoing narrative. Like Bishop, Lowell in the 1950s was discovering through his work in prose a new way of writing poetry.

4 / Under a Reading-Glass

Elizabeth Bishop came to New York in April 1957 partly to go over the proof of her translation of *The Diary of "Helena Morley."* This trip to the United States made possible, among other things, her first meetings with Lowell in seven years, and they saw one another at least three times in Boston and Castine, the village in Maine where the Lowells had begun to spend their summers. Both the tenderness and competitiveness of their letters were aggravated in these encounters. In one sense Bishop became part of a drama already under way in Lowell's career; in another sense her presence contributed to, if it did not precipitate, a crisis.

Lowell had traveled to the West Coast in late March of 1957 for some readings, one or more a day. In the wake of the Beats his old poems seemed stiff and heavy to him, "like prehistoric monsters dragged down into the bog and death by their ponderous armor"—and under the pressure of reading aloud he found himself simplifying the poems, adding or dropping a few syllables for the sake of clarity. And then of course these were his "old New Criticism religious, symbolic poems, many published during the war." ("I've done so few poems in the last five years," he'd written to Bishop.) The regular meters troubled him, and when he came back to Boston he tried poems in looser rhythms and a new style. "No poem, however, got finished and soon I left off and tried to forget the whole headache. Suddenly, in August, I was struck by the sadness of writing nothing, and having nothing to write, of having, at least, no language."

The frustrations were not new, but events of the past few months had thrown them into new relief. By the time he returned from the West Coast he had seen W. D. Snodgrass's "Heart's Needle" and had written admiringly to Bishop that though personal it was also "like Vaughan and Traherne with a Laforgue-like wit and a perfect ear." Snodgrass, who had been a student of Lowell's at Iowa, had written about his divorce and his child in "expert little stanzas," something Lowell would speak of as a "new kind of poetry" that avoided the pitfalls of comparably direct poems which were too often slack and without vibrance. "His experience wouldn't be so interesting and valid if it weren't for the whimsy, the music, the balance, everything revised and placed and pondered. All that gives light to those poems on agonizing subjects comes from the craft." The trick was to skirt sentimentality, the inflated emotion, and give value—as he felt Snodgrass and Laforgue did—to tender emotions, pathos, and fragility.

And then there was, as always, the challenge of Bishop, the simplicity of the surface but the exploratory suggestive symbolic underpinnings of her verse that he had been among the first to discern. Not the sort of symbolic poetry that, once unwound, is only skin-deep. "She seldom writes a poem that doesn't have that exploring quality; yet it's very firm, it's not like the beat poetry, it's all controlled."

Lowell and many of his critics have written extensively and eloquently about the energies he was trying to incorporate into verse—and about the importance of Bishop's verse, of Snodgrass's verse, of his own prose efforts. The way the dammed-up impulses were released is equally revealing. Lowell has said that "Skunk Hour"—the first of the *Life Studies* series to be completed—"became my test of what I somewhat grandiosely felt was my battle with the impossible." Not only was the poem

dedicated to Bishop, but it was intricately bound up with the
anticipation and excitement of her visit. In Boston, in late May
or early June, he heard her read "Sunday, 4 A.M.," which he
admired for its "surrealism of everyday life," and "The Armadillo," a poem that became for him a talisman. He carried
it around with him in his billfold for several months. "I think
I read your work with more interest than anyone now writing,"
he wrote Bishop. " 'The Armadillo' is surely one of your three
or four very best." At first he thought the title mistaken, "a
Moore name for an out-of-doors personally seen and utterly
un-Moore poem." But "Armadillo" was right, he said, "for
the little creature, given only five lines, runs off with the whole
poem."

The appeal of the mailed armadillo for Lowell is suggestive,
partly because of the animal's eventual importance for "Skunk
Hour"—the vital and obvious reason—but partly because Lowell at the time thought of his writing as encased in armor when
he compared it with Bishop's: "Rereading her I couldn't understand why my own style was so armored heavy and old-
fashioned. A partial [imitation] of her tone, rhythms, imagery,
stanza construction, etc. seemed to give me the means for a
break-through from my fortifications."

In late July and early August, Bishop and Lota de Macedo
Soares were with the Lowells in Castine. For Lowell, who had
already been attaching excited importance to Bishop's presence,
gathering tensions came to a head. He claimed her visit to Boston in June had brought more peace to his house than in ages,
thought of spending July alone in New York, and was determined, much to Bishop's alarm, to come by himself to see her
in Brazil. Things went so badly in Castine—Lowell termed it
his "slip into the monstrous"—that Bishop and Lota cut short
their stay. Bishop, a friend of hers recalled years later, felt that
Lowell was getting sick and that he "was getting very amorous
with her. There was this reawakened interest in her as someone
he was in love with." The day before she left he gave her a
two-volume edition of Herbert that he had recently found in

storage, his grandfather's copy, dated 1859. In Lowell's awkward printing he inscribed

THESE TWO VOLUMES

GIVEN ONE AUGUST MORNING

WITH <u>ALL</u> HIS HEART BY

ROBERT T. S. LOWELL (4TH)

TO

ELIZABETH BISHOP

Robert Lowell

8/8/57

("THE MOUTH WAS OPEN, BUT THOU COULDST

NOT SING.")

Back in New York, Bishop chose to respond only obliquely to the incidents of Castine and the inscription's allusion to his failed proposal of nine years before. She thanked him for the Herbert (it was the first time she'd ever traveled without a copy of his poems) and, deflecting the cause to drinking, allowed Herbert to speak for their embarrassments:

We should have read H's translation of Cornari's (whoever he was) "Treatise of Temperance & Sobriety" out loud to each other. It begins "Having observed in my time many of my friends, of excellent wit & noble disposition, overthrown and undone by Intemperance; who, if they had lived, could have been an ornament to the world and a comfort to their friends. I thought fit to discover in a short Treatise, that Intemperance was not such an evil, but it might easily be remedied . . ."

Dear Cal, do please take care of yourself and be an ornament to the world (you're already that) and a comfort to your friends . . . Sobriety & gayety & patience & toughness will do the trick. Or so I hope for myself and hope & pray for you, too.

But Lowell, the very day she left, had already written to apologize in a letter that makes their drinking irrelevant as an explanation:

I see clearly now that for the last few days I have been living in a state of increasing mania—almost off the rails at the end. It almost seems as if I couldn't be with you any length of time without acting with abysmal myopia and lack of consideration. My disease, alas, gives one (during its seizures) a headless heart.

The next day he adds:

Gracelessly, like a standing child trying to sit down, like a cat or a coon coming down a tree, I'm getting down my ladder to the moon . . . I love my lovely family again.

He promises that he'll make no "solo descents" on her either in New York or in Brazil, and assures her that he'd always wanted to give her the Herbert volumes. "Perhaps you can add some stumbling block of humor to the dedication."

Bishop replies only cautiously to his directness, her affection a little gingerly and forbearing. For one thing, she's somewhat fearful, and insistent that he shouldn't come to Brazil by himself. He'll be bored in the country and restless after a few days in Rio. Best to come for a long stay *en famille*, with their own apartment and time to get acquainted with the country. Meanwhile, she is trying to get information about doctors he might consult in Boston. And: "Maybe I shd. add to the inscription in the Herbert 'E.B. "the 1st" ' (but I shan't, of course). I do hope and pray you are feeling better and please write me whenever you feel like it."

Her concern is tempered by her lack of experience with Lowell's illness and by her trying to keep him at arm's length. Meanwhile, he had taken another step in trying to understand what had obsessed him for years—the "might have been" of the Stonington experience nine years before.

———

Only a few days after Bishop left Castine, Lowell began feverishly writing poems, some of which would find their way into the autobiographical sections of *Life Studies*. The activity was bound up with an equally intense absorption with Bishop, an attempt to sort out once and for all the feelings that gathered nine summers before in Maine. He writes and rewrites the story of Carley Dawson and of how her "banishment" paved the way for a day alone with Elizabeth Bishop. He drafts soliloquies for Bishop, dialogues between the two of them, lines *for* Elizabeth Bishop prompted by his remembrance of her retreating figure when he took her to the Bangor airport. Almost all these drafts and poems hark back to 1948, and are haunted by what Lowell had learned from and about her then and in Castine. ("Before she had gone," he would write to Randall Jarrell, speaking of the Castine visit in 1957, "we had told each other almost everything that had ever happened to us. She really has risen from the ocean's bottom.") On August 15 he wrote her, in the hope that he would not be "forever in exile," the long and moving letter in which he tried to purge once and for all his romantic confusions and to seal off their friendship upon firmer ground:

Also I want you to know that you need never again fear my overstepping myself and stirring up confusion with you. My frenzied behavior during your visit has a history and there is one fact that I want to disengage from all the harsh frenzy. There's one last bit of the past that I would like to get off my chest and then I think all [will] be easy with us. Do you remember how at the end of that long swimming day and sunning Stonington day (the water was too cold for us) after Carlie's removal by Tommy, we went up to, I think, the relatively removed upper Gross house and had one of those real fried New England dinners, probably awful. And we were talking about this and that about ourselves and I was feeling the infected hollowness of the Carlie business draining out of my heart, and you said rather humorously—yet it was truly meant, "When you write my epitaph,

you must say I was the loneliest person who ever lived." Probably
you forget, and anyway all that is mercifully changed and all has come
right since you found Lota. But at the time everything, I guess (I
don't want to overdramatize), [in] our relations seemed to have
reached a new place. I assumed that it would be just a matter of time
before I proposed and I half believed that you would accept. Yet I
wanted it all to have the right build-up. Well, I didn't say anything
then. And of course the Eberharts' in-laws wasn't the right stage-
setting, and then there was that poetry conference at Bard and I
remember one evening presided over by Mary McCarthy and my
Elizabeth was there, and going home to the Bard poets' dormitory,
I was so drunk that my hands turned cold and I felt half-dying and
held your hand. And nothing was said, and like a loon that needs sixty
feet, I believe, to take off from the water, I wanted time and space,
and went on assuming, and when I was to have joined you at Key
West I was determined to ask you. Really for so callous (I fear) a man,
I was fearfully shy and scared of spoiling things and distrustful of
being steady enough to be the least good. Then of course the Yaddo
explosion came and it was all over. Yet there were a few months. I
suppose we might almost claim a something like apparently Strachey
and Virginia Wolf [*sic*]. And of course there was always the other side,
the fact that our friendship really wasn't a courting, was really disinterested (bad phrase) really led to no encroachments. So it is. Let
me say this though and then leave the matter forever. I do think free
will is sewn into everything we do. You can't cross a street, light a
cigarette, drop saccarine [*sic*] in your coffee without really doing it.
Yet the possible alternatives life allows us are very few, often there
must be none. I've never thought there was any choice for me about
writing poetry. No doubt if I used my head better, ordered my life
better, worked harder, etc, the poetry would be improved and there
must be many lost poems, innumerable accidents and ill-done actions.
But asking you is *the* might have been for me, the one towering
change, the other life that might have been had. It was that way for
those nine years or so that intervened. It was deeply buried, and this
spring and summer (really before your arrival) it boiled to the surface.
Now it won't happen again, though of course I always feel a great
blytheness [*sic*] and easiness with you. It won't happen. I'm really

underneath utterly in love and sold on my Elizabeth and it's also a great solace to me that you [are] with Lota, and I am sure it is the will of the heavens that all is as it is.

However resolved the letter was, the poems about Bishop which Lowell was drafting at the same time show a more complex struggle to sort out his feelings. The account of the Dawson incident in the poems is much less balanced. His amorous interest in Bishop was colored by attempts to identify himself with her and by competitive feelings as well. Published years later as part of a four-sonnet sequence about Bishop, the final forms of these poems—"Water" and "Flying from Bangor to Rio 1957"—betray very little of their original intensity and confined occasion. Would we even know—if he had not added her name to it—from the published versions that "Water" was written earlier for and about Bishop? "Water" was the opening poem of *For the Union Dead* (1964), the book that followed *Life Studies*, and appears to pick up the rhythms of "Skunk Hour," in quirkily rhymed short-lined stanzas that use the coast of Maine and its lobster towns as a landscape of regret:

> It was a Maine lobster town—
> each morning boatloads of hands
> pushed off for granite
> quarries on the islands,
>
> and left dozens of bleak
> white frame houses stuck
> like oyster shells
> on a hill of rock,
>
> and below us, the sea lapped
> the raw little match-stick
> mazes of a weir,
> where the fish for bait were trapped.

But before it became a relatively impersonal Arnoldian poem of parting, "Water" passed through several stages. It is clear that at the time Lowell began it he was rereading Bishop's letters from Stonington nine years before. The drafts pick up her phrasing, and the poem, first entitled "Gulls," began in various attempts as a letter in Bishop's voice or as a dialogue between the two of them. A constant element in several early versions was the mermaid that figured in one of Bishop's letters from Stonington: "I've just been indulging myself in a nightmare of finding a gasping mermaid under one of these exposed docks—you know, trying to tear the mussels off the piles for something to eat—horrors." Lowell makes it barnacles—even more extreme—instead of mussels:

> I had a dream:
> I was a mermaid clinging to a wharf-pile,
> and trying to tear
> off the barnacles with my hands.

At the end of a poem spoken entirely by the Bishop figure this had a hysterical ring—an exaggeration of Bishop's tone. When Lowell sent her the poem a few years later, she short-circuited some of the drama by connecting the dream to a parody of Edna St. Vincent Millay she'd recited on the day he was recalling:

> I want to be drowned in the deep sea water,
> I want my body to bump the pier.
> Neptune is calling his wayward daughter,
> "Edna, come over here!"

And by then Lowell had considerably tempered the emotional key by giving the poem to the male speaker, by making the dream only an episode, not the inescapable conclusion of the poem, and by distancing the dream a little from the day they shared together—not "that night I had a dream," but "one night." The changes are quiet ones, but they transform the poem from one of an entrapment and thwarted passion attributed to Bishop into a poem of erosion and frustration experienced by the two of them, something more like "To Marguerite" or "Dover Beach," two of Lowell's favorite poems. The lovers on their "slab of rock," in their physicality, their subjection to time are like the "dozens of bleak / white frame houses stuck / like oyster shells / on a hill of rock." Against the barnacled nature of which the lovers appear to be part, he poses an evanescent image of desire:

> We wished our two souls
> might return like gulls
> to the rock. In the end,
> the water was too cold for us.

Lines from "Water" were first intertwined with another poem, "For Elizabeth Bishop Flying to Rio de Janeiro" (finally published in *History*, much revised, as "For Elizabeth Bishop 2: Castine, Maine"), which also began as a soliloquy for her. But here he attributed to Bishop, in their parting at Bangor, words that didn't entirely please her:

> Starlike the eagle on my locket watch,
> Mother's sole heirloom. I hear her, "All I want
> To do is kill you!"—I, a child of four;
> She, early American and militant.

Bishop wrote to him immediately: "If you ever do anything with the poem about me—would you change the remark my mother was supposed to have made? She never did make it; in fact I don't remember any direct threats, except the usual maternal ones—her danger for me was just implied in the things I overheard the grown-ups say before and after her disappearance. Poor thing, I don't want to have it any worse than it was."

In these drafts Lowell takes some pleasure in exaggerating Bishop's already quite real solitude and displacement as a child and young woman. The drama ranged from small things (the

mother's *sole* heirloom) to larger ones (the alleged threat of the
mother to kill Bishop)—in one version: "Mother's sole relic,
where she lay in jail / After her tries to kill me not yet four").
He suggests, with careful ellipses, that there was a time—"Two
years out of Vassar, Elizabeth, a frantic / anchor unsecured by
any hope . . ."—when Bishop was close to suicide. At first, he
thinks of her wanderings, her inability to settle on a place to
live as a kind of insanity.

> Half Nova Scotian, half New Englander,
> Wholly Atlantic, I would drift and hear
> My genius begging for its cap and bells,
> And tears bedewed my flat, untasted beer—
> Key West, the Village, our Atlantic Coast
> Then Nova Scotia—there was nowhere else;
> Yet both my countries gave me up for lost.

The "cap and bells" ended up in a later version as the regalia
of George III, to whom Bishop's Nova Scotian forebears had
remained loyal—"mad King George." ("Poor puffing pig, he
only hurt himself, / his periwigged face was like a shaving
mug.")

In the draft soliloquy Lowell has Bishop thinking of Dorothy and William Wordsworth:

> One reads his "Dearest friend, my dear, dear friend,"
> And weeps for Wordsworth, yes, and Dorothy—
> All that dry, horselike, Viking energy—
> How soldierly their Northumberland reserve
> Defied the Walsung's incest! . . . I will serve
> England's true genius, I desire to bend
> With humorous awe to love's contingency,

> Yet cringe disloyally from their fierce joy—
> Even Victoria in all her glory

Is less Olympian. Poor Wordsworth's sorry
Lightning-rod figure and sublimity
Say little after forty . . . The marvelous boy
Still (thirty) guides his sister to the sylvan Wye,
Mirrors the shooting lights in her wild eye!

It is easy to see why this particular poetic tack was abandoned. The identifications are too confused. Were Dorothy and William meant to be prototypes of the young Bishop and Lowell? And if so, at some points Bishop is poet and at others dedicated sister. The nineteenth-century pair represent a kind of stalwart Viking entanglement which Bishop and Lowell had now left behind, and its rejection is something the poem sees, hazily, as a key to Bishop's humanity. However elliptically, the stanzas gloss Lowell's letter of August 15 and his efforts to set himself and Bishop free; they also reveal an entangling feeling of rivalry, a quickly suppressed attempt to imagine Bishop less as an equal and more as an adoring companion. ("The marvelous boy / Still . . . guides his sister to the sylvan Wye, / Mirrors the shooting lights in her wild eye!")

Read guardedly, these drafts usually are of help in understanding the emotional field within which Lowell was operating when he wrote a poem, the charged particles before the magnet has drawn them firmly into place. Lost love, rival, adoring friend, suffering youth doomed to poetry—Bishop is in these poems more as a locus for Lowell's feelings than as her historical self. In their first stages the poems are both a way of reaching out to another figure and of appropriating others' experiences or projecting some of Lowell's own extreme feelings upon them. So, for example, in the case of Bishop's "murderous mother," Lowell exaggerated beyond what Bishop had told him the parental violence which sets a child adrift. He made Bishop a counterpart to the figures he cut for himself in his own autobiographical pieces. One of them, the hound House on Fire, the bull terrier whose mother had been deserted by his father, yearns to grow up "to be a champ so that I can kill my father." "My own father," Lowell wrote, "was a gentle, faithful, and dim man. I don't know why I was agin him. I hope there will be peace." To discover family violence elsewhere—and, exaggerating Bishop's case, in the comforting reversal of a parent harming a child, may have allowed him to feel less monstrous about his own wishes. In any event, the mixture of curiosity and projection characterized many of his "portraits." They were slightly crazed mirrors which allowed him both to feel kindred and to appropriate a less guilt-ridden, more vital persona.

The poems about Bishop are emotionally charged in another way. Ian Hamilton, in his biography of Lowell, has traced the alarming regularity with which Lowell's manic attacks were accompanied by infatuations outside his marriage, fantasy desertions of his wife which would allow him a clean slate, a feeling of being purged. In 1957 the high amorous signs and mania were also accompanied by intense poetic activity. The early drafts of one of the *Life Studies* poems, "Waking in the Blue," were disoriented love poems addressed to Ann Adden, a "psychiatric fieldworker" from Bennington College whom Lowell met when he was finally hospitalized in December. Ann Adden was soon out of his life, and once the generating energy of his affair had been absorbed, she was out of his poem as well. What was left was a disciplined and harrowing poem about life in McLean Hospital, now shorn of its fantasy Muse and of the possibilities of escape and self-deception that Ann Adden represented. There are no signs of Ann Adden in it, and yet in some way the energy she released is part of the poem.

Lowell's attachment to Bishop was richer and more complicated than any such evanescent affair. Still, Bishop's visit to Castine did prompt his amorous attentions—and there was the noticeable speeding up that August, though this time he recovered quickly (only to suffer a severe breakdown in December). His immediate apologies, his understanding letter after her visit show how eager he was to free their friendship of any confusing romantic fantasies. The yearned-for "other woman" was a very small part of what he felt for her, but it did contribute to the snarl of motives and of responses to Bishop and her poetry. However confused his feelings about her, the *act* of trying to disentangle them released energies that were part of one of the most intense moments in his writing career.

———

Lowell always spoke of August and September of 1957 as a turning point in the writing of *Life Studies*. "I've been furiously writing at poems," he wrote to Bishop,

and spent whole blue and golden Maine days in my bedroom with a ghastly utility bedside lamp on, my pajamas turning oily with sweat, and I have six poems started. They beat the big drum too much. There's one in a small voice that's fairly charmingly written I hope (called Skunk Hour, not in your style yet indebted a little to your Armadillo). If I can get two short lines and a word, I'll mail it to you. The others, God willing, will come to something in the course of the winter. At least I feel I have armloads of lines and leads.

Lowell could be professorial later on about his debt in "Skunk Hour" to "The Armadillo": "[I] was now intent on copying its form. Both poems have an ambling structure, little stanzas and the final natural but charged image that gives the poem its conclusion and title." At the time, of course, the atmosphere was more fraught; he felt himself engaged in a "battle with the impossible." What was important about the poems *about* Bishop was that for the moment he discarded them. He found more release in writing a poem in her manner than in making use of her autobiography—and, above all, in writing a poem which, however metaphorically, accounted for their differences rather than trying to appropriate her character. "A skunk isn't much of a present for a Lady Poet," he wrote jokingly to her about the dedication, "but I'm a skunk in the poem." The substitution of the fearless unretreating little outcast for Bishop's more armored fleeing beast was the enlivening discovery of "Skunk Hour." Lowell wrote these last stanzas first, and the image of the skunks fiercely parading down the center of the New England village must have alleviated some of the feelings of disruption and guilt which his illness and his behavior toward Bishop and his family brought on.

There were deeper connections to Bishop's work. For a time, Lowell had the last four stanzas of the poem in close to their final form but with nothing before them, and he began to be repelled, he says, by their "bleak violence":

I began to feel that real poetry came, not from fierce confessions, but from something almost meaningless but imagined. I was haunted by an image of a blue china doorknob. I never used the doorknob, or knew what it meant, yet somehow it started the current of images in my opening stanzas. They were written in reverse order, and at last gave my poem an earth to stand on, and space to breathe.

The descriptive styles which called into question the confessional cast of his last stanzas prompted the milder landscapes of the opening he added to "Skunk Hour"—and of course his prized antagonist in those styles was Bishop, one of whose entirely descriptive poems, "Cape Breton," "contains" a china doorknob:

> . . . the closed schoolhouse,
> where today no flag is flying
> from the rough-adzed pole topped with a white china doorknob.

In Lowell's first draft of the notes on "Skunk Hour," it was a white china doorknob, not a blue, whose image released the flow of images in his opening stanzas.★

"Skunk Hour," then, was more than superficially Bishop's poem. Dedicated to her, stimulated by her visit and her "Armadillo," it was a successful poem in her vein completed amid a frustrating series of attempts to write poems *about* her. Dealing

---

★The passage in Lowell's draft notes for "On 'Skunk Hour' " reads: "After getting a version of the last four stanzas, I began to recoil from their violent and personal force. For several days, I was haunted by the idea that some deep personal experience might have less poetic truth in it than a description of a china doorknob. The image of the white doorknob remains with me, though it never got into my poem and never revealed its meaning. Instead my first four stanzas, rewritten more or less in reverse order, gave me space to breathe and a freedom from significance."

with many of the pressures Lowell was feeling that summer in Castine, "Skunk Hour" was in part nourished by Lowell's confused feeling for Bishop as admired writer, rival poet, unattainable and renounced love, and fantasy Muse.

Prompted by Bishop's poems, Lowell has written a very different, a much more *historical* poem. Whatever gestures he was making toward descriptive styles, toward Bishop's habitual coolness of tone, "Skunk Hour" never claims to be "receptive," to be merely open to the givens of time and place. Bishop's poem begins "This is the time of year . . ." It gives itself over to the pleasures of observing the fire balloons on St. John's Eve and only as those begin to spend themselves investigates their consequences. She must by the end reinterpret her scene. Lowell's "time of year" is more deliberately chosen, its features more purposefully symbolic from the start: "The season's ill . . . A red fox stain covers Blue Hill." The symbolic creatures in each poem—the skunk, the armadillo—serve each poet as a resolving force. But Lowell's skunk, with its multiple meanings, can't help but refract his human situation, become part of his autobiography. (As he pointed out, all too simply, "I'm a skunk in the poem." And elsewhere: "I like the language of my new poems, but feel fatigued by their fierceness, my old serpent in the perfect garden. I wish I could be described as stubborn, hopeful, summery, utilitarian.")

Bishop's armadillo is viewed from a greater distance, is more creaturely, a part of the whole natural scene rather than the human and historical one. She documents a prior creation, in contrast to Lowell's stubborn and impressive refusal to believe in a world prior to his own. In "Skunk Hour" the physical world is drawn into a historical drama of Lowell's re-enacted helplessness. In "The Armadillo," the panorama is one of great attraction to and compassion for the physical world of which the spectator-poet is only a small part. However much Lowell needed a descriptive style as ballast, it is incidental, not central to his poem; the scene's repeated monosyllables are only tolling to prepare the "hell" and "ill" of the close. It is interesting how uncomfortable Lowell was with sustained description, how deftly he turns it to narrative, even in his comments on Bishop's poem: "Weak and armored, I suppose he [the armadillo] is those people carrying balloons—illegal—to their local saint." Bishop's poem makes no mention of "those people" and gives the fire balloons their own hypnotic entrance and momentum:

> This is the time of year
> when almost every night
> the frail, illegal fire balloons appear.
> Climbing the mountain height,
>
> rising toward a saint
> still honored in these parts,
> the paper chambers flush and fill with light
> that comes and goes, like hearts.

"The Armadillo," and Lowell's attendant feeling for and rivalry with Bishop, liberated him, were part of the impulse for his *Life Studies* poems. Yet "Skunk Hour" is quite different from the poems he completed soon after, the family poems. In "Skunk Hour" he separated himself poetically from Bishop, as he had personally in his letter of apology in August of 1957. Testing himself against her as well as learning from her, he made the poem a way of confirming his historical—as distinct from descriptive—vantage point, and also a way of renouncing grandiosity. In that sense "Skunk Hour" is pivotal for his book—placed last, but really the poem that launched him into his true subject, investigation of the debilitated historical and personal forces that had shaped his life.

"My darling receding Elizabeth," Lowell wrote, mimicking Miss Moore's expressive salutations. Bishop was on a month-long freighter trip, returning to Brazil. In certain ways their friendship resumed its old tenor. "I really glory in the memory of your visit and miss you terribly," he wrote in December. When she left he had given her a Christmas present which she could not resist opening because of its label, *lava cameo*. Two weeks before the holiday, she thanked him:

Sydney Smith speaks somewhere of an Englishman dancing at court in Naples, wearing "volcanic silk with lava buttons," and I'd wondered what it meant—it sounded slightly Emily-Dickinson-ish for Mr. Smith. Now I think I know—perhaps "volcanic silk" was shot silk, or else just scarlet—but I think the buttons, like your cameo, must be straight from Vesuvius, don't you? It's really a marvellous, curious, quaint, and evocative piece of workmanship and I am crazy about it . . . It makes me think of the Brownings, "The Marble Faun," "Roderick Hudson," and my own strange stay in Naples. Did you notice the high point of the carving—that one romantic curl that you can see through? I also like the other cruder curls of the gold, which remind me strongly of sucked dandelion stems; but I'm getting altogether too Marianne-ish about this, I'm afraid—you can see I am very much taken with it. It is really pure 19th-century romanticism, late—do you know anything about where it came from and if I am right?

Bishop's precision, their high romantic pleasure in Victorian echoes—these were constants in their relationship, a grounded exaltation. But in other ways Lowell's achievement in and absorption by *Life Studies* subtly adjusted their friendship. Bishop couldn't help but feel challenged by the energies released in the midst of one of Lowell's most unstable periods. "The whole phenomena [*sic*] of your quick recovery and simultaneous productivity seems to me in looking back to be the real marvel of the summer." Bishop probably saw "Skunk Hour" for the first time in Boston in late September when she took a weekend trip to say goodbye to Lowell. He had gone there from Castine, still working on poems "like a skunk, doggedly and happily," as he wrote Jarrell. Bishop also saw a few "family poems" and was to see more of them in a manuscript Lowell mailed to Brazil. It contained at least "My Last Afternoon with Uncle Devereux Winslow," "Commander Lowell," "Terminal Days at Beverly Farms," "Sailing Home from Rapallo," "Memories of West Street and Lepke," "Man and Wife," " 'To Speak of Woe That

Is in Marriage,' " and, of course, "Skunk Hour." Bishop's full reaction was delayed. She sent a telegram which Lowell carefully preserved and marked "from Brazil": POEMS LOVELY HAVEN'T FORGOTTEN YOU / ELIZABETH. But it wasn't until December 11 that she finally wrote him, puzzled herself about why she had uncharacteristically waited a month. The letter is long, was written over two or three days, and circles Lowell's new poems appreciatively and cautiously. The *Life Studies* poems—which he continued to send her over the next year— proved the occasion not only for praise but for a reconsideration of her own work. She'd been working on her "Letter to Two Friends" (Moore and Lowell) and finding it rather light:

Oh heavens, when does one begin to write the *real* poems? I certainly feel as if I never had. But of course I don't feel that way about yours— they all seem real as real—and getting more so—

To his compliment that he'd "broken through" to where Bishop had always been, she could only reply, "I haven't got anywhere at all, I think—just to those first benches to sit down and rest on, in a side-arbor of the maze."

"Skunk Hour" is still her favorite—and Lota's too—yet "I suppose it's exercises compared to the other ones." The family group was "more brilliant." The comment is telling and characteristic of the way, in the next two years, she keeps turning Lowell's poems over in her mind. What interested her was not the poem most indebted to her own work, nor did she respond to any single poem so much as to the ensemble.

I find I have here surely a whole new book of poems, don't I? I think all the family group—some of them I hadn't seen in Boston— are really superb, Cal. I don't know what order they'll come in, but they make a wonderful and impressive drama, and I think in them you've found the new rhythm you wanted, without any hitches. Could they have some sort of general title?

She did not like the title "Life Studies" that he eventually gave to the group of autobiographical poems in his book as well as to the book itself. But it was the notion of a sequence or series that, from the first, apparently challenged and drew her. The family poems, she writes in the same letter,

have that sure feeling, as if you'd been in a stretch . . . when everything and anything suddenly seemed material for poetry—or not material, seemed to *be* poetry, and all the past illuminated in long shafts here and there, like a long-waited-for sunrise. If only one could see everything that way all the time! It seems to me it's the whole purpose of art, to the artist (but not to the audience)—that rare feeling of control, of illumination—life *is* all right, for the time being. Anyway, when I read such an extended display of imagination as this, I feel it *for* you.

The tightrope of envy and generosity is striking in Bishop's long letter, as she tries to translate Lowell's accomplishment into serious questions about her own:

I must confess (and I imagine most of our contemporaries would confess the same thing) that I am green with envy of your kind of assurance. I feel that I could write in as much detail about my Uncle Artie, say—but what would be the significance? Nothing at all. He became a drunkard, fought with his wife, and spent most of his time fishing . . . and was ignorant as sin. It is sad; slightly more interesting than having an uncle practising law in Schenectady maybe, but that's all. Whereas all you have to do is put down the names! And the fact that it seems significant, illustrative, American, etc. gives you, I think, the confidence you display about tackling any idea or theme, *seriously*, in both writing and conversation. In some ways you are the luckiest poet I know!—in some ways not so lucky, either, of course. But it is hell to realize one has wasted half one's talent through timidity that probably could have been overcome if anyone in one's family had had a few grains of sense or education . . . Well, maybe it's not too late!

I'm not really complaining and of course am not really "jealous" in any deep sense at all—I've felt almost as wonderful a sense of relief since I first saw some of these poems in Boston as if I'd written them myself and I've thought of them at odd times and places with the greatest pleasure every single day since, I swear.

I have quoted at length from her letter of December 1957 to suggest the seriousness from the very start of Bishop's engagement with *Life Studies*. It continued through the publication of the book—for which Bishop wrote the jacket blurb—in April 1959. She had been "craving something new," she wrote Lowell in the fall of 1958, and now, when she read American poetry—she was going to give a talk on American literature in Rio—she found she had "new ideas." The terms Bishop uses in her letter are interesting: the poems make an impressive *drama*; she plans to talk about "Democracy": Concord's, a little like a Greek city, and then "Whitman's steamy variety," Amherst's variety, and "your interest in character will be stressed—after all, I can't think of any English poet who writes about *people*, the way you do any more." She is constantly weighing the claims and possibilities of narrative against her ingrained resistance to narrative styles. ("I just read, for the first time, 'The White Peacock' and you have no idea how refreshing and wonderful all that long-winded nature-description seemed.") What impresses her about Lowell's narrative style is its pared-down manner, presentation without editorial interpretation—the "strangely modest tone" no matter how personal, how autobiographical the material. More, that everything or anything seems not simply *material* for poetry, but to *be* poetry. Such terms are ones that could more comfortably bring narrative close to descriptive poetry—poetry documenting a prior creation, the kind of poetry that allowed her to enter, self-effacing, and lay claim to a pre-existing world. And it is when, writing the blurb for the first edition of *Life Studies*, she seeks a figure for the transforming energy in Lowell's verse that she turns to that image of her grandfather's Bible under a reading-glass:

As a child, I used to look at my grandfather's Bible under a powerful reading-glass. The letters assembled beneath the lens were suddenly like a Lowell poem, as big as life and as alive, and rainbow-edged. It seemed to illuminate as it magnified; it could also be used as a burning-glass.

Bishop's reactions to Lowell's work allowed her to come to terms with a mixture of impulses in her own recent writing. She had not—contrary to the impression her letters give—been unproductive during the years since she had come to Brazil. She had, indeed, completed what was for her a very substantial amount—a dozen poems, two stories ("Gwendolyn" and "In the Village"), and the translation of *The Diary of "Helena Morley."* Among the poems were both descriptive pieces— "Questions of Travel," for example—and anecdotal character sketches ("Manuelzinho"). There was a strong autobiographical bent now in Bishop's writing, and *Life Studies* only encouraged it. But this new work of Lowell's, with its mixture of poetry and prose, with its intense effort at self-presentation, raised a more serious issue for her. Did the disparate poems and stories she was writing cohere, in their own way, as self-presentation? Did her work in these years amount to something as sustained as Lowell's recent work appeared to be?

5 / Questions of Travel

For New Year's Day in 1959 Bishop sent Lowell a poem, "Brazil, January 1, 1502," that she had completed a few months before. "Jungle into picture into history and then jungle again" was Lowell's way of characterizing it. "I think it is a bit artificial," she said, "but I finally had to do something with the cliché about the landscape looking like a tapestry, I suppose." The triggering epigraph ("embroidered nature . . . tapestried landscape") was from Sir Kenneth Clark's *Landscape into Art*, and the poem is in part a comment on such passive notions, a rededication to what Brazil had confirmed in her preferences for descriptive encounter over historical experience:

> Januaries, Nature greets our eyes
> exactly as she must have greeted theirs:
> every square inch filling in with foliage—

The energies of the crescent jungle dwarf those of Brazil's first Christian settlers, as they are also a potential reproof of the zealous poet just entering the country. However much tropical luxury encourages the picture-making pleasures—the sky a "simple web," rocks "worked" with lichens, the jungle like a tapestry from its frame—it has also an independent force that makes Nature in the poem (very much a "she") as elusive as the Indian women who continually lead on and escape the early Christian invaders.

That Bishop saw this as an analogue of her own experience, her own writing efforts in Brazil, is made clear by the position she gave the poem in her next collection, *Questions of Travel* (1965). She had already printed in *A Cold Spring* her first Brazilian poem, "Arrival at Santos," but would choose to reprint it as the opening of *Questions of Travel* with the added legend, dating her arrival, *"January, 1952."* Her New Year's poem, "Brazil, January 1, 1502," which follows immediately, picks up and generalizes the perils of that arrival: "Januaries . . ." And, in fact, it was not long after writing the poem that she began thinking of her new collection under the title *January River.* A set of linked poems, very different from *Life Studies,* was emerging from her Brazilian experience: her geographical way of locating herself rather than Lowell's historical progression. She was not writing, as Lowell did, in the shadow of a family, present and past, but rather almost the reverse, almost as a lone individual entering into and acquiring attachments, tentatively, but more completely than she ever had before, out of a need to gain a world rather than to lose one. The shape of the book crystallized over the years rather than being strictly calculated. But it came eventually to represent the deepening stages by which Brazil reconciled her to her presence in the world—from the superficial observations of the arrival at Santos through a mythological identification with the spirits of the Amazon. In February 1960 she actually took a trip up that river. "I suppose I should be studying the stones of Florence," she wrote Howard Moss that spring, "but geographic curiosity leads me on and on and I can't stop. Last night I dreamed there was a narrow road that began at Tierra del Fuego and went straight north, and I had started to walk it, quite cheerfully. —A large primitive stone coffin was being carried on mule-back alongside of me, ready for me when I gave out—the mule driver had a toothache. (I can't understand that part.)" And even before her Amazon trip she had written a poem of expectation, "The

Riverman," based on details from Charles Wagley's *Amazon Town*. It's told in the first person, the growing obsession of a man in a remote Amazon village who decides to be a witch doctor working with water spirits:

> Look, it stands to reason
> that everything we need
> can be obtained from the river.
> It drains the jungles; it draws
> from trees and plants and rocks
> from half around the world,
> it draws from the very heart
> of the earth the remedy
> for each of the diseases—
> one just has to know how to find it.
>
> . . .
>
> The river breathes in salt
> and breathes it out again,
> and all is sweetness there
> in the deep, enchanted silt.

Lowell promptly drew some autobiographical conclusions for her. "The Riverman" was "the best fairy story in verse I know. It brings back an old dream of yours, you said you felt you were a mermaid, scraping barnacles off a wharf-pile. That was Maine, not Brazil." Certainly "The Riverman" is worlds away from the deprivation reflected in the "nightmare" she reported to Lowell more than a decade before. But Bishop had her own way of intertwining her Brazilian experience with the further reaches of memory. She seemed to sense more and more clearly that her deepening assimilation to Brazil not only recalled her Nova Scotia childhood but helped her recapitulate and reclaim it. Her poems about Brazil take on an air of mysterious and festive progress. For the first time, as we have seen, she had succeeded in writing directly about Nova Scotia and her childhood losses in "Gwendolyn" and "In the Village," and, in the latter story, about the enabling elements in her Great Village life. Her fascination in translating *The Diary of "Helena Morley"* had to do with such restorative powers, as well as with the fact that this was "a real, day-by-day diary, kept by a real girl." Bishop writes in her introduction to the *Diary*:

> The more I read the book the better I liked it. The scenes and events it described were odd, remote, and long ago, and yet fresh, sad, funny, and eternally true. The longer I stayed on in Brazil the more Brazilian the book seemed, yet much of it could have happened in any small provincial town or village, and at almost any period of history—at least before the arrival of the automobile and the moving-picture theater. Certain pages reminded me of more famous and "literary" ones: Nausicaa doing her laundry on the beach, possibly with the help of *her* freed slaves; bits from Chaucer; Wordsworth's poetical children and country people, or Dorothy Wordsworth's wandering beggars. Occasionally entries referring to slavery seemed like notes for an unwritten, Brazilian, feminine version of Tom Sawyer and Nigger Jim.

Many of the remarks Bishop delighted in ("Your father was always a good five years older than I was") carried her back to Nova Scotia. "I'm sure I've heard most of them before." The links between her adopted new life and the springs of childhood observation puzzled and encouraged her, as if they were somehow a key to writing and resilience.

Shortly after she saw Lowell in 1957, her Aunt Grace sent her a matched pair of family portraits she'd known as a child: her mother, "Gertie," about nine, leaning on a "red-plush-hung-table" and, leaning on a red plush chair, her mother's brother Arthur, "Artie," aged twelve, painted with legs crossed like his sister's but in the opposite direction. This was the same Uncle Artie she had told Lowell of, saying that writing in detail about Uncle Artie, a drunkard and as ignorant as sin, would be utterly without significance. Yet not many years later, Bishop is beginning a story about Uncle Artie (one she wouldn't publish until 1977, because his wife was still alive)—a story that she makes resonant in her own particular way.

"Memories of Uncle Neddy," as it was eventually called, begins with the arrival of the matched portraits in a rainy Rio, where everything is damp and moldy. The "ancestor-children," clean and glossy as almost never again in life, are in constant danger from the mildew that "appears overnight on dark surfaces, like breath on a mirror." With that arresting image, conflating the perfect dead with the vibrant decaying living, Bishop concentrates the force of her story at the end: the preserved and static past continually challenged by active change and decay; the interpenetration of childhood and ripening life. The small Northern figures stare into her adopted tropical world, posing questions about the links of her present and past.

Uncle Neddy will continue to exchange his direct, bright-hazel, child's looks, now, with those of strangers—dark-eyed Latins he never knew, who never would have understood him, whom he would have thought of, if he had ever thought of them at all, as "foreigners." How late, Uncle Neddy, how late to have started on your travels!

Uncle Neddy is a figure against whom Bishop implicitly measures herself. In the real Uncle Artie—the child in the portrait—she saw a physical resemblance. In the fictional Uncle Neddy she imagined, and has imagined over the years, a kind of devil, "not a violent, active Devil, but a gentle black one, a devil of weakness, acquiescence." Uncle Neddy's life and marriage are blighted by drink and irresponsibility in ways that Bishop obviously identified with her own anarchic side. The story both embraces and separates itself from this figure, especially in its understanding of the difference Bishop's travels have made—both her appetite for travel and the imaginative exercise it afforded her.

"Memories of Uncle Neddy," though unfinished at the time, is unique among her works in the sixties because it attempts in fictional form the montage of Nova Scotia and Brazil which Bishop felt as a fact of her daily life in the Southern Hemisphere. Her Aunt Grace had sent her some Great Village historical publications which were a help in writing "Uncle

Artie" and in describing the Nova Scotia village of her youth. And she had been reading Lucy Larcom's *A New England Girl-hood*—"fascinating . . . Beverly in 1830 was very much like Great Village in 1920." Now, of course, TV aerials rise from the Great Village shingles. "The dying out of local cultures seems to me one of the most tragic things in this century." She finds it happening in Brazil, too. Bishop's interest in her past is double: for one thing, she is probing the secret resilience of her childhood, the unresolved, undetermined nature of childhood perception. But she is also probing the degree to which her way of perceiving the world is bound up with village life— where, if anywhere, one can discover the waywardness, the unpredictability of what may appear, on its surface, to be altogether simple. And the experience of village life, as I have said, held for her one of the secrets of vitality—a language, open-eyed, that is unembarrassed by anomaly.

In April of 1962, while she was in the middle of writing "Uncle Artie," Bishop received from Lowell a short stanzaic version of her memoir story "In the Village." "I don't know why I bother to write 'Uncle Artie,' really," she wrote Lowell in response. "I shd. just send you my first notes and you can turn him into a wonderful poem—he is even more your style than the Village story was." She went on to praise his poem: "The Scream really works well, doesn't it—the story is far enough behind me so I can see it as a poem now. The first few stanzas I saw only my story—then the poem took over—and the last stanza is wonderful. It builds up beautifully, and everything of importance is there. But I was very surprised." However equable Bishop tries to be, she was clearly thrown off balance, especially about the memoir she was now writing. Lowell picked up the anxiety in her letter, hoped that "The Scream," as he titled it, hadn't annoyed her; it was just a footnote to her story. Bishop smooths this over in her reply: "NO —I was very pleased with 'The Scream.' I find it touching to think you were worried for fear I might be annoyed . . . All letter-writing is dangerous, anyway—fraught with peril." The ripple of misunderstanding comes at a time when Lowell was about to visit Brazil and when, eager as she was for his visit, Bishop has to explain her own relative anonymity in Brazil: "They think if I were any good I'd be at home." Lowell is coming officially and is a MAN. Lady poets in Brazil are the male poet's mistress: "He writes his poems for her."

The real issue vis-à-vis Lowell's versing of "In the Village" has to do with his appropriations of Bishop's experience and her own efforts to write a level autobiography. His "borrowing" prods her awareness, throws into relief the differences in their self-presentation. With "The Scream" he had sent her a final version of "Water," the poem remembering Stonington in 1948: "More romantic and gray than the whole truth," Lowell remarked, "for all has been sunny between us." His adaptation of "In the Village" was more elegiac as well. It, by his account, makes something small and literary out of something "much larger, gayer, and more healthy." Even his choice of title suggests the melodramatic view he was taking of Bishop's story. He had added significantly to the details he quoted from Bishop. When the young girl's mother disappears for good, he has her say something he claims to have heard from his young daughter Harriet: "But you can't love everyone, / your heart won't let you." The last stanza, according to Lowell, is just Bishop's prose in three-beat lines:

> A scream! But they are all gone,
> those aunts and aunts, a grandfather,
> a grandmother, my mother—
> even her scream—too frail
> for us to hear their voices long.

But in Bishop's story that last phrase is part of a question, not a statement: "Are they too frail for us to hear their voices long, too mortal?" And the voices, apart from the scream, belong not to people but to things: "clothes, crumbling postcards, broken china; things damaged and lost, sickened or destroyed; even the frail almost-lost scream." Her question is about the artifacts from which she has imagined her own losses, artifacts whose subsequent loss she has herself survived. Lowell concentrates on the vanished ancestors; Bishop mixes elegy with an edge of resilience. Her story ends with the *clang* of the blacksmith's forge, the sound that fuses the scream with ongoing life: "It is the elements speaking: earth, air, fire, water."

Eventually, when he put "The Scream" into *For the Union Dead*, Lowell placed it just after "Middle Age," a poem in which, at forty-five, he meets his father at the same age, who, though he "never climbed / Mount Sion, yet left / dinosaur / death-steps on the crust, / where I must walk." He would have imagined it, very probably, as a pendant piece to the poem in Bishop's voice about the scars of her mother's death and insanity. Both "The Scream" and "Water" were tempered versions of Lowell's need to identify Bishop with his own experience, however much he darkened what she had written and what they had shared. Nor did Bishop call attention to his shadings, except perhaps by taking a measured tone that suggested she'd been caught off guard—"very surprised" by "The Scream" and almost treating "Water" as if it were about someone else, preferring to account for the mermaid episode by a reference to the parody of Edna St. Vincent Millay. She praises the "color" stanzas (4 and 5), the rock "the color / of iris, rotting and turning purpler." And, apologizing for her "George Washington handicap," she suggests "lobster town" instead of Lowell's "It was a Maine fishing town," and "fish for bait" to clarify Lowell's draft "where the fish were trapped." He promptly accepted both "corrections."

What she does admit later in the letter—he had sent her at least five poems—is that she feels challenged to write a lot immediately, yet worries that her verses "would come out, if at all, sounding like you. But . . . if after I read a poem the world looks like that poem for 24 hrs. or so I'm sure it's a good one—and the same goes for paintings . . . Recently here I saw a Jules Bissier show (do you know his paintings?—slight, maybe, but beautiful)—and the world looked all like Bissiers for a long time, here, there, and everywhere. *Your* scenery comes and goes, half-real and half-language, all the time."

During these years Bishop's tone toward Lowell is a strange mixture—sometimes intimidated, sometimes excited by his intensity of self-presentation and his appetite for experience. She is gingerly too, uncertain about her own independence but solicitous as well about Lowell's health. His breakdowns came with brutal regularity at least every two years, and the friendship with Bishop—so removed from the scene and the fray—had special easing powers. With her as with Peter Taylor, he writes, he never has to be diplomatic—there is "no one else I can talk to with confidence and abandon and delicacy." She was witness to the ups and downs of his poetic ambitions, to their disturbing side, too closely associated with his illnesses. He wrote her in July 1959 that "in the hospital I spent a mad month or more rewriting *everything* in my three books. I arranged my poems chronologically, starting in Greek and Roman times and finally rose to air the present [sic] with *Life Studies*. I felt I had hit the skies, that all cohered. It was mostly waste." He describes the seesaw of breakdown and recovery in similar terms over and over: "One is left strangely dumb, and talking about the past is like a cat's trying to explain climbing down a ladder." A few years later he tells her, "I don't seem able to use that much remembrance anymore." He announces that his "old Bible," *The Education of Henry Adams*, now bores him:

I think his tone is a state anyone from our background should go through to be honest and alive, and then drop. I suspect anyone who hasn't been that bitter. Still, staying there is like calling malaria life. I guess what I mean is that there was real malaria under the jokes, exaggerations, and epigrams, a sort of Baudelairean gallantry. But who could *want* what Empson says somewhere *to learn a style from a despair?*

The feeling of exhaustion with his own voice (this is Lowell's phrase) was one that had already prompted him to begin, soon after he finished *Life Studies*, a set of translations. Writing his poems could seem "distasteful," but doing what became his *Imitations* seemed "like living in someone else's house and being carried by their framework." If Bishop was troubled by his borrowings of *her* voice and *her* experience, she also had ample evidence in his letters of Lowell's fatigue, of his strenuous casting about for other voices. This spending of oneself in one's writing was an experience foreign to Bishop but vividly present in Lowell's example—against which Bishop, looking not within herself but to a creation outside herself, would slowly define her own poetic practice in these years as she put into her own kind of order the poems she had completed since coming to Brazil.

———

Some of their differences were made sharply apparent, in fact, not by poems relating to Bishop, but by Lowell's translations of French poetry. Translations had always been a resource for Lowell—or rather versions of the sort he did even before his first book, some of which turned up in *Lord Weary's Castle*, poems "after" Rilke, Valéry, Dante, Villon, for instance—ways of varying and extending his voice. In the 1950s, reading a parallel French translation of Rilke's "Orpheus. Eurydice. Hermes," he felt challenged to do a better job of it in English. Later, as relief from "the longer, less concentrated problems of translating Racine's *Phèdre*," he worked at Baudelaire to give himself practice in quatrains and couplets. While he was in the hospital, and at the same time that he was plotting the grandiose chronological collection of his own poems, he did several translations of Heine and Baudelaire. Admiring Montale, he discovered how well that poet emerged in English free verse. Such efforts, "written from time to time when I was unable to do anything of my own," eventually resulted in the collection to be published as *Imitations*, which he proposed to dedicate to Bishop. She must have received the manuscript just after New Year's in 1961, and sent Lowell a telegram: TRANSLATIONS ABSOLUTELY STUNNING. PROUD AND PLEASED. But it wasn't until the first of March that she finally sent off a letter about them. In an earlier letter, evidently lost in the Brazil–New York post, she had already praised Lowell's *Phaedra* as a tour de force, noble, natural, "pure, but undated." She had more trepidations about the short poems—or at least the French poems, which she knew best. The dedication "of course made me shed tears." But once Bishop begins to study the French poems, she gets very nervous about them—so nervous, probably, that she delayed writing, then put her letter through a number of drafts, all of which appear to have been sent eventually to Lowell.

Once again, her tone toward him is mixed, even confused—sometimes solicitous, sometimes disagreeing, then embarrassed by the sharpness of her disagreements. First of all she is protective of him, of his "reputation for solid, severe, painstaking workmanship" and doesn't want him to be attacked.

Your star is so very high now . . . and to publish things open to misunderstanding might produce a lot of foolish jealous haggling and criticism that you could easily avoid.

What will the French say? What will the "niggling" London *Times* say? Or Eliot? Or perhaps he should consult Eliot before publishing these. But her concern runs deeper. The test cases are the Rimbaud poems, several of which Bishop had spent a month translating, alone one summer in Brittany. With both Baudelaire and Rimbaud, Lowell has made changes that *sound* like *mistakes*, she argues; sometimes he even has the poet say the opposite of what is said in the original. "The Rimbaud and Baudelaire poems are all so well known that I don't think you should lay yourself open to charges of carelessness or ignorance or wilful perversity." Baudelaire, she finds, is more suited to Lowell's temperament, manner, and rhythms. But several of the Rimbaud poems he has chosen—early sonnets—sound in the original "so gay and *healthy* and normal beside Baudelaire." Lowell has somehow darkened them.

At the risk of sounding schoolmarmish, Bishop not only makes corrections but makes a series of literal translations of

Rimbaud for him. She saves him, or tries to save him, from errors. The last lines of "At the Green Cabaret"—"et m'emplit la chope immense, avec sa mousse / Que dorait un rayon de soleil arriéré"—should be "and filled up an immense stein for me, with its foam gilded by a ray of *late* sun" where Lowell had mistaken *arriéré* for *behind*. "The *late* seems very important, fixing the atmosphere of fatigue, late afternoon, peacefulness." And *tartines* are not tarts but the little pieces of bread and butter given to French schoolchildren. Lowell took the first suggestion, didn't bother with the second. Or in "On the Road"— his translation of Rimbaud's fantastical "Ma Bohème": Lowell has the carefree poet with "the rain's cheap wine . . . splashing on my face" where Rimbaud has simply "drops of dew" ("des gouttes de rosée"). And where Rimbaud has his poet plucking the elastics on his ragged shoes as if they were the strings of a lyre, holding one foot near his heart, Lowell has merely "one foot pressed tight against my heart," ignoring the fanciful lyre entirely and with it the bravura parody of Apollo serenading the Muses. Bishop's literal "corrections"—Lowell did not change his version of "Ma Bohème"—slip quickly over into questions of tone. Compared to Lowell's version, Rimbaud's poem is more consistently "delicate, gay, unreal—*humming*— like in The Tempest songs—"

"I feel I am running an awful risk and I am suffering, writing this," Bishop says of her revised and rerevised responses to the *Imitations*. What must have made her anxious, poem after poem, were the issues that always kept drawing themselves between her and Lowell: the question of a, by her lights, "healthy" view of the world and the related question of "fact," of misappropriating creations and lives not one's own. Without putting it so heavily or abstractly, she bridled at his Rimbaud poems: "I just can't decide how 'free' one has the right to be with the poet's intentions." "La Maline"—Lowell's "A Malicious Girl"—strikes her as "so much more light-hearted than you've made it, and the girl, fussing with plates to make an opening for conversation, is feminine, flirtatious, untidy, by implication young and pretty, 'naughty'—but not sordid or dirty. Although he [Rimbaud] likes to go in for adolescent shock, a lot of these early poems seem quite gay in spite of formal perfection." In "At the Green Cabaret" there is a more slatternly serving girl of whom Lowell says, "But it was terrific when the house-girl / with her earth-mother tits and come-on eyes . . ." Bishop recommends introducing the girl's entrance simply with "And it was adorable when . . ." And she points out that Rimbaud's soldier "studies" the naïve pictures while Lowell has him laughing at them. "I feel as if you've spiked it with alcohol," she remarks.

Again, in "The Sleeper in the Valley," she finds Lowell's language pressing too hard. For "c'est un petit val qui mousse de rayons" why add a simile as Lowell did—"The *whole* / valley bubbled with sunbeams like a beer-glass"—when Rimbaud does it all with a present-tense verb? "The little valley foams with sunbeams," Bishop suggests. Rimbaud's poem is a kind of delicate pastoral trick, a picture whose peace is broken only at the very end by a single outrageous detail. A soldier in a soothing landscape sleeps, like a tired sick child napping. Only in the last phrase are we shown that he is dead, two red holes in his side. Lowell early on gives him bruises; his "white eye rolls" (later his "blue eye rolls") in the next-to-last line. It spoils Rimbaud's joke, Bishop says, gives his show away "by bringing in his horrors too soon." But Lowell has upped the ante from the start, made his landscape more portentous than lulling. His river is "swollen." Instead of fragrances that might "make nostrils quiver" (the Wallace Fowlie translation) he has flowers that "no longer make his hot eyes weep."

What disquiets Bishop over and over is the force and scale of Lowell's language, and the word she keeps coming back to is "over-riding." She means not only the movement of Lowell's poems but their relation to the French originals. And, of course, Lowell, whether making mistakes or willful alterations, is perfectly aware of what he is doing. "This book is partly self-sufficient and separate from its sources," he would write in his introduction, "and should be first read as a sequence, one voice running through many personalities, contrasts and repetitions

. . . The dark and against the grain stand out . . ." What doesn't ring true for Bishop is his claim that though "reckless with literal meaning," he has "labored hard to get the tone." Their disagreement about tone, about the autonomy of the original texts, is almost a parody of their temperamental differences about poetry. Increasingly after *Life Studies* Lowell's appetite was for the poetic sequence which would amplify and explain the single life. The hospital fantasy of arranging all his poems chronologically beginning with Greek and Roman times was symptomatic, and would one day be realized in *History*. The narrative frame of *History*, however embracing, is, as Stephen Yenser pointed out, also *his*-story—the kaleidoscope arranging and rearranging the materials of his and other lives so that they make his own seem comprehensible and whole. Even the translations were to be read as the refraction of one voice playing through and appropriating what seemed the relevant experience of others. Years later, Bishop would connect Lowell's temperamental needs with certain habits of style. She spoke of the prodigious assortment of adjectives in his prose and his conversation as well as in his poetry—mostly referring to people rather than things. The attempt to be all-inclusive (in language, literature, even with women) extended down even to modifying a noun, a simple noun that perhaps didn't need to be modified at all. She detected—from the vantage point of his last book, *Day by Day*—an increasing eagerness in his work to pile up these adjectives, a habit that destroyed rather than enhanced their precision. One couldn't insert a small wedge of common sense or contradiction between them or ask *why*. Often the adjectives canceled each other out, and this led to flatness and deadness in spite of Lowell's attempts at brilliant effects.

Bishop's preternatural sense of the outside world as a separate and discrete creation was never Lowell's; it disturbed her that he often failed to observe the distinction between self and world, between writing and life. Poetry for Bishop was, in James Merrill's words, "a life both shaped by and distinct from the lived one." To Lowell's driven nature writing—never complete, always rearranged and rearrangeable—was by and large the only bearable way to experience life. It was *the* lived life. As he would say yearningly in one of his last poems, "Shifting Colors":

> I seek leave unimpassioned by my body,
> I am too weak to strain to remember, or give
> recollection the eye of a microscope. I see
> horse and meadow, duck and pond,
> universal consolatory
> description without significance,
> transcribed verbatim by my eye.

> This is not the directness that catches
> everything on the run and then expires—
> I would write only in response to the gods,
> like Mallarmé who had the good fortune
> to find a style that made writing impossible.

Bishop found the last lines "weird."

Bishop had a hard time explaining her attraction to Lowell's work as she became more intensely aware of their differences. She felt comfortable with *Life Studies* because she could think of the poems as modest, "gentle really," like a muted trumpet or a cello. She made a strained comparison to moderns she admired, such as Webern and Klee: "modesty, care, *space*, a sort of helplessness but determination at the same time." "Helplessness" and "space" are key words here and have to do with the self-effacing imagination which records and arranges but does not editorialize, and so allows the reader space for interpretation. Indeed, Bishop resolutely disassociated herself from other autobiographical poets, writers Lowell himself praised. She disliked W. D. Snodgrass's *Heart's Needle* for its self-congratulatory "I do all these awful things but don't you think I'm really nice." It seemed to her the male equivalent of a habit she disliked in Anne Sexton and other female writers.

That Anne Sexton I think still has a bit too much romanticism and what I think of as the "our beautiful old silver" school of female writing which is really boasting about how "nice" *we* were. V. Woolfe [*sic*], K.A.P., Bowen, R. West, etc.—they are all full of it. They have to make quite sure that the reader is not going to misplace them socially, first—and that nervousness interferes constantly with what they think they'd like to say . . .

"You *tell* things," Bishop wrote to Lowell, "but never end up with your own darling gestures."

Lowell defended Sexton—but not wholeheartedly—as a writer of books that can be remembered: "She's more inspired than she knows how to be . . . I don't really like the tone underneath, or care much about the experience, or rather the experience's impact on A.S." But Bishop, however much she found Sexton "good in spots," thought her work, by comparison with *Life Studies*, "egocentric—simply that." She lets you know too much about her. Lowell, on the other hand, made egocentricity "intensely *interesting* and painfully applicable to every reader." It's clear that Bishop is walking a critical tightrope in part out of simple affection for Lowell and because she was more interested in the details of *his* life than she was in those of Snodgrass's or Sexton's. But it's also clear that she experienced a shock of pleasure at the fantasy power Lowell found in the familiar trappings of New England life. For example, reading "Fall 1961," a poem about a grandfather clock and nuclear war:

> Your poem is haunting me—I find I have it almost memorized
> We had a clock that had a ship that rocked back and forth, and another
> one that showed something moving on the window of the house on
> a green hill—I always thought it was someone shaking out the sheets.

Lowell's clock face had a moon, confounded later in the poem with one that "lifts, / radiant with terror"—a touch Bishop praises, as she also praises "the old sayings used in ghastly new contexts." ("Nature holds up a mirror. / One swallow makes a summer.")

Lowell's imagery also prodded her, as it had years before with "The Prodigal," to explore a disordered side of herself she did not usually touch in her poetry. (She would even begin a poem about *his* Muse—"She looks rather like an aunt of mine by marriage—tough, red-headed, illegitimate!") He was writing a poem called "The Drinker" and Bishop asked specially to see it; she had a "sort of sonnet" called "A Drunkard." Lowell's "drinker" is debilitated and urban, deserted by a wife or mistress, mocked by his surroundings ("The cheese wilts in the rat-trap, / . . . car keys and razor blades / shine in an ashtray"). "His despair has the galvanized color / of the mop and water in the galvanized bucket." The "most awful line" for Bishop was Lowell's grim response, "even corroded metal somehow functions," to the drinker's exclusion from even the grimmest city sensations ("Her absence hisses like steam, / the pipes sing . . ."). The poem's sense of time she found "terrifying— have hours gone by, or one awful moment?" At the end

> two cops on horseback clop through the April rain
> to check the parking meter violations—
> their oilskins yellow as forsythia.

"The cops at the end are beautiful, of course," Bishop commented, "with a sense of release that only the poem, or another fifth of Bourbon, could produce." She obviously understood the vicarious pleasure one might take in Lowell's final glimpse of fanciful guilt and punishment.

As Elizabeth Hardwick put it, Bishop "knew also the weight of drinking and the weight of the years of not drinking." But Bishop's own "Drunkard" took a very different line from Lowell's. It is hard to know whether she worked on the poem only in response to his, or whether it was one of those poems to which she kept returning over the years. All we have is a fragment that never reached print; it begins as a first-person narrative done from a young child's point of view, in short rhythms close to the movements of a child's voice. She is three years old, standing in her crib watching a gigantic fire across the harbor in Salem. Cinders are raining down on them and everything is dyed red by the reflecting sky—even the white dress of her mother on the lawn. The child is thirsty, but calls in vain to her mother busy helping escapees arriving on their beach. Next day the fires are still burning in the sunlight and the child is walking on a beach strewn with charred fragments.

> I picked up a woman's long black cotton
> stocking. Curiosity. My mother said sharply
> *Put that down!* I remember clearly, clearly—
> But since that day, that reprimand
>   that night that day
> I have suffered from abnormal thirst—
> I swear it's true—and by the age
> Of twenty or twenty-one I had begun
> to drink and drink—I can't get enough
> and, as you must have noticed,
> I'm half-drunk now . . .
> And all I'm telling you may be a lie . . .

The poem has little to do with Lowell's except for the provocation to work on it, and the treatment is much more like what Bishop attempted in prose. The fragment is too skeletal to say whether it would have made a good poem or not—what we have is a strong image and, for Bishop, at the end a surprisingly explicit "explanation." Like the memoir of her Uncle Artie that she began to write in the sixties, it tried to clarify the relations of present and past in a single frame. Though it is more "exposed" than most of Bishop's work, I think that was less a reason to drop the poem than the fact that it gave itself too simply, too schematically to narrative "explanation."

Bishop seems, then, to have taken "A Drunkard" up as part of a dialogue with Lowell and to have dropped it when it didn't work out well. She had a competitive streak that at times threw her off balance, and she would point out agitatedly in her letters to Lowell, as she had done in her letters to Moore, that she had an unfinished poem on a similar subject or was using a similar image. "I have a poem that has a galvanized bucket in it, too," she told Lowell after reading "The Drinker." "It is one I started in Key West—and I think I even used the phrase "dead metal," oh dear—but it has nothing to do with my Drunkard one." Her sensitivity, her nervousness about what Lowell was doing were the negative side of the stimulation his work provided—for *Life Studies* challenged her to winnow out her own work and shape her next collection as self-presentation. Distinct in feeling as it was from Lowell's book, Bishop's *Questions of Travel* would be all but unthinkable without it.

———

When it came time for Bishop to collect the poems for *Questions of Travel*, she inserted, almost at the last minute, "In the Village." It was a double-edged decision, in part a bow to Lowell, who had included his prose memoir, "91 Revere Street," in *Life Studies*, and in part a way of reclaiming her own story after Lowell's "versification" of it as "The Scream" in *For the Union Dead*, which he had just published. "In the Village" provided a context for several of the Nova Scotia poems— "Sestina" and "First Death in Nova Scotia" among them—that she planned to include, and invited the reader to think of the book, though less insistently so than *Life Studies*, as an auto-biographical whole.

But what *kind* of self-presentation did Bishop have in mind? She had been reading and commenting on Lowell's poems in *For the Union Dead* as they appeared in magazines or as he sent them to her. They became a sounding board for her, a way of defining the feelings that had been generated by *Life Studies*. Poems such as "Night Sweat," "The Flaw," "The Old Flame," and "Those Before Us" spoke for a Lowell she found immensely human and appealing ("sympathetic" in the French sense). She envied him image after image: the summer rain that "fell in pinpricks"; the snowbound couple "simmering like wasps / in our tent of books"; the "looping shore / of nature's monotonous backlash." But she also resisted certain details in ways that helped her see her own book more clearly. "My passion for accuracy may strike you as old-maidish—but since we do float on an unknown sea I think we should examine the other floating things that come our way very carefully; who knows what might depend on it? So I'm enclosing a clipping about raccoons. But perhaps you prefer mythology." The occasion was "July in Washington," a poem that brought back "all my feelings of misery and horrid anxiety there—only I could never put it into words like that. The image of the eyelids is lovely—and the 'delectable mountains'—but the first two stanzas really hit the target. Maybe it's because I feel it so strongly that I want to pick on it—(but I know you are not morbid about these things)." Besides Lowell's details about the raccoons, Bishop wanted to correct his phrase "rings on a tree." Wasn't it more accurately "*in* a tree"? "The *on* gave me an unfortunate deck-quoits picture before I realized what you meant . . . *in* suggests the un-knowing-ness of the line before ('We cannot name their names, or number their dates')." Lowell did not take up either of these suggestions, but he did accept others—that the garden statuary in "Neo-Classical Urn" would be cast stone not plaster, as he first had it; that certain card tables would not be "tin" ("Those Before Us") or that "as full of holes as a fishnet" was an "unlikely" image. These comments might have been merely fussy on Bishop's part, except that she saw Lowell's carelessness as part of an elegiac version of self that she found disquieting in his poems: "Please don't age yourself that way in advance, à la Eliot. It doesn't look well saying you're 'fragile,' and so on!"

It is precisely on this matter that she parted company with him, in one of those arguments which goes on throughout eternity. Bishop simply felt not only that the outside world was often being absorbed and distorted by Lowell's autobiographies (and she was right) but that he was "mythologizing" his life in a dangerous way, that the present was cripplingly shadowed by the burden of the past.

Bishop's *Questions of Travel*, published in 1965, was a curious combination of self-assertion and guardedness. The poems fell into two sections, "Brazil" and "Elsewhere," separated by the prose narrative "In the Village." "Elsewhere" is principally the Nova Scotia of her childhood, and is strictly cordoned off from the Brazil of the opening section. However autobiographical the book declared itself to be, Bishop makes no attempt to interweave her two worlds, as she did frequently in her letters and as she had in her drafts of the memoir of Uncle Artie and "A Drunkard." The story of her childhood and its potential crippling force is told in "In the Village" and refracted in poems such as "Sestina" and "First Death in Nova Scotia." The reader is free to draw whatever connections he likes between the orphaned child in Nova Scotia and the adult observer in Brazil. But the Brazilian poems themselves resist narrative explanations and links between present and past. The poems record an awakening to a world almost as if Bishop had no previous history; they are "life studies" in a new transparent key, the bright C major of discovery in the present tense. The first three poems are explicitly poems of method, shucking off habitual notions of culture and history. It is for this reason that Bishop reprints "Arrival at Santos" from her previous volume and follows it with a poem that suggests tropical reproof for conventional European notions of conquest and possession. "Questions of Travel," the poem that follows, falls back on minute discriminations, the anthropologist's technique, the awakening to a world question by question ("Never to have studied history in / the weak calligraphy of songbirds' cages"). Discomfort and disorientation ("There are too many waterfalls here . . . / Is it right to be watching strangers in a play / in this strangest of theaters?") undermine habit. The life explored in these poems is both intimate and mysterious. Human figures are at home in this landscape almost because it makes them aware of their limitations. Several of the poems celebrate the Petrópolis house that Bishop shared with Lota de Macedo Soares. "Song for the Rainy Season" begins:

> Hidden, oh hidden
> in the high fog

the house we live in,
beneath the magnetic rock,
rain-, rainbow-ridden,
where blood-black
bromelias, lichens,
owls, and the lint
of the waterfalls cling,
familiar, unbidden.

As in "The Armadillo," part of the appeal of the poem lies in the easy passage from human to creaturely world, the mixture of comfort and surprise, even danger. In its last lines, "Song for the Rainy Season" suddenly leaps forward to imagine a world without rain:

. . . For a later
era will differ.
(O difference that kills,
or intimidates, much
of all our small shadowy
life!) Without water

the great rock will stare
unmagnetized, bare,
no longer wearing
rainbows or rain,
the forgiving air
and the high fog gone;
the owls will move on
and the several
waterfalls shrivel
in the steady sun.

The poem is followed ritualistically by the full address of the house ("*Sítio da Alcobaçinha / Fazenda Samambaia / Petrópolis*"), as in those childhood chartings that go in precise stages from street to city to state to nation to world.

215]

Bishop's self-location in many of these poems is a triumph of syntax, as in lines like these, from "Song for the Rainy Season," that enclose parasites within the parentheses of human pleasure:

> House, open house
> to the white dew
>
> and the milk-white sunrise
> kind to the eyes,
> to membership
> of silver fish, mouse,
> bookworms,
> big moths; with a wall
> for the mildew's
> ignorant map;
>
> darkened and tarnished
> by the warm touch
> of the warm breath,
> maculate, cherished,
> rejoice!

It is hard to separate the decay from the breath that gives it life or to disentangle the syntax enough to know what is cherished— the mildew or the house. Bishop's language has a special transparence in many of these poems: the "house" that protects is also part of the phrase "open house" that introduces what feeds upon it.

Or, again, in "Squatter's Children," part of the ease and tenderness of the poem comes from the fact that it embraces in a single stanza, which is also a single sentence, the delicate montage of home and exposure ("the threshold of the storm . . . rooms of falling rain") which accords with Bishop's sense of where we are, with how much frailty we belong in the world:

Children, the threshold of the storm
has slid beneath your muddy shoes;
wet and beguiled, you stand among
the mansions you may choose
out of a bigger house than yours,
whose lawfulness endures.
Its soggy documents retain
your rights in rooms of falling rain.

"Squatter's Children" is unique in the way it turns at the close and passes on its benediction, even if it is a benediction of vulnerability, to a younger generation. But several of the poems in the "Brazil" section are in the optative mood: invocations, promises, exclamations—poems whose conclusions in one way or another include the future. Others identify or try to identify with figures of Brazilian life: the humble Manuelzinho, the mythological Riverman, figures pendant to one another. Part of the point of "Manuelzinho" is the distance between the Brazilian landholder and her "half squatter, half tenant." Anomalous, fanciful, undependable, Manuelzinho is a constant spur and tease to her imagination mysterious and, from any practical point of view, a disaster. He comes to settle the accounts

with two old copybooks,
one with flowers on the cover,
the other with a camel.
Immediate confusion.
You've left out the decimal points.
Your columns stagger,
honeycombed with zeros.
You whisper conspiratorially;
the numbers mount to millions.
Account books? They are Dream Books.
In the kitchen we dream together
how the meek shall inherit the earth—
or several acres of mine.

Through "The Riverman," by contrast, the speaker desires to be, and succeeds in becoming, completely identified with the surroundings, a figure who after years will have all the secrets of the deep by literally submitting to total immersion in the world.

The "Brazil" section of *Questions of Travel* is remarkable in Bishop's work for the process it represents, the acts of self-location. It begins on the margin and ends in a rounded participation in the world. Against its adult reawakening are poised the other sections of the book, prose and poetry remembering Nova Scotia and a more shadowed entry into the world. But "In the Village" and such poems as "Sestina" and "First Death in Nova Scotia" are told resolutely from the child's point of view. There is no overlapping of histories—the constant explanations of the present in terms of the past that were Lowell's genius (even if cause and effect were constantly being revisited and revised in his poems). By comparison with *Life Studies* and the books of Lowell's that followed it, *Questions of Travel* has a curiously incomplete or pregnant quality, depending on the reader's angle of vision and expectations. The questions of how the child survived or "learned" to be the adult of Brazil are too mysterious to be answered or even asked. The yawning gap between past and present in the book can seem a triumph of repression, yet repression in Bishop's case appears deeply linked to the capacity for discovery and, almost by reflex, for pleasure in the present. Take "First Death in Nova Scotia," which owes some of its impulse to that poem of Lowell's Bishop so admired, "My Last Afternoon with Uncle Devereux Winslow," which is on a similar subject—a child's first encounter with death. Lowell wrote with reciprocal admiration of Bishop's "First Death in Nova Scotia" that it was the "best thing in the language of its kind"—a real child, memorialized from Bishop's own memories. "Your little child is caught in all its childish, fairy story pomp and simplicity, and pushing in like black prongs are the years, autumn and maturity." But the last phrase is more descriptive of the five-year-old Robert Lowell in his own elegy for his dying uncle. Uncle Devereux literally and figuratively stands behind the boy in this poem. The child's identification with the doomed uncle is far more complete than the young Bishop's distanced and distracted view of the corpse of her young cousin. In Lowell's poem the death of Uncle Devereux is his first taste of his own fate. In Bishop's version the child Arthur's death is a barely assimilated fact of life. Lowell's poem is massively circumstantial. The impedimenta of Edwardian life—the ritual boys' clothes from Rogers Peet's, seasons in Boston's Symphony Hall, Alpine cuckoo clocks—overshadow the actual "living." The world of his grandfather—pleasurable, eccentric, decaying—has preempted the experience of the adult remembering it. Even as a child he recalls moving among figures already frozen into commemorative attitudes: "my models" in the display windows of Rogers Peet's; Symphony Hall, death-like in summer, its "naked Greek statues draped with purple / like the saints in Holy Week"; the poster figures of Mr. Punch and *La Belle France* and the rest, which seem to say between them everything one need know about drinking, having an Edwardian mistress, sports and war; and, the ultimate model, Uncle Devereux, dying of Hodgkin's disease, already himself a poster "animated, hierarchical, / like a ginger snap man in a clothes-press."

Similar commemorative figures appear in Bishop's elegy for her young cousin—chromographs of Edward, Prince of Wales, with Princess Alexandra, of King George with Queen Mary, look down on the "frosted" coffin of the dead child. But they are not there as historical figures overshadowing the poet's present. They are part of the child Elizabeth's fantasy that the doll-like dead Arthur has been invited to be "the smallest page at court." The attendant rituals—the royal icons, the laying out of the corpse—seem no more mysterious, and no less, than the loon, shot and stuffed by Arthur's father, on the marble-topped table beneath the royal likenesses. The young girl is equally absorbed or perhaps more so by that figure:

> His breast was deep and white,
> cold and caressable;

his eyes were red glass,
much to be desired.

. . .

Arthur's coffin was
a little frosted cake,
and the red-eyed loon eyed it
from his white, frozen lake.

In its tempting icy solitude that red-eyed loon belies domestic rites and comforts: imagined on a "frozen lake" merely parodied by the "frosted cake" of the coffin; on ice rather than icing; its red glass eyes open, the dead child's "real" eyes closed. In some canny haunted way, the young Elizabeth is drawn to the loon, more inclined to cast a cold eye than accept the fairy-tale explanations with which one yearning side of her invests the dead child. The loon sits there—immune, final, cold, caressable—an utterly inexplicable, erotically tinged image of what enables the young girl to survive.

In the potentially shattering moments of these pieces about Bishop's early life, the girl's attention and feelings are constitutionally *deflected* from unsettling events. Objects hold radiant interest for her precisely because they help her absorb numbing or threatening experiences—the loon in the poem, or the shop window and the blacksmith's in "In the Village."

No wonder that *Questions of Travel* is, as a whole, an unsettling book. The materials of autobiography are there, but Bishop refuses to connect them. The book is even less "explanatory" than *Life Studies*. Lowell did not mean to draw conclusions about the interweaving of present and past, but his book makes one feel that there are mysterious disabling links between them, too charged to be further explored. His poems are shadowed by history, personal and general, and he is more faithful to the narrative spirit of Freud and the nineteenth-century novelists than Bishop is. The "Brazil" section of *Questions of Travel* sees geography as history, description as autobiography; it is a sequence about participation rather than memory. Its discovery of a new world is fresh and resilient,

while Bishop's accounts of childhood are problematic, self-protective treasuries of deflected and redirected feeling. The two
parts of the book—North and South—answer to one another,
but do not interlace. They are about the ample and inexplicable
powers of recovery; repression and impression are the twin
reflexes they explore. For Bishop in this book, what's past is
past. To quote her "Sestina": "*Time to plant tears*, says the
almanac."

6 / Questions of Memory

With *Questions of Travel* Bishop had found the blend of description and self-presentation toward which her poems had long tended and toward which Lowell's example had encouraged her. As he had before with Bishop's work, Lowell discovered the right formula with which to approach it, felt that it read something like a sequence: "with the steady excellence of some perfect short story, say my beloved Coeur Simple." He saw the deepening force of the sequence—that, for example, "The Riverman" was "a very powerful initiation poem that somehow echoes your own entrance into Santos." With this, her third book, Bishop's *literary* relationship to Lowell—the debts and the differences—had been clarified.

The old personal dependencies on both sides, but especially on Bishop's, of course continued. Bishop, in her years of correspondence with Lowell, had spoken of hers freely. "Please never stop writing me letters," she would say. "They always manage to make me feel like my higher self (I've been rereading Emerson) for several days." Or again:

You have no idea, Cal, how really grateful to you I am and how fortunate I feel myself in knowing you, having you for a friend— When I think how the world and my life would look to me if you weren't in either of them at all—they'd look very empty, I think. —I am awfully happy with Lota, odd as it is in some ways, and with living in such a hopeless, helpless country, too—I don't seem to need or enjoy a lot of intellectual society—but I certainly need you.

As in the past, Lowell did a great deal of "literary" living for her. For years, he had served as a kind of mediator, not just sending her magazines and material she would not otherwise have seen, but countering her ingrained resistance to most new poetry. Bishop confessed after seeing a lot of poets in London:

Oh so many poets—all the names at the bottoms of columns in those reviews, or at the bottoms of reviews—and most of whose poetry I can't tell apart. And all I'm afraid not terribly interesting. —I'm afraid you're the only poet I find very interesting, to tell the truth! There is a deadness there—what is it—hopelessness . . . That kind of defiant English rottenness—too strong a word—but a sort of piggish-ness! —As if they've thrown off Victorianism, Georgianism, Radicalism of the '30s—and now let's all give up together. Even Larkin's poetry is a bit too easily resigned to grimness don't you think? —Oh I am all for grimness and horrors of every sort—but you can't have them, either, by shortcuts—by just saying it.

Lowell "helped" her with their most gifted contemporaries; she felt somewhat out of tune even with those she recognized as among the best, Berryman and Jarrell. He had prepared her in a way for *77 Dream Songs*, describing Berryman to her as

utterly spooky, teaching brilliant classes, spending weekends in the sanitarium, drinking, seedy . . . going into the seventh year of a long poem that fills a suitcase and is all spoken by John's first son (seven) from his second marriage. The poem is spooky, a maddening work of genius, or half genius, in John's later obscure, tortured, wandering style full of parentheses, slang no one ever spoke, jagged haunting lyrical moments etc.

Bishop replied that she'd never met Berryman but "one has the feeling a 100 years from now that *he* may be all the rage—or a 'discovery'—hasn't one?" When the *Dream Songs* appeared, she asked Lowell for a copy of his review of the book: "I'm pretty much at sea about that book—some pages I find wonderful, some baffle me completely. I am sure he is saying *something* important—perhaps sometimes too personally? I also feel he's probably next-best to you." And elsewhere she wonders why the indulgence in baby talk? Lowell, in his pioneering review of the *Dream Songs*, praised them in part *because* "the voice of the man becomes one with the voice of the child here, as their combined rhythm sobs through remorse, wonder, and nightmare. It's as if two widely separated parts of a man's life had somehow fused." But Bishop's suspicion of this habit of fusing past and present as an enemy of adult resilience had led her to keep the child's *voice* relatively separate in her work—for her a necessary defense.

With Jarrell, her relationship had always been problematic. He had consistently admired and praised her poetry, but since about 1948, when he sent her "The Night before the Night before Christmas," she had had her doubts about his. Much of it seemed limp to her, the material better suited to short stories. And once Jarrell had introduced her to Lowell, their relationship had been somewhat short-circuited. She preferred Lowell, and Lowell's poetry, and the conspiratorial air with which Lowell told her endless tales of Jarrell's sacred critical rages. She visited Jarrell on the Cape during his first marriage, then drifted away after his divorce and her own move to Brazil. There was something of a rift when Jarrell published his novel, *Pictures from an Institution*, in 1954. "I was vexed at your letter about *Pictures*," he wrote her, "which is to me a serious book not about Mary McCarthy." But their lack of contact owed more to their falling out of the habit of writing to each other—or, as Jarrell put it, to "just ordinary or extraordinary neurotic behavior." They did meet on Bishop's visit to the States in 1957, while Jarrell was Consultant in Poetry at the Library of Congress. Jarrell began to be more attentive, and in the next few years wrote to praise individual poems as they appeared. Of her "Sestina," he remarked, "I like your poetry better than anybody's since the Frost-Stevens-Eliot-Moore generation; so I looked with awed wonder at some phrases feeling to me a little like some of my phrases, in your poem; I felt as if, so to speak, some of my wash-cloths were part of a Modigliani collage, or as if my cat had got into a Vuillard." He liked her work better than Marianne Moore's now, he said, much as he continued to like Moore: "But life beats art, so to speak, and sense beats eccentricity, and the way things really are beats the most beautiful unreal visions, half-truths one can fix up by leaving out and indulging oneself. This, too, is just half the truth about her, but I've written the other half at great length."

Bishop, on her side, thanked Jarrell for "The Breath of Night," a poem that helped her, she wrote him, with "The Armadillo." But she continued to have mixed feelings, even about Jarrell's much-praised last book, *The Lost World*. Once again Lowell had tried to broaden her sympathies. In the spring of 1963 he reported to Bishop that Jarrell "really in his way seems to have reached a gentle honest and inspired state of life." And two years later, when Randall removed his beard:

One can talk more easily of Randall, now that he has shaved and walks the same earth we do. Gone the so noble air of pained, aloof nobility. Something touching and imposing to look at is gone, but what a relief for his friends! I'm afraid I like the perverse savage new poems best: In Montecito and Three Bills, and of the straight serious poems, Next Day. Most of the opening poems except the long Lost World are good . . . His worst fault is the repetition of a style and subject, as though Houseman [*sic*] had written rather voluminously and slopped up his meter, and strung individual poems out. Endless women, done with a slightly mannered directness, repeated verbal and syntactical tricks, an often perverse and sadistic tenderness—but I am getting into clichés in describing. I like him better than any of us except you when he is good.

Bishop agreed that Jarrell was better than almost any other living poet one might read; she had written Jarrell "all the compliments I could truthfully pay." But Jarrell's "women" always rankled her. She disliked even more than Lowell did those poems addressed to or spoken by women ("Next Day," in the final book, was an example—a *memento mori* spoken by a suburban housewife). She wonders "where he *gets* these women—they seem to be like none I—or you—know." "His worst flaw," Lowell tried to explain, "was forcing his wives into becoming false assents to himself, agreeing on everything . . . making them dishonest, as one of his poems even says." "I just never did like," Bishop wrote disapprovingly of Jarrell's introduction to poems of Eleanor Ross Taylor, "his *understanding* and sort-of-over-sympathizing with the lot of women—but this would take explaining and is NOT just Women's Lib." Her reaction was not unrelated to a complaint she made to Lowell against remarks of his in an interview: "Perhaps I shouldn't say this—but it antedates all Female Lib-ism by 40 years—I'd rather be called *"the 16th poet"* with no reference to my sex, than one of 4 women—even if the other 3 are pretty good . . ."

Bishop's insistence on detouring around women's issues sounds a little like special pleading, but in a sense she was more concerned with ingrained attitudes, and she preferred not to link these with gender. Jarrell's aging and disappointed women (his Marschallin, his Woman in the Washington Zoo) disturbed her partly because like Auden's poems of the early 1960s and Lowell's a little later they seemed to project and indulge a premature old age. Lowell, with his broader literary sympathies, appeared to preside over a world predominantly masculine and self-destructive, for whom the act of writing had become narrowly elegiac. "Being a poet is one of the unhealthier jobs," Bishop wrote. The sixties had seen so far, among poets of the then middle and younger generations, the death of Theodore Roethke, the suicide of Sylvia Plath, the growing drunken debilitation of John Berryman, and then, most perplexing of all, the death of Jarrell in October 1965. "I think suicide, but I'm not sure," Lowell wrote Bishop shortly after attending the fu-

neral, "and Mary's version, the official version, is accident."
Earlier that year Jarrell had been hospitalized for a manic-
depressive attack and, according to Lowell, a previous suicide
attempt had been hushed up. That fall Mary Jarrell was in California; the Peter Taylors were convinced that she and Randall
were headed for divorce. Jarrell was at Chapel Hill undergoing
hospital treatment for a residual wrist injury (he had put his
hand through a window that spring). The first report was that
he had lunged in the path of a car as he was walking along a
main highway near a bypass, and that a bottle of Demerol had
been found in his pocket. "Oh, but he was so absolutely gifted,
and [a] noble man," Lowell wrote Bishop, "poisoned and killed,
though I can't prove it, by our tasteless, superficial, brutal
culture."

"I felt awful about Randall. We had just seemed to be
getting in touch again, too, after a long silence," Bishop replied,
and then, with a characteristic deflection, "I feel it must have
been an accident of an unconscious-suicide kind, a sudden impulse when he was really quite out of his head—because surely
it was most unlike him to make some innocent motorist responsible for his death—I feel sorry for whoever it was . . .
Demerol is a *strong* drug." (The doctor in charge of the autopsy
told the media some weeks after the accident that he found
"reasonable doubt about its being a suicide": Jarrell was struck
by the side of the car—a glancing blow—and not run over, and
there were no drugs in his body; he had only the prescription
for Demerol in his pocket, unfilled.)

In those years, there was evidence of waste everywhere in
the world of poets. The survivors elegized the literary dead and
then themselves dropped away. Lowell in his sonnets and Berryman in his *Dream Songs* became the memorialists of their own
and preceding generations: Pound, Eliot, Frost, Delmore
Schwartz, Plath, Jarrell. Bishop must have felt as threatened as
the rest. She singled out and paraphrased a sentence of Roethke's
that hit close to home: "I know my drinking hides the will to
die." Yet she refused to think of herself as leading what Lowell
spoke of as

the same life,
the generic one
our generation offered
(*Les Maudits*—the compliment
each American generation
pays itself in passing)

She had, in the sixties, followed a different train of life and had different expectations of writing. "I feel we must beware of the easiness of the catastrophe—the catastrophic way out of every poem," she wrote to Lowell. "But how can one help but be gloomy and take a gloomy outlook?" The thread she had taken up was that of the Brazilian encounters which opened *Questions of Travel*; it was broken by the death, in the fall of 1967, of Lota de Macedo Soares. Until then, Bishop's life and work were intimately and positively bound up with the imaginative possibilities of travel and a "new world." Her next project was to be a prose collection she wanted to call either *Black Beans and Diamonds* (an old projected title for her translation of *"Helena Morley"*) or *Brazil-Brasil: A Scrapbook*. (A few years before, she had written a book on Brazil for a Time-Life series; it had been so heavily revised and banalized by the editors that Bishop did not speak of it as her own.) Lowell was one of the advisers to the Rockefeller Foundation and suggested for her a grant that she was able to use in 1966 and the first months of 1967. The book was to be a mixture of pieces—memoir, life stories, short stories, popular music, and reports of places where journalists rarely, if ever, go, "where life is pretty and unchanged but bound to change very fast very soon." Writing on South America, and especially Brazil, had gone down badly in the past hundred years; the only good things, according to Bishop, were the old naturalists and, recently, Lévi-Strauss. Judging from the pieces she began or even brought close to completion, this was to be a book about fresh starts, where the air is one of expectation: accounts of a trip down the Amazon and a later trip, in 1967, down the Rio São Francisco, and accounts of shorter sorties like those in "To the Botequim & Back" and "A Trip to Vigia."

Such writing was one with her settled/unsettled experience of Brazil. She much preferred the relatively isolated mountain house in Petrópolis to their apartment in Rio. In the mid-1960s she bought herself another house, seventeenth-century, in Ouro Prêto—the baroque city, nine hours from Rio, that was once the capital of the interior state of Minas Gerais, where she spent as much as two months at a time while Lota was working in Rio. "I like Ouro Prêto because everything there was made on the spot, by hand, of stone, iron, copper, wood—and they had to invent a lot—and everything has lasted perfectly well for almost three hundred years now. —I used to think this was just sentimental of me—now I'm beginning to take it more seriously." The air of improvisation, the pressure to cope with the *present*, was a model for writing and a confirmation or fulfillment of deep-seated impulses, as old as a notebook entry from 1934. She had, back then, been visiting a friend on Cuttyhunk Island off the coast of Massachusetts and noted how much she liked island life: "You live all the time in this Robinson Crusoe atmosphere, making this do for that, and contriving and inventing." As early as the mid-sixties she was working on "Crusoe at Home," a poem that would see the light ten years later as "Crusoe in England." Crusoe—not just as a castaway, but as a type of the writer—was to have played a central part in her preface to *Brazil-Brasil*: She had planned to talk about her maternal great-grandfather whose ship went down off Cape Sable Island, Nova Scotia, and about her own early wish to be a sailor; about her reading of South America in magazines and how she was especially drawn to it by E. Lucas Bridges's *Uttermost Part of the Earth*, that book she found comparable to *Robinson Crusoe* in its "suspense of strangeness and ingenuity and courage and loneliness."

The constellation is striking: the strangeness; the practicality of Crusoe; the moral strenuousness linking ingenuity, courage, and loneliness. It suggests how fortunately, for a few years, Bishop's active and fantasy and writing lives were fused.

But everything depended on a balance of circumstance that in Brazil in the sixties was quite precarious: Bishop found the city of Rio and the turmoil of Brazilian politics more and more trying, and especially so as they put Lota de Macedo Soares under growing pressure. Lota had been named head of a commission overseeing the construction of a vast public park full of highways, public beaches, and playgrounds, to be established on a landfill that stretched for three miles along the waterfront in Rio—a task that made her, in Bishop's words, "a mixture . . . of Mumford, Galbraith, and perhaps Mayor LaGuardia." The park was a triumphant success and Lota became a popular hero. "Every time we turn on the (maid's) TV—someone is talking about her," Bishop wrote a friend, "and people in passing cars, when we're driving, recognize her and shout out, 'Bravo for the new park, Dona Lota!'—honestly." But the strain on both women was great, and for Lota there was little relief. Bishop managed to get her out of Brazil for a brief trip to Italy in the summer of 1964, and then it was "back to the Brazilian madhouse."

Bishop's own "escapes" from Rio with its revolutionary coups and political betrayals could be more frequent; the alternatives were Ouro Prêto and her "ideal" Brazil, or Europe and America, where she could get back in touch with a rational—or rationalized—culture. In the winter of 1965–66, against Lota's wishes and with doubts and fears of her own about leaving Lota alone for even this short period, she accepted a job teaching writing for one semester at the University of Washington in Seattle, the old Roethke position. When she returned things were worse. Lota was in bed for a month ("what they used to call a 'nervous breakdown' "), and then Bishop took her to Europe—the Netherlands and London—in the hope of hastening her recovery. The trip was a failure, Lota hating London, hating everything. They cut their stay short by two or three weeks. "She has had this breakdown coming on for a long time, the drs. assure me—she looked dreadful when I got back in July," Bishop wrote Lowell in the spring of 1967. "But [she] can't stop blaming me for going away in the first place, even if I thought I had to, to get out of the atmosphere here for a while—& this makes me feel guilty. She was in a clinic here for two stretches—then finally I gave out, too." Bishop had her "most spectacular" attack of asthma in years and spent a month in the same clinic as Lota. Later that year, in July, taking advantage of a free apartment in New York, Bishop went there for a few months, leaving Lota in the care of her doctor and a trusted maid, and hoping that Lota would join her in America. They would return to Brazil together in September. Lota did come to New York and died there, a suicide.

It was effectively the end of Bishop's Brazilian life. She still owned the Ouro Prêto house and returned there regularly for several years trying to make it her home, but the loving tie that bound her to Brazil was broken and in the most devastating fashion. The life that once seemed to remind her of the way an orphaned child survived in Nova Scotia now reminded her only of her great losses. Their mutual friends in Rio refused to receive her, as if to say she had abandoned Lota; relatives sued to gain the properties Lota's will had denied them. Bishop lost the house in Petrópolis. She began living with a young woman she had met in Seattle. They took an apartment in San Francisco and spent part of the year in Ouro Prêto. Bishop loved the house there, which she called Casa Mariana in honor of Moore, but was robbed blind by contractors and domestics in the course of trying to restore it and keep it going. "I suppose I had Lota for so long to intervene for me, in Petrópolis, at least—and I really was happy there for many years," she wrote Lowell in December 1969. "Now I feel her country really killed her—and is capable of killing anyone who is honest and has high standards and wants to do something good . . . and my one desire is to get out. But How to LIVE?" Or again, a few weeks later, of Lota: "I miss her more every day of my life. This is one of the reasons I want to leave Brazil (forgive me)."

She had abandoned *Brazil-Brasil*. The book's worth for her had been as exploration—as a talisman for improvising life in the present and the future. Her thoughts of it now must have been bitter indeed, and her stay in Brazil, in one light, must have seemed bracketed by loss. The end of her Brazilian life also marked the end of her chance to define her life as a poet separately from literary establishments and from the doom-laden, predominantly masculine poetry world. She would begin to teach at Harvard. She would give readings and be visible to the poetry audience as she had not previously been. And she would take up the poetry of memory and elegy as she had never needed to do before.

———

At about the time Elizabeth Bishop began her North American life, Lowell was interrupting his. He was in England, first at All Souls, Oxford, in the spring of 1970 and then in the fall at the University of Essex. Bishop taught her first semester at Harvard while he was away. They largely alternated teaching the advanced Harvard poetry courses and during these years were frequently on opposite sides of the Atlantic. The seventies began with emotional upheavals for both of them. Bishop accepted the Harvard job in the wake of the breakdown of the young woman with whom she had been living after Lota's death. "It is all too much like my own early days—but I had loving grandparents and aunts at least." She had already determined to leave the Ouro Prêto house—sell it if she could find a buyer—and live by herself in America. But her young friend's breakdown left her numbed and feeling powerless: "I lost my mother, and Lota, and others, too—I'd like to try to save somebody, for a change." Lowell, in England, became involved with Lady Caroline Blackwood, with whom he had a son. He eventually divorced Elizabeth Hardwick to marry Blackwood and, apart from the intervals at Harvard, lived abroad with her in Kent and London and Ireland.

The friendship of Bishop and Lowell, quite stable for twenty years, was inevitably on a different footing as their lives shifted ground. With new homes, new anxieties, new and unfamiliar loves, they did not always recognize in one another the figures they felt they knew. There were unexpected abrasions. With Bishop in America, questions of her recognition as a poet were less veiled by the distances and delayed posts of Brazil.

Much praised, winner of new prizes (a National Book Award, a Critics Circle Award, the *Books Abroad*/Neustadt International Prize for Literature), she could still feel that as a woman—and a woman who had spent much of her life outside the United States—she was in Lowell's professional shadow. His sponsorship, indispensable in the past, had its drawbacks when they were in the same arena. Lowell was instrumental in getting her to Harvard, but she feared he would reclaim his full position at some point and that she would be left with none. Not that she fully lost perspective, but that being in New England, on what seemed Lowell's home ground and without a substantial income or pension or health insurance, she naturally felt vulnerable. Friends noticed from time to time an edge of irritability when she spoke of Lowell. But as she wrote to him: "Don't let the academic stuffiness come between us. I think we both need to keep our old friends—for the rest of our lives . . . don't you?"

The friendship did, indeed, remain sustaining in the decade which proved the last of their respective lives. The fact that Bishop and Lowell were both now "senior" poets at the height of their reputations put a different light on what they could do for one another. Bishop was less dependent upon Lowell, and Lowell, with a new family and with the return of his manic attacks, was perhaps only intermittently attentive. They were, in their geographical and professional orbits, closer together; psychologically, they were probably farther apart. Their temperamental and literary differences, though more than outweighed by an instinctive sympathy, would be more apparent in these years. But only because of the uncertainties and newness of their lives, as tremors disclose a geological fault.

———

Lowell wrote Bishop in the autumn of 1967, shortly after Lota's death: "It's been a joy to sit chatting with you, even in this sad time—all the more perhaps because the sorrow can be shared a little. You make most people, even the most charming, seem as if seen through a glaze, as if they lived in a glaze. And your poems and prose animals have the same freshness, the wood is exposed, clean and genuine." It was a tribute to the power she retained to at least mime the movements of life. But her letters over the next three years bear witness to her misery. "Well, you are right to worry about me," she wrote to Lowell from Ouro Prêto early in 1970, "only please DON'T!—I am pretty worried about myself. I have somehow got into the worst situation I have ever had to cope with and I can't see the way out." Readers of Lowell's work will recognize the words; they are incorporated, all but verbatim, into one of the four sonnets about Bishop that Lowell included in his revised *Notebook* of 1970. It was with this group of poems, which both paid tribute to Bishop and somewhat unwittingly exposed their differences, that Lowell brought to a head his continuing, frustrated effort to write about her.

Three of the poems, meant to be at least emblems for a life bound up imaginatively with Bishop for close to twenty-five years, were among the loose sonnets he brought together for the revised *Notebook*. They had begun as long, struggling pieces worried early out of telling moments in their relationship, then years later compacted to lyrics a little edgy and oblique. The first was the poem "Water" in *For the Union Dead*, now recast as a sonnet, whose subject dates back to 1948 and their day alone together in Stonington. The second, Bishop's favorite, drew on the ill-fated visit to Castine in 1957. It had begun as a somewhat overwrought description prompted by Bishop's departure—"Flying from Bangor to Rio"—but in its final form as a sonnet was a relatively pleasant character sketch of Bishop. A third poem, "Calling," started out to describe the shared assumptions of their writing and ended admiringly—and probably to Lowell's surprise—by isolating their differences. "I hope they roll up to something more passionate than any of the parts," he wrote when he sent the three sonnets to her in Ouro Prêto, in February of 1970. Bishop replied immediately, before the end of the month. Characteristically, Lowell made a fourth from her reply, then revised all four again two years later for *History*.

The additional poem, "Letter with Poems for Letter with

Poems" (last to be written but next to last in the printed arrangement), is made up, except for one line, of passages from
Bishop's letter quoted with very little change. He wrote later
to apologize

for versing one of your letters into my poems on you in Notebook.
When Lamb blew up at Coleridge for calling him 'Frolicsome Lamb'
Coleridge said it was necessary for the balance of his composition. I
won't say that, but what could be as real as your own words, and
then there's only a picture that does you honor. Still, too intimate
maybe, and if so I humbly ask pardon.

Bishop's reply, if she made one, is not among their letters. But
his publishing this picture of her distress couldn't have pleased
her. He had taken one of the few moments in which she had
indulged some sense of urgency, even despair, in her letters—
excerpts from the very letter in which she thanked him for the
ostensibly complete series of three poems about her; and he had
printed the sonnet before the year was out. Bishop's letter had
talked mostly about her difficulties in Ouro Prêto and with her
young friend.* Lowell quoted two striking passages, one from

*The relevant passages are these (the ellipses are Bishop's):
  Well, you are right to worry about me, only please DON'T!—I am pretty worried
about myself. I have somehow got into the worst situation I have ever had to cope
with and I can't see the way out. If I could trust anybody in this town, I'd close up
the house and leave, or leave a maid or two in it —but that would just mean coming
back again, sooner or later, and although it would be a tremendous relief to get away—
I don't want to do that. I am trying to sell the house, as I think I wrote you—have
had several nibbles, but nothing at all certain yet. I am trying just to get everything in
working order, go through all the books, papers, letters, and so on—(about 3,000 or
more books here) so that I can leave if the chance comes. But it may take months or
years; meanwhile it is too damned lonely and disagreeable and I have not been able to
work. Just the last two weeks I've done a little, but very little—there are endless, endless
interruptions, noise, confusion, thefts (you wouldn't believe how much has been stolen,
a lot of it somehow right under my eyes . . .), trips to Belo Horizonte for building
materials, hiring, firing, re-hiring, re-firing. It's a terrible tale of woe. Another problem
is that Roxanne likes it here and doesn't want me to sell the house—and this makes for
difficulties, naturally. The saddest part of all is that I really love my house and would
like to stay in it, if—if—if things were different—but the only solution seems to be to
sell it and get out. The very thought of all the packing and expensive shipping makes

the opening, one from the close, and by omitting some of the leavening center of the letter, the small talk, made it sound more desperate than it was. This is his final version, published in *History* in 1973:

> "You are right to worry, only please DON'T,
> though I'm pretty worried myself. I've somehow got
> into the worst situation I've ever
> had to cope with. I can't see the way out.
> Cal, have you ever gone through caves?
> I did in Mexico, and hated them.
> I haven't done the famous one near here. . . .
> Finally after hours of stumbling along,
> you see daylight ahead, a faint blue glimmer;
> air never looked so beautiful before.
> That is what I feel I'm waiting for:
> a faintest glimmer I am going to get out
> somehow alive from this. Your last letter helped,
> like being mailed a lantern or a spiked stick."

Lowell made only small changes in Bishop's language, but enough so that it was no longer altogether her own. Bishop's "daylight . . . never looked so wonderful before" became "air

---

me sick—and then, where to go? How to live? I am thinking of New York—and then Dr B[aumann] writes me she thinks San Francisco is better for me! But what does she know about it? I liked the flat there—now sub-let—but again, the living arrangements just didn't work, and if I go back there I'd have to find another place, or two other places, preferably . . . I want to live alone, dismal as it is. (But please don't refer to this when you write.) Well, all I can do is to try to get ready, and endure it here, and try to work a little while I endure, and pray to get away as soon as possible . . .

[And after four paragraphs on other matters—publications, the prospect of a National Book Award, Lowell's trip to Italy, his Oxford appointment—]

Have you ever gone through caves? —I did once, in Mexico, and hated it so I've never gone through the famous ones right near here. Finally, after hours of stumbling along, one sees daylight ahead—faint blue glimmer—and it never looked so wonderful before. That's what I feel as though I were waiting for now—just the faintest glimmer that I'm going to get out of this somehow, alive. Meanwhile—your letter has helped tremendously—like being handed a lantern, or a spiked walking stick— Write when you have time—I do know how busy you are—

never looked so beautiful before." And Bishop had written: "Your letter has helped tremendously—like being handed a lantern, or a spiked walking stick."

As Lowell's sheepish apology suggests, it was hard for him to see the difference between the trust his poem movingly authenticates and the trust that publishing it betrays. The line between the "real" and the "private" was one that Lowell and Bishop had clashed over twenty years before when William Carlos Williams incorporated the intimate letters of a young woman he had known in *Paterson*, and it was an issue that would divide them deeply again when Lowell quoted directly from Elizabeth Hardwick's letters in *The Dolphin*—an instinctive disagreement about what constitutes the "usable self" in poetry. These later, almost dramatic rifts only reflected a continuing tension, inseparable from something that bound them. What Lowell admired and envied in Bishop's work, what he tried to emulate, was a naturalness of tone, a truthfulness, which often in his own writing became associated with anxiety and an unslaked appetite for new versions of experience. "Accident threw up subjects," he said of his sonnets in *Notebook*, "and the plot swallowed them—famished for human chances." If for Bishop the life of poetry and the life one lived were interrelated but distinct and to be kept separate, Lowell could only partly make that separation. Peter Taylor remembers a Sunday-morning walk with Lowell in Boston the year the poet died, Lowell gleefully leading him around the landmarks of his childhood. Taylor has written that it wasn't a "memory bath"—Lowell's phrase—but more of a primarily literary experience. "At some point he had come to terms with his fictional character, his public self, and achieved the oneness he had wanted. I told him then what my impression was. I quoted to him a sentence from *The Lesson of the Master*, 'What's art but an intense life?' " For Lowell things became real as he got them into verse on the page—hence the urgency, the appetite to do so. Bishop had a more submissive mentality; the page and the experience were separate realities.

In "Calling" (the original title was "Vocation"), the final

sonnet in the series addressed to Bishop, Lowell tried to write about the poetic assumptions the two of them held in common. It mattered to him that his friends shared a distinctive "postmodern" style, one John Berryman had once identified as "casual in tone and form, frightening in import." Yet Lowell kept sifting the idea of the casual as he tried to describe it for Bishop, and "Calling" finally takes the measure of what would always divide them.

One of the germs of the poem must have been its closing picture of Bishop herself at work:

> Do
>
> you still hang your words in air, ten years
> unfinished, glued to your notice board, with gaps
> or empties for the unimaginable phrase—

Lowell wanted to link Bishop at the outset of the sonnet to painters who have to "live on iron rations, / rushed brushstrokes." Their common enterprise was one of accomplished recklessness, an art that lives on nerves. "But who is destroyed if we destroy ourselves," he wrote at first, and for the final version: "Who is killed if the horseman never cry halt?" The contrast is with the heavily worked painting of Albert Ryder, who

> let his crackled amber moonscapes
> ripen in sunlight. His painting was repainting,
> his tiniest work weighs heavy in the hand.

It took a while for Bishop's role in this poem to come into focus. Lowell must eventually have realized that what he was claiming in the name of an implied "we" was primarily self-description. In draft after draft one sees a new figure of Bishop emerging almost of its own will. At first Bishop has a "casual" Muse who calls on her "uneasy friend," then an "uneasy Muse" for a casual friend. Out of the variations comes one of those amazing transformations when a desired word emerges unexpectedly from the husk of another. The *uneasy* Muse, no longer wooed by Bishop but instead identified with her as Lowell's Muse, becomes the "unerring Muse who makes the casual perfect." You can hear the gesture of abandon in that last line. Bishop comes forth at the end, his serene antagonist. They share the element of risk, but those empty spaces on Bishop's board, empty for years, suggest a moment of rest when finally life and observation will provide the missing detail, the inner premonition will find a confirming external response from a mysterious, enduring, independent outer world. Lowell was never that patient or submissive. His own life was so turbulent that he never waited for it to compose definitively, never expected to make the casual perfect, kept arranging and rearranging in order to "explain" his life to himself. Even this small series to Bishop bristles with irreconcilable energies. Complete, then revised; identifying himself with her, then almost by accident exposing their differences. And having done so, in "Calling," having set her against the unslakable moderns, he then turned around and wrote a poem, "Letter with Poems for a Letter with Poem," which deliberately turns his own aesthetic against her.

———

At about the time that Lowell was apologizing for "versing" one of Bishop's letters, he was also involved in a literary and personal tangle that saw him doing the same with pained communications from Elizabeth Hardwick. The detailed scenario of Lowell's affair and marriage with Lady Caroline Blackwood and the birth of their son is told in Ian Hamilton's biography of the poet. Almost from the beginning Lowell was writing out, in sonnets that would become *The Dolphin*, his attraction to Lady Caroline, his confusions, and his indecisions about leaving wife and daughter. At first it seemed unlikely that he could or would publish them, though he had shown them to close friends like Frank Bidart as early as December 1970. It was only in 1972 that it became clear Lowell would make a book out of them, and not until then that Bishop saw the collection in manuscript. Her reaction was predictable—perhaps Lowell waited so long to send the poems to her for that very reason. But the intensity of her response was unexpected. Bishop's letter of March 21, 1972, begins, as did her letter about Lowell's *Imitations*, fearfully—not wishing to hurt him: "DOLPHIN is magnificent poetry. It is also honest poetry—*almost*." But the letter must be read at length to sense its growing anger and, for Bishop in dealing with Lowell, boldness ("I feel sick for *you*"):

Dearest Cal, I've been trying to write you this letter for weeks now, ever since Frank [Bidart] & I spent an evening when he first got back, reading and discussing THE DOLPHIN. I've read it many times since then & we've discussed it some more. Please believe I think it is wonderful poetry. It seems to me far and away better than the NOTE-BOOKS; every 14 lines have some marvels of image and expression, and also they are all much *clearer*. They affect me immediately and profoundly, and I'm pretty sure I understand them all perfectly. (Except for a few lines I may ask you about.) I've just decided to write this letter in 2 parts—the one big technical problem that bothers me [concerning the "plot"] I'll put on another sheet—it and some unimportant details have nothing to do with what I'm going to try to say here. It's hell to write this, so please first do believe I think DOL-PHIN is magnificent poetry. It is also honest poetry—*almost*. You probably know already what my reactions are. I have one tremendous and awful BUT.

   If you were any other poet I can think of I certainly wouldn't attempt to say anything at all; I wouldn't think it was worth it. But because it is you, and a great poem (I've never used the word "great" before, that I remember), and I love you a lot—I feel I must tell you what I really think. There are several reasons for this—some are worldly ones, and therefore secondary . . . but the primary reason is because I love you so much I can't bear to have you publish something that I regret and that you might live to regret, too. The worldly part of it is that it—the poem—parts of it—may well be taken up and used against you by all the wrong people—who are just waiting in the wings to attack you. —One shouldn't consider them, perhaps. But it seems wrong to play right into their hands, too.

(Don't be alarmed. I'm not talking about the whole poem—just one aspect of it.)

Here is a quotation from dear little Hardy that I copied out years ago—long before DOLPHIN, or even the *Notebooks*, were thought of. It's from a letter written in 1911, referring to "an abuse which was said to have occurred—that of publishing details of a lately deceased man's life under the guise of a novel, with assurances of truth scattered in the newspapers." (Not exactly the same situation as DOLPHIN, but fairly close.)

"What should certainly be protested against, in cases where there is no authorization, is the mixing of fact and fiction in unknown proportions. Infinite mischief would lie in that. If any statements in the dress of fiction are covertly hinted to be fact, all must be fact, and nothing else but fact, for obvious reasons. The power of getting lies believed about people through that channel after they are dead, by stirring in a few truths, is a horror to contemplate."

I'm sure my point is only too plain. Lizzie is not dead, etc.—but there is a "mixture of fact & fiction," and you have *changed* her letters. That is "infinite mischief," I think. The first one, page 10, is so shocking—well, I don't know what to say. And page 47 . . . and a few after that. One can use one's life as material—one does, anyway—but these letters—aren't you violating a trust? IF you were given permission—IF you hadn't changed them . . . etc. But *art just isn't worth that much*. I keep remembering Hopkins' marvellous letter to Bridges about the idea of a "gentleman" being the highest thing ever conceived—higher than a "Christian," even, certainly than a poet. It is not being "gentle" to use personal, tragic, anguished letters that way—it's cruel.

I feel fairly sure that what I'm saying (so badly) won't influence you very much; you'll feel sad that I feel this way, but go on with your work & publication just the same. I also think that the thing could be done, somehow—the letters used and the conflict presented as forcefully, or almost, without changing them, or loading the dice so against E. It would mean a great deal of work, of course (but you're a good enough poet to write *anything*—get around anything—after all)—and perhaps you feel it is impossible, that they must stay as written. It makes me feel perfectly awful, to tell the truth—I feel sick for *you*. I don't want you to appear in that light, to anyone—E, C, —me—your public! And most of all, not to yourself . . .

In general, I deplore the "confessional" —however, when you wrote LIFE STUDIES perhaps it was a necessary movement, and it helped make poetry more real, fresh and immediate. But now—ye gods—anything goes, and I am so sick of poems about the students' mothers & fathers and sex-lives and so on. All that *can* be done—but at the same time one surely should have a feeling that one can trust the writer—not to distort, tell lies, etc.

The letters, as you have used them, present fearful problems: what's true, what isn't; how one can bear to witness such suffering and yet not know how much of it one *needn't* suffer with, how much has been "made up," and so on.

I don't give a damn what someone like Mailer writes about his wives & marriages—I just hate the level we seem to live and think and feel on at present—but I DO give a damn about what you write! (Or Dickey or Mary . . .) They don't count, in the long run. This counts and I can't bear to have anything you write tell—perhaps— what we're really like in 1972 . . . perhaps it's as simple as that.

Bishop is disturbed enough to shift ground—from the narrower issue of confounding fact and fiction, deceiving the reader, to the whole question of privacy, the relation of writing to self and other selves: "But *art just isn't worth that much.*" For several months letters went back and forth between them, and, triangularly, to and from Frank Bidart, who was a friend of both. "I feel like Bridges getting one of Hopkins's letters, as disturbed as I am grateful," Lowell remarked in partial response to her charge of cruelty, of preferring his own writing to being, in Hopkins's high and special terms, a "gentleman." To Bidart he characterized Bishop's letter as "a kind of masterpiece of criticism, though her extreme paranoia (For God's sake don't repeat this) about revelations gives it a wildness. Most people will feel something of her doubts." It was the most powerful criticism he had ever received from her, and he was daunted enough to say that he was determined to publish *The Dolphin* in good form, that he was in "no hurry for time." But the argument was their old disagreement, weary and abraded but still passionate, about fact and fiction—a subject rehearsed first in reaction to William Carlos Williams using the young woman's letters, then reborn over *Life Studies* and, above all, *Imitations* and the sonnet using Bishop's own despairing letter.

Lowell countered in a letter at Easter, rephrasing her objections: "It's the revelations (with documents?) of a wife wanting her husband not to leave her and who does leave her. That's the trouble, not the mixture of truth and fiction. Fiction—no one would object if I said Lizzie was wearing a purple and red dress, when it was yellow. Actually my versions of her letters are true enough, only softer and drastically cut. The original is heartbreaking, but interminable." He tried to throw the burden on technical problems: how could the story be told at all without the letters? But the strong objections of Bishop among others made their mark: he would quote in italics and attribute many of the lines, changed, to himself.

"The problem of making the poem unwounding," he continued, "is impossible, still I think it can be made noticeably milder without losing its life. It might be much better, for who can want to savage a thing. How can I want to hurt? Hurt Lizzie and Harriet, their loving memory? Working my poem out is a must somehow, not avoidable even though I fail—as I must partially." One set of changes took up Bishop's suggestions in the second part of her letter that the "plot" was not clear. The announcement that Caroline and Lowell were to have a child seemed too abruptly and melodramatically introduced to close the book at the end of a Christmas visit to Lizzie and Harriet in New York. And she objected to the title "Burden" and the phrase "Have we got a child?" as too Victorian. Lowell decided to shift the birth of his new son to before the New York visit. That falsified the real time sequence but would get rid of the callous happy ending and soften Lizzie's role in the New York poems. "She seems rather serenely gracious (I overstate) about my visit after the birth. I can go this far but won't bring any post facto business about the baby into the New York section . . ." "Foxfur" and "Messiah" would become gentler with the reader assuming the child was born.

Outlining these changes to Bidart a few weeks later, he concludes:

Now the book must still be painful to Lizzie and won't satisfy Elizabeth. As Caroline says, it can't be otherwise with the book's *donnée*. However, even fairly small changes make Lizzie much less a documented presence. A distinct, even idiosyncratic voice isn't the same as one, almost fixed as non-fictional evidence, that you could call on the phone. She dims slightly and Caroline and I somewhat lengthen. I know this doesn't make much sense, but that's the impression I get reading through the whole. Then Sheridan is somewhat a less forced and climactic triumph; as E's problem of the getting back to England and into pregnancy is gone; and the very end of Flight, with the shark, is less Websterian and Poeish.

Oddly enough, Bishop had no objections, even praised Lowell's rearrangements of the final poems of *The Dolphin*, though they falsified the true time sequence. But as late as July she was still sending him quotations about the mixture of fact and fiction. Why does one kind of fictional rearrangement—being false to the real time scheme—not disturb her while another—altering Hardwick's letters—is constantly offensive? One answer is that the former changes damp down the pain of the poem from Hardwick's point of view, while altering the letters can only heighten her discomfort. Furthermore, it touches Bishop's deepest fears about the intersection of suffering and the written word: "How one can bear to witness such suffering and yet not know how much of it one *needn't* suffer with, how much has been 'made up.' " In those comments, the passage of "suffering" from subject to reader is alarmingly direct. The association of the written word with pain reaches deep back into Bishop's life and especially to the years after her tormented mother was taken away from her. For Bishop, as Lee Edelman has pointed out, writing must document the literal truth; Bishop would insist on this, with a scientific tone to her voice. But part of her meaning was that such "literal" representation kept almost inconceivable pain within bounds. The child in "In the Waiting Room," a poem Bishop was writing just about the time that Lowell sent her *The Dolphin*, having become aware of grotesque and reductive representations of women's suffering, falls back with relief to dates, places, objects—the fifth of February 1918, her name, her age, the copy of *National Geographic* she holds in her lap.

"In the Waiting Room" (1971) is a key text in understanding Bishop's treatment of suffering. A first feint at presenting this memory comes in the story "The Country Mouse," probably written ten years before the poem and published only after her death, in the volume of her collected prose. Her aunt asks her to accompany her to the dentist. While the child remains in the waiting room she is overcome by a "feeling of absolute and utter desolation." It would, in a few days, be her seventh birthday. "I felt *I, I, I,* and looked at the three strangers in panic I was *one* of them, too, inside my scabby body and wheezing lungs." When she retells the story in verse she finds or remembers a detail—the scream—that pulls the episode taut and transforms it from a vague initiation into a fearful recognition of her link to the suffering women:

> Suddenly, from inside,
> came an *oh!* of pain
> —Aunt Consuelo's voice—
> not very loud or long.
> I wasn't at all surprised;
> even then I knew she was
> a foolish, timid woman.
> I might have been embarrassed,
> but wasn't. What took me
> completely by surprise
> was that it was *me*:
> my voice, in my mouth.

The mysterious suggestiveness of "from inside" turns the scream—not even mentioned in her story—into a condition. Does it mean simply, at the narrative level, that the young girl "learns" from hearing her aunt scream? Or, more eerily, that she herself screams, in a moment of involuntary identification? The indeterminacy of reference gives the poem its air of menace and complicity. When I said this in print some years ago, Bishop actually took the trouble of a long-distance call to say that "inside" did *not* have a multiple reference and that perhaps rather than mislead readers she should change the line. Like her insistence that details in her poems were literally true, her announced suspicion of ambiguity was more a writerly device, a trope, than a fact. As several "investigators" have pointed out, the issue of the *National Geographic* Bishop cites does not in fact contain all the African material mentioned in her poem, nor is it to be found in another issue of the magazine which she cited when the disparity was pointed out to her. Nor does this matter in our reading of the poem. The point is the presence of the magazine at all and the vital role it plays in the child's awakening and distress. Its subject matter prompts and contributes to her vertigo, but the physical print, the mere literalness of the magazine with its date and familiar yellow and black are an anchor, as definite, and reductive, as her own name. For Bishop, the unknown, the unspeakable, may give a poem its power, but what is printed must be trusted as literal, must not be indistinct lest it work mischief on the reader and the writer. Lowell's overriding appetite for the absolute had never pleased her. For Bishop, the actual existences that lie outside the self—geography, other minds, the world as prior creation—are like life rafts, respite and rescue from guilt. And she insists on literal accuracy not merely because she believes it is "true" but because it is *literal* in the root sense—of the letter. The printed word asserts a frail bond between self and world.

The differences between Lowell and Bishop here center, finally, on guilt. Lowell's conviction was that the written word could convey and explore it; Bishop's settled position was that writing countered it, channeled energies in new and healing directions. "In general, I deplore the 'confessional,' " she had written him. For Lowell, confession seemed at times to be an absolute necessity. "My immorality, as far as intent and skill could go," he wrote her in July 1973, "is nothing in my book [*The Dolphin*]. No one, not even I, is perversely torn and twisted, nothing's made dishonestly worse or better than it was. My sin (mistake?) was publishing. I couldn't bear to have my book (my life) wait inside me like a dead child." (The image is telling—is it the waiting that kills the child? Is the child already dead and so forcing the delivery? I think that Lowell means the former: not just that art participates in life as it did for Bishop, but that art *is* life and displaces it.) "One life, one writing!" he says in a poem that earlier explored that image of aborted life: "Always inside me is the child who died, / always inside me is his will to die— . . . in this urn / the animal night sweats of the spirit burn." The insistent linking of self-consumption and writing is far too explicit for Bishop. In reply to Lowell's July letter, she is oblique but instinctively marking off private guilt from the daytime activity of writing poems: "We all have irreparable and awful actions on our consciences—that's really all I can say now. I do, I know. I just try to live without blaming myself for them *every* day at least—every *day*, I should say— the nights take care of guilt sufficiently."

In 1974 Bishop bought an apartment in a recently renovated dock building on Lewis Wharf in Boston. It marked her choice to stay at Harvard and her commitment to Alice Methfessel, a younger woman who had been her close friend since 1971. What she saw from her window was hardly a seascape but, rather, the kind of mixed view she liked—tankers and container ships passing along the Boston harbor, the low stretching point of East Boston in the distance, and, oh yes, an extensive parking lot. When Elizabeth Spires sent her a draft for what eventually became her *Paris Review* "Writers at Work" interview, Bishop characteristically—and à la Marianne—rewrote the description of the living room:

The room itself is spacious, with wide-planked polished floors, two old brick walls and one wall of books, a beamed ceiling and glass doors opening onto the balcony. Beside some comfortable modern furniture, the room includes a wildly baroque Venetian mirror, a jacaranda rocker and other old pieces from Brazil, two paintings by Loren MacIver, a giant Horse Conch, from Key West, and a Franklin stove with firewood in a donkey panier, also from Brazil. (I *do* like antiques, and I don't think an ordinary rug needs mention—of course there's also fire-wood on the floor but that's because I have a lot. I'm just trying to put in the more interesting, possibly, items.) And then, of course, there are the twin paintings of Bishop's mother and Uncle Arthur, posed in canon to one another—the portrait centerpieces of her story "Memories of Uncle Neddy."

This was the most settled period in her life since the death of Lota some seven years before. She and Alice both loved the out-of-doors, made trips to spots as remote as the Galápagos, did cross-country skiing, spent long stretches at John Malcolm Brinnin's house on the shore at Duxbury, and in the summer on the wild and beautiful North Haven Island in Maine. She taught a series of gifted young poets, among them Brad Leithauser, Jane Shore, Jonathan Galassi, Dana Gioia, and Katha Pollitt. It was a rich time for poetry at Harvard, what with Lowell returning for a semester several times and the possibility of taking workshops alternately with each of them.

This was not a period in which her friendship with Lowell notably deepened. Bishop had her own "American" life: prizes, judgeships, a circuit of readings about which she was always reluctant. She became visible in ways she had never been when she was the mysterious talented writer who lived in Brazil and the facts of whose life no one exactly knew. Now the newspapers could say that she "taught at Harvard," was a well-known literary figure in Boston, and make it sound as if she were just another great gray poet ensconced in the academy. (Alice Methfessel, after seeing Bishop engaged in hours of conversation with a woman on a train in Finland, asked if she had told the woman she was a poet. "Why ever would I" was

Bishop's response.) But James Merrill spoke more accurately of her

instinctive, modest, lifelong impersonations of an ordinary woman, someone who during the day did errands, went to the beach, would perhaps that evening jot a phrase or two inside the nightclub match-book before returning to the dance floor. Thus the later glimpses of her playing was it poker? with Neruda in a Mexican hotel, or pingpong with Octavio Paz in Cambridge, or getting Robert Duncan high on grass—"for the first time"—in San Francisco, or teaching Frank Bidart the wildflowers in Maine.

Lowell, in the 1970s, was leading a much more turbulent life. The last pages of Ian Hamilton's biography show him an ill, restless transatlantic traveler. After four years on lithium, relatively free of trouble, he began to have regular breakdowns, which exhausted the patience and emotional resources of his new wife, herself often unstable and even hospitalized. Toward the end of his life, it became clear that he wanted to return to Hardwick, and in the last summer of his life they spent peaceful months together in Castine. He saw Bishop on his trips to America and she was cordial to his new family the few times he resettled them in Cambridge. After their *Dolphin* quarrel and Bishop's fears, for a time, that he was trying to displace her at Harvard, the two resumed an equable tone. "Talking with you in Cambridge was somehow like the old days in Stonington," Lowell wrote her in May of 1974, "a lovely warmth . . . No need to stop talking, and always when the talk stops it starts." Or again, in June: "I feel our friendship has passed out of some shadow."

What disturbed Bishop was Lowell's insistent talk of old age. For a long time now he had cast himself as the elegist of his generation and, more and more, of his own life. Bishop, too, was turning toward the past; Moore had died in 1972 and Bishop was engaged in writing the memoir of her she had had in mind for many years. But the spirit was different from Lowell's in approaching such work. She seemed to enjoy the project enormously, though she never completed it altogether to her satisfaction. Lowell's talk about old age troubled her (he was only fifty-eight at the time, while she was sixty-four). It was something like Stonington thirty years before, when they were both unhappy bachelor poets. And now, as then, she found herself assuming a cheerful pose to counter Lowell's melancholy. She tells him of a friend in Florida who remarried—for the third time—at seventy-six, walks hand in hand with her husband on the beach, "happy as clams." "Of course," she continues, "it's different for a writer, I know—of course I know!—nevertheless in spite of aches and pains I really don't feel much different than I did at 35—and I certainly am a great deal happier, most of the time . . . I just *won't* feel ancient—I wish Auden hadn't gone on about it so his last years, and I hope you won't."

. . .

Afterword

David Kalstone, in a note for his unfinished final chapter, calls *Geography III* Elizabeth Bishop's "last and, in many senses, greatest book." I would like to suggest briefly, without presuming to complete that chapter myself, why my friend thought so. His pages on Bishop in *Five Temperaments* (1977) provide some helpful clues:

> Her "questions of travel" modulate now, almost imperceptibly, into questions of memory and loss. Attentive still to landscapes where one can feel the sweep and violence of encircling and eroding geological powers, poems such as "Crusoe in England" and "The Moose" pose their problems retrospectively. Crusoe lives an exile's life in civilized England, lord in imagination only of his "un-rediscovered, un-renamable island." In "The Moose" we are city-bound, on a bus trip away from Nova Scotia, and the long lean poem reads like a thread the narrator is laying through a maze—to find her way back?

In the chapter David would almost certainly have included readings of those two poems, along with more than a glance at "The End of March," "One Art," the later "Santarém," "North Haven," and the posthumous "Sonnet." There would have been some graceful tying up of loose threads, perhaps a last glimpse of Miss Moore. Nothing is lost by guesswork except the author's own touch.

A further clue surfaces in his working notes to the present book:

> The Real Problem for Bishop: How to turn the descriptive poem into a narrative—while keeping it descriptive in nature. (This is a main thread.)

Whether or not Bishop herself felt the problem hardly matters. Her lifelong devotion to narrative—to Chekhov, to Helena Morley's diary, to aspects of Lowell's own work—was bearing fruit in this late collection. True, some earlier poems had told a story, like the faintly eucharistical "A Miracle for Breakfast" or "The Burglar of Babylon"—though that ballad rides to safety on a raft of pastiche and does not foreshadow the denser narratives in *Geography III*.

Beyond the turning point of the icy promenade in "The End of March" stands a curious green-shingled, boarded-up house—"my crypto-dream-house." Into it Bishop projects a whole lazy self-indulgent life, reading, drinking, talking to herself. "Spring tides"—whose latest victim, a "man-size . . . sodden ghost" of string, she has just now encountered on her walk—threaten the house, but it is protected from them by "a palisade / of—are they railroad ties? / (Many things about this place are dubious.)" The parenthesis alerts us to a double meaning. Railroad ties? Well, yes and no.

The poems in *Geography III*, David writes, "revisit her earlier poems as Bishop herself once visited tropical and polar zones, and . . . they refigure her work in wonderful ways." The early poem here revisited is "Chemin de Fer":

> Alone on the railroad track
> I walked with pounding heart.
> The ties were too close together
> or maybe too far apart.

Anyone who has walked on a railroad track knows at least this; and to anyone who has known love the merest hint of ties grown unmanageable will suffice. As the narrator advances into the poem's "impoverished" scenery a "dirty hermit" bursts from his cabin and fires his shot-gun. A tree shakes, a hen clucks, and

> "Love should be put into action!"
>   screamed the old hermit.
> Across the pond an echo
>   tried and tried to confirm it.

An Elizabethan poet would have quoted the echoing syllable. Bishop leaves it to the mind's ear: action! . . . shun . . . shun . . . shun. For love's sake, the hermit's cracker-barrel version of an Elizabethan dandy has withdrawn into the wilderness. Now, as "The End of March" opens, *withdrawn* is the key word: "Everything was withdrawn as far as possible, / indrawn." Bishop's dream house fantasy is not, however, "put into action." She imagines it lingeringly, then dismisses it: "perfect! But—impossible." Just as the railroad ties here echo those in "Chemin de Fer," so they combine with the word *impossible* to recall Marvell's "Definition of Love"—"begotten by Despair / Upon Impossibility." Marvell's own proleptic railroad track appears in his two lovers' feelings which, being "so truly parallel, / Though infinite, can never meet." For Bishop, the ties themselves create the impossibility, her own ties to the world, to the friends walking the beach along with her, to all the dubious claims of responsibility and affection. There is accordingly a return to some livable house. The tide also will have turned. The mystery of certain giant paw-prints and that corpse of sodden string ("A kite string?—But no kite") is about to be, however provisionally and fancifully, solved:

> On the way back our faces froze on the other side.
> The sun came out for just a minute.
> For just a minute, set in their bezels of sand,

the drab, damp, scattered stones
were multi-colored,
and all those high enough threw out long shadows,
individual shadows, then pulled them in again.
They could have been teasing the lion sun,
except that now he was behind them
—a sun who'd walked the beach the last low tide,
making those big, majestic paw-prints,
who perhaps had batted a kite out of the sky to play with.

Emerging from drabness, cold, apathy, emblems of death, this moment easily outdoes the imagined perfections of the dream-house. The stones, at first withdrawn like the hermit in "Chemin de Fer" or like uncommunicative mental patients coaxed out of themselves, behave as souls in Dante do (the suicides' moaning trees, the talking lights in *Paradiso*) and for something of the same reason: their quickened relation to a generative source. For by now the sun is, both from an earthly viewpoint and in an odd sense of approbation, "behind" the stones, as if the whole scene were somehow *better* thanks to Bishop's turning back. (The Christmas trees in "At the Fishhouses" are also, David noted, "behind us" in more than one sense.) That the moment is handled lightly or "teasingly" diminishes its splendor not one bit. David once remarked that both Lowell and Bishop were at heart theological poets. He must have had a passage such as this in mind.

The neatly handled, explicit plot of "The End of March" represents a late achievement for Bishop. Whereas "At the Fishhouses," a poem not dissimilar in length and dramatic apparatus, can be resolved only through an extended alchemical rhapsody, every descriptive touch in the lines just quoted answers to the "inside story" they conclude.

"Crusoe in England" is the longest, funniest, and finally bleakest of these late narratives. Written as from the vantage of her return to New England, using the famous fiction as a mask and a visit to the Galápagos as a field trip, Bishop mythologizes the cheerfulness and awfulness of her own self-imposed years in the tropics. (Or so one might imagine. In fact, the poem must have been written off and on in Brazil. A 1965 letter to Howard Moss says that it needs "a good dusting." And the Galápagos trip came after its publication in 1971.)

New islands, Crusoe tells us without excitement at the start, keep being born; *his* island, however, remains "un-rediscovered, un-renamable." The lavish description of the next hundred or so lines suggests why.

> Well, I had fifty-two
> miserable, small volcanoes I could climb
> with a few slithery strides—
> volcanoes dead as ash heaps.

Dead? Presently we read: "The folds of lava, running out to sea, / would hiss." Of course it's the usual rain hissing, or else the giant local turtles sounding like the teakettle Crusoe would "have given years" for. Then smoke appears, on inspection turning out to be the sea up-spiraling within the waterspouts' "glass chimneys." Amid so much elemental confusion it is hard to bear in mind that the volcanoes haven't come back to life— as Crusoe has, warming to his story. The more he tells, the more dreamlike and elusive the island grows. Small wonder no one has found it. It is turning before our eyes to language, having already—its fifty-two volcanoes weeks of the year?— turned to time, time spent, depleted and shrunken like Crusoe's old clothing. Or as Bishop puts it elsewhere ("Poem"): "Life and the memory of it so compressed / they've turned into each other."

Defoe's Crusoe, we recall, kept an obsessive calendar, and named his companion for the day they met. Bishop's Crusoe, whose island leaves not a wrack behind, is nonetheless able to *date* the keenest of his losses: "And Friday, my dear Friday, died of measles / seventeen years ago come March." So Geography bows to History.

> The sun set in the sea; the same odd sun
> rose from the sea,
> and there was one of it and one of me.
> The island had one kind of everything . . .

The sun is odd because singular, a solitary like Crusoe, and also because it keeps—playfully? irresolutely?—rising and setting. Instead of being teased, like the sun by the stones in "The End of March," Crusoe's sun appears to be teasing *him*. A certain volcano gets christened either *"Mont d'Espoir* or *Mount Despair* / (I'd time enough to play with names)." The berry juice used to dye a baby goat red merges a few lines later with the blood from a baby goat's slit throat. These details glint cheerful-awful like shot silk. How small are the volcanoes, really?

> I'd think that if they were the size
> I thought volcanoes should be, then I had
> become a giant;
> and if I had become a giant,
> I couldn't bear to think what size
> the goats and turtles were . . .

Throughout her work Bishop loves juggling relative sizes. In "Jerónimo's House" a chair "for the smallest baby" had "ten big beads." The vast and ominous moonscape in "12 O'Clock News" is a view of the writer's desk. Her dexterity has never been more sinister than here. Crusoe's flute appropriately plays "the weirdest scale on earth."

According to David, "play of curiosity" and "joy" pervade the poem. He acknowledges Crusoe's recurrent nightmare of "being trapped on infinite numbers of islands, each of which he must in painful detail explore. Back in England the nightmare is just the opposite: that such stimulation, imaginative curiosity and energy will peter out." I would like to suggest (if my friend were still reachable by telephone) that Crusoe's nightmares are waking ones too, and include the maddening blanks and queasy uncertainties that beset all but the last pages of his account. For here those various oscillations come to an abrupt halt.

> Just when I thought I couldn't stand it
> another minute longer, Friday came.
> (Accounts of that have everything all wrong.)
> Friday was nice.
> Friday was nice, and we were friends.
> If only he had been a woman!
> I wanted to propagate my kind,
> and so did he, I think, poor boy.
> He'd pet the baby goats sometimes,
> and race with them, or carry one around.
> —Pretty to watch; he had a pretty body.

> And then one day they came and took us off.

Like stepping ashore from a rocking boat, this language shocks by its flatness: no description, no double takes, no thickening of the plot. Was Friday then neither soulmate nor servant, lover nor cannibal—just another teenager cavorting on the beach at Rio? I once idiotically asked the author, on being shown this poem before publication, if there couldn't be a bit more about Friday? She rolled her eyes and threw up her hands: Oh, there used to be—*lots* more! But then it seemed . . . And wasn't the poem already long enough?

Despite its concluding lines, "Crusoe in England" is an elegy less for Friday than for the young imagination that running wild sustained itself alone. Friday's role is to put an end to the monologue. Until he appears it is chiefly resourcefulness and bravado—reinventing the parasol, making home-brew, playing word games, breeding hallucinations—that keep Crusoe going in his solitary realm. Friday confirms the scale of things: a stabilizing figure and a silencing one. The story goes underground. It will remain only for Crusoe to describe the trappings of old age on another island which "doesn't seem like one, but who decides?"

————

In 1983 David's friend Svetlana Alpers published *The Art of Describing*, a study of seventeenth-century Dutch painting. The book struck him as bearing uncannily upon his own. In particular the polarity between Dutch painters and those of the Italian Renaissance, the latter felt by historians even in our time to be somehow more "important" than the genial naturalists beyond the Alps—couldn't this be fruitfully applied to a view of Bishop and Lowell?

The Dutch manner "will appeal to women"—a slur attributed to Michelangelo. Indeed, Bishop was Dutch in her love of curiosities locatable in time and place (a hen run over, in summer, on West 4th Street); of genre scenes (Faustina and her mistress, the "Filling Station" attendants) or single figures at their daily tasks (the "sad seamstress," the boy Balthazár, the old netmender outside the fishhouses); of microscopic close-ups and lucid distances ("I can make out the rigging of a schooner / a mile off"); of maps, which, as Alpers puts it, show us "not land possessed but land known in certain respects"; and in her general avoidance of allegorical framework as well as of the rhetoric that corresponds, perhaps, to those wonderstruck figures gesturing from the edge of a nativity or a martyrdom, as if the viewer wouldn't otherwise know where to look or what to feel.

Turning from Bishop's open-air naturalism to Lowell can be like entering a hall full of tortured gods, wounded Gauls, patricides, massacres of the innocents. This last subject, Alpers writes, "with its hordes of angry soldiers, dying children, and mourning mothers was the epitome of what [in the Italian tradition] pictorial narration and hence painting should be." As Lowell himself must often have felt: "Always within me is the child who died." Always upon him was the pressure, in David's words, "to make the poem *signify*," the "rhetorical effort to amplify events, to see them as part of the patterns of the past." Hence the revision of *Notebook* into *History*. This urge is central to Lowell's genius; he could never resist it for long. "In truth I seem to have felt mostly the joys of living," he admits in his "Afterthought" to *Notebook*; "in remembering, in recording, thanks to the gift of the Muse, it is the pain." Can it be the same Muse who, given the raw materials of Bishop's life, worked so countervailing an alchemy?

———

"Crusoe in England" is an exception to Bishop's preference for the happy ending, or the ruefully cheerful one. (Marianne Moore made no bones about *her* preference. "Like John Cheever," she confided to the editor of *Writer's Digest*, " 'I have an impulse to bring glad tidings.' ") So "The Moose" reverts to type, culminating in a wave of joy "we all feel" at the sight of the great, mysterious animal.

The poem has begun with a "Dutch" catalogue of ravishing pictorial details—landscapes, cottages with figures, flower-pieces or vegetable-pieces—glimpsed from an old-fashioned bus traveling from Nova Scotia to Boston (the alpha and omega, virtually, of Bishop's own life). Between this opening passage and the appearance of the moose occurs a haunting slow movement during which—now that night has fallen and the supremely interesting outside world become an "impenetrable wood"—the poet, *faute de mieux*, finds herself attending to History. Voices "back in the bus" begin "Talking the way they talked / in the old featherbed, / peacefully, on and on" until "it's all right now / even to fall asleep / just as on all those nights." David Kalstone suggests that "this discourse and its kinship to her own powers, the storyteller's powers handed down, summon up the strange vision which stops the bus . . . The moose seems both to crystallize the silence, security, and awe of the world being left behind and to guarantee a nourishing and haunting place for it in memory."

But those voices, however mild and sleep-inducing, have painful—or once painful—tales to tell:

> deaths, deaths and sicknesses;
> the year he remarried;

the year (something) happened.
She died in childbirth.
That was the son lost
when the schooner foundered.

He took to drink. Yes.
She went to the bad.
When Amos began to pray
even in the store and
finally the family had
to put him away.

Death, remarriage, alcoholism, manic spells, the asylum—
where have we most recently heard all that? Why, right here,
in and between the lines of Robert Lowell's and Elizabeth Bishop's own lives. The themes which in "The Moose" seem so
general are in fact achingly particular. Yet Bishop, even as she
introduces these "confessional" elements into the poem, consigns them ("not concerning us") to the back of the bus. That
is *her* Muse's way with Lowell's kind of subject matter. Eloquent
at many other levels, "The Moose" can still be read as part of
"one of those arguments that goes on throughout eternity"—
or so David puts it, looking back on the differences between
the two poets.

In that argument there is, mercifully, no last word intended
either by him or in this postscript. Instead . . . a handful of
memories?

—I saw Miss Moore at the end of her life, accompanied
by a nurse, settled in the front row at the Guggenheim Museum.
That evening Elizabeth was reading, among other poems, her
"Invitation to Miss Marianne Moore," published decades earlier, in 1948. A year later, its dedicatee had written with characteristic self-belittlement: "We are called poets, Elizabeth, and
one of us is." Now here they were, face to face, ceremonially,
for perhaps the last time.

—Back then in 1948 I was teaching at Bard College when the legendary Poetry Weekend took place. Cal and Elizabeth (as I wouldn't have dared to call them at the time) were together at one of the parties, delightedly drinking each other in. A colleague—who, lucky man, knew them both—wondered if this intimacy mightn't *lead to something*. A romance? Only now do I realize how young they were. "The Quaker Graveyard" and "Florida" had been written, but not "Skunk Hour" or "The Armadillo." Or "The Moose." Those poems, of course, are what the intimacy led to.

—The phone rings. It is David, in 1984, wanting to talk about "The Moose." I mention the stanza that evokes a household at night, the kitchen where a dog sleeps, tucked in his shawl. "Tucked in *her* shawl," David corrects, the smile audible.

Brief, threadbare impressions at the time. It would take all my friend's sympathy and scholarship to place them in a fuller, truer light. Let me try to do as much for that assertion.

In the famous sonnet already partly quoted Cal is still marveling at Elizabeth's patience:

> Have you seen an inchworm crawl on a leaf,
> cling to the very end, revolve in air,
> feeling for something to reach something? Do
> you still hang your words in air, ten years
> unfinished, glued to your notice board, with gaps
> or empties for the unimaginable phrase—
> unerring Muse who makes the casual perfect?

That inchworm is a haunting *trouvaille*. Elizabeth, in her elegy "North Haven"—her only poem addressed to Cal—also finds in nature a poignant and oddly appropriate image, whereby his lifelong recyclings of earlier work come to seem not so much tortured as instinctive, part of a serene Arcadian world:

> The Goldfinches are back, or others like them,
> and the White-throated Sparrow's five-note song,

pleading and pleading, brings tears to the eyes.
Nature repeats herself, or almost does:
repeat, repeat, repeat; revise, revise, revise.

. . .

You left North Haven, anchored in its rock,
afloat in mystic blue . . . And now—you've left
for good. You can't derange, or re-arrange
your poems again. (But the Sparrows can their song.)
The words won't change again. Sad friend, you cannot change.

It should not be surprising that two brilliant, complex, and often self-destructive people late in life chose to depict one another as bent, like those fragile totem creatures, unambiguously upon survival. Amid the human welter what remained constant in the poets was their incapacity not to reach out for words, not to revise their songs. Their feelings, too, of mutual protectiveness. It is what happens when friends persist in seeing each other's best, and it is a note on which to let this book break off. By concentrating on the language used, the clear-eyed readings (or misreadings) of poems sent back and forth, the letters exchanged, and the climate of faith and gratitude that against all odds prevailed in them, our critic has been able to broach at once the mysteries of affinity and those of making.

James Merrill

Appendix

Notes

Index

Appendix

This is the version of Elizabeth Bishop's "Roosters" made by Marianne Moore and her mother, transcribed from the original typescript in the Rosenbach Museum and Library and published with the kind permission of the Marianne Moore Estate.

THE COCK

At four oclock
In the gun metal half blue dark
We hear the first crow of the first cock.

And below
the window that is metal blue also,
an immediate echo

in the distance;
from the backyard fence

from the broccoli patch.
All over town the flare begins to catch.

In the blue blurr
as rustling wives admire,
the roosters brace their feet and glare

with eyes
unseeing as from their beaks rise
uncontrolled outcries. Confusion multiplies

deep from protruding chests
in green gold medals dressed
to terrorize the rest

who lead hen's lives
of being courted and despised.

From strained throats
a senseless order floats

across fastidious beds,
from rust-discolored sheds,
from makeshift pens and bedsteads

fenced and crazily conjoined across white churches
on which the golden rooster perches;

in brave sallies
from the muddy alleys
that form maps like Rand McNally's.

The warring throats of true
glass pin-head colors,

golds, coppers, greens,
anthracite blues, alizarins,
scream, "This is where I live."

Cocks, what are you projecting?
Greek sacrificial cocks
tied to a post to struggle,
whom we label

fighting-cocks, what right have you to give
commands, and tell us how to live?—

cry "Here," "Come here,"
and wake us where are
irrelevant love, conceit, and war?

The crown of red
set on your little head
is charged with all your fighting-blood.

Yes, in mid air
by twos they fight. Another
feather joins the first flame feather,

floats and falls; the plucked body defying
even the sensation of dying.

He lies in dung,
with open bloody eyes
as his metallic feathers oxidize.

St. Peter's sin
was worse than that of Magdalen
whose sin was of the flesh alone.

Of spirit, Peter's
among "servants and officers."

Holy sculpture
sets it all together:
one scene, past and future,

Christ amazed,
Peter, saint,—two fingers raised,

a little cock is seen
carved on a dim column in the travertine,

explained as "Gallus canit;
"*Flet Petrus*" underneath; the pivot.

["*Gallus canit*" explains why.
The words are "*Gallus canit*."]

Yes Peter's tears
at cock-crow, gemming a cock's spurs.

A new weathervane
On the basilica,
outside the Lateran.

There was always to be
a bronze cock on a porphyry
pillar so that people and Pope might see

that the Prince
of the apostles
was forgiven; to convince

them that "Deny deny deny"
is now [*sic*] now as it was, the rooster's cry.

In the morning
a low light is floating

From underneath
the broccoli stems, leaf by leaf,
gilding the lines of pink in the sky,

the day's preamble
like wandering lines in marble;

And climbing in to see the end,
The faithful sin [*sic*] is here,
as enemy, or friend.

Notes

ABBREVIATIONS

In the source notes the following abbreviations have been used:

For the correspondents:
EB   Elizabeth Bishop
MM   Marianne Moore
RL   Robert Lowell

For the manuscript holdings:
(H)   Houghton Library, Harvard University
(R)   The Rosenbach Museum and Library,
       Philadelphia, Pennsylvania
(V)   Vassar College Library
(W)   Washington University Libraries,
       St. Louis, Missouri:
       Olin Libraries Special Collections

Where there is no indication of manuscript location, the letter is in private hands.
Passages quoted from Elizabeth Bishop's poems are taken, unless another source is given in the notes, from *The Complete Poems, 1927–1979* (New York: Farrar, Straus and Giroux, 1983).
Letters begun on one day and completed on a later one are given both dates: January 8/20, 1964.

x. "After a poem is published": EB, interview with Ashley Brown, *Shenandoah* 17, no. 2 (Winter 1966), p. 15.

xi. "two of my favorite poets": EB to Anne Stevenson, January 8/20, 1964 (W). When Ashley Brown visited Bishop in Brazil in 1966, he noticed photographs of Baudelaire, Marianne Moore, and Robert Lowell near her worktable.

ELIZABETH BISHOP AND MARIANNE MOORE

1/FROM THE COUNTRY TO THE CITY

3. the long memoir . . . that has since appeared: See Elizabeth Bishop, *The Collected Prose*, ed. Robert Giroux (New York: Farrar, Straus and Giroux, 1984), pp. 121–56. This chapter draws on the memoir for many of its details.

3. "Everyone has said that": EB to MM, October 24, 1954 (R).

4. "As for indebtedness": MM to EB, September 21, 1959 (V).

4. "subliminal glimpse": Bishop, *Collected Prose*, p. 156.

5. "otherworldly": Bishop, *Collected Prose*, p. 137.

5. "uplifted, even inspired": Bishop, *Collected Prose*, p. 137.

5. that she ever deliberately tried to meet a "celebrity": EB to Anne Stevenson, March 23, 1964 (W).

6. copied out in longhand "The Jerboa": EB, notebook (V).

6. So, it turned out, would Eliot: In his introduction to Moore's *Selected Poems* (1935).

6. "a tall, eagle-nosed, be-turbaned lady": Elizabeth Bishop, "A Sentimental Tribute," *Bryn Mawr Alumnae Bulletin* 43 (Spring 1962), p. 2, quoted in Elizabeth Spires, "An Afternoon with Elizabeth Bishop," *Vassar Quarterly* 75 (Winter 1979), p. 5.

7. Mickey Rooney: "When one day I told her she looked like Mickey Rooney, then a very young actor (and she did), she seemed quite pleased." Bishop, *Collected Prose*, p. 133. Mickey Rooney, at the age of fourteen, had played Puck in the movie version of *A Midsummer Night's Dream* (1935).

7. "Miss Moore, indeed": Yvor Winters, review of "The Shorter Poems of Robert Bridges," *The Hound and Horn* 5, no. 1 (October–December 1931), p. 322.

7. "poor, sick, her work practically unread": EB, notebook (V).

7. "a flicker of impudence": Marianne Moore, *The Complete Prose of Marianne Moore* (New York: Elisabeth Sifton / Viking, 1986), p. 328.

8. "All dedications are dowdy": Bishop, *Collected Prose*, p. 142.

8. "Dedications imply giving": Marianne Moore, *Selected Poems* (New York: Macmillan, 1935), p. 108.

8. "double or triple negatives": Bishop, *Collected Prose*, p. 129.

8. She could hear Mrs. Moore: EB to MM, October 9, 1944 (R).

8. has the effect of a dialogue: EB to MM, December 8, 1944 (R).

8. "anarchic order": Marguerite Young, "An Afternoon with Marianne Moore (1946)," in *Festschrift for Marianne Moore's Seventy-seventh Birthday*, ed. Tambimuttu (New York: Tambimuttu & Mass, 1965), p. 65.

Notes

8. "very serious": Bishop, *Collected Prose*, p. 129.

9. "Her manner toward Marianne": Ibid.

9. "I should say, in candor": MM to EB, December 17, 1936 (V).

9. "Why had no one ever written": Bishop, *Collected Prose*, p. 123.

9. "of such a ritualistic solemnity": Elizabeth Bishop, "As We Like It," in the Marianne Moore issue, *Quarterly Review of Literature* 4 (Spring 1948), p. 131.

9. "For a mind of such agility": T. S. Eliot, introduction to Marianne Moore's *Selected Poems*, p. xi.

10. "the necks set": MM to EB, January 31, 1942 (V).

10. "course of study": MM to EB, April 26, 1936 (V).

10. "every bit of pictorial evidence": EB to MM, May 2, 1936 (R).

10. "our degradation of after-illness": MM to EB, March 22, 1936 (V).

11. "snakes in alcohol": MM to EB, March 14, 1936 (V).

11. at work in June: EB to MM, April 4, 1936 (R).

11. "in bad repute": MM to EB, January 31, 1936 (V).

11. "less driven into desperate straits": Randall Jarrell, "The Poet and His Public," *Partisan Review* 13, no. 4 (September–October 1946), p. 499; Randall Jarrell, *Poetry and the Age* (New York: Knopf, 1953), p. 234.

11. made her passive: EB to Anne Stevenson, March 23, 1964 (W).

11. "Miss Moore's 'architectural' method": EB, notebook (V).

12. "the soft combed and carded look": EB, notebook (V).

12. "Along the street below": Unless otherwise noted, passages quoted from Bishop's poems are taken from *The Complete Poems, 1927–1979* (New York: Farrar, Straus and Giroux, 1983).

13. "the poems I like best": EB to Anne Stevenson, March 23, 1964 (W).

14. "The window this evening": EB, notebook (V).

14. one of her favorite poets: EB to Anne Stevenson, January 8/20, 1964 (W). Bishop writes, "Two of my favorite poets (not best poets) are Herbert (I've read him steadily almost all my life), and Baudelaire. I can't attempt to reconcile them."

14. a dream . . . in which George Herbert appears to her: EB, notebook (V).

15. "using the poet's proper material": EB, notebook (V).

16. "There is no 'split' ": EB to Anne Stevenson, January 8/20, 1964 (W).

18. "it is in the city alone": EB, notebook (V), entry dated May 19, 1935.

19. "looked into the inside of a small mask": EB, notebook (V).

20. "as insincere as poison": EB, notebook (V).

20. "These are *men on rafts*": EB, notebook (V).

21. "overtaken by an awful awful feeling": EB, notebook (V).

22. the poet's own sense of place: Anne Stevenson, *Elizabeth Bishop* (New York: Twayne, 1965), p. 43.

22. "She lived until 1934": EB to Anne Stevenson, January 8/20, 1964 (W).

23. "intelligent and resourceful": Helen Sanderson to Anne Stevenson, January 19, 1963 (W).

23. "enormously cagey": Barbara Swain to Anne Stevenson, March 22, 1964 (W).

23. "apparently unchronological incidents": EB, notebook (V).

23. Bishop, "Dimensions for a Novel": *Vassar Journal of Undergraduate Studies* 8 (May 1934), pp. 95–103.

23. "If I suffer a terrible loss": Ibid, pp. 100–1.

24. "The crises of our lives": Ibid, p. 100.
24. "a drop of mercury": Ibid, p. 103.
24. Bishop herself believed: EB to Anne Stevenson, May 5, 1964 (W).
25. "don't think I dote on it": EB to Anne Stevenson, March 23, 1964 (W). Most of the details that follow are taken from this letter.
25. "all hope was abandoned": EB to Anne Stevenson, May 5, 1964 (W).
27. "The Bishops were horrified": EB to Anne Stevenson, March 23, 1964 (W).
27. "suffer acutely": Ibid.
27. "Mrs. Sullivan Downstairs": EB, draft (V).
28. "She looked remarkable": Frani Blough Muser, quoted in Robert Giroux's introduction to Bishop, *Collected Prose*, pp. xii–xiii.
28. "girls who were as clever": EB to Anne Stevenson, March 23, 1964 (W).
29. a guest in other people's houses: "But my relationship with my relatives—I was always sort of a guest, and I think I've always felt like that." EB, interview with Elizabeth Spires, *Paris Review* 80 (Summer 1981), p. 75.

2 / TRIAL BALANCES

30. "a little more money than I had": EB, "The U.S.A. School of Writing," *Collected Prose*, p. 35.
30. "puritanically pink": Ibid.
31. "colored our air": EB, "A Brief Reminiscence and a Brief Tribute," *Harvard Advocate* (Auden issue, 1975), p. 47; repr. *Elizabeth Bishop and Her Art*, ed. Lloyd Schwartz and Sybil P. Estess (Ann Arbor: University of Michigan Press, 1983), p. 308.
31. "His then leftist politics": Ibid.
31. "so few people do": EB to MM, September 15, 1936 (R).
32. "My friendly circumstances": EB, journal (V).
32. "I envy the mind": Mary McCarthy in a symposium, "I Would Like to Have Written . . . ," *New York Times Book Review*, December 6, 1981, p. 68; repr. *Elizabeth Bishop and Her Art*, p. 267.
34. "The Baptism": Bishop, *Collected Prose*, pp. 159–70.
35. like Hans Christian Andersen's: EB to MM, October 18, 1936 (R).
35. "Then Came the Poor": The story appeared first in *Con Spirito* (Vassar) 1 (February 1933), and then in *The Magazine: A Literary Journal* (California) 1, no. 4 (March 1934), pp. 105–10. The principal editors of *Con Spirito*—the title, suggesting "conspiracy" as well as "with spirit," was Bishop's idea—were Bishop, Mary McCarthy, and Eleanor Clark.
36. as Bonnie Costello points out: In her *Marianne Moore: Imaginary Possessions* (Cambridge, Mass.: Harvard University Press, 1981), p. 67.
36. "known only to a musician": MM to Edward Aswell, October 29, 1935.
36. "Rhythm, of course": T. S. Eliot, *The Dial* 75 (December 1923), pp. 595–96.
37. "Snow sown by tearing winds": Marianne Moore, "Those Various Scalpels," *The Complete Poems of Marianne Moore* (New York: Macmillan, 1967), p. 51.
37. "the releasing, checking, timing": This and the quotations from her article that follow are from Elizabeth Bishop, "Gerard Manley Hopkins: Notes on Timing

in His Poetry," *Vassar Review* 23 (February 1934), pp. 5–7; repr. in part in *Elizabeth Bishop and Her Art*, pp. 273–75.

37. His musical ideas: EB to MM, April 2, 1935 (R).

37. Their purpose: M. W. Croll, "The Baroque Style in Prose" (1929); repr. *Style, Rhetoric and Rhythm: Essays by Morris W. Croll*, ed. J. Max Patrick *et al.* (Princeton, N.J.: Princeton University Press, 1966), p. 210.

39. "sprung rhythm . . . is the nearest": Gerard Manley Hopkins to Robert Bridges, August 21, 1877, in *The Letters of Gerard Manley Hopkins to Robert Bridges*, ed. C. C. Abbott (London: Oxford University Press, 1935), p. 46.

40. "I do just for fun": EB to T. C. Wilson, August 14, 1934.

40. The occasion was an anthology: *Trial Balances*, ed. Ann Winslow (New York: Macmillan, 1935).

40. a remarkably prophetic note: *Trial Balances*, pp. 82–83; repr. *The Complete Prose of Marianne Moore*, pp. 327–29.

40. "like the vegetable-shredder": Ibid.

40. "Some feminine poets": Ibid.

41. "less driven into dens of innocence": Randall Jarrell, "The Poet and His Public," *Partisan Review* 13, no. 4 (September–October 1946), p. 499; Randall Jarrell, *Poetry and the Age* (New York: Knopf, 1953), p. 234.

41. "One asks a great deal": Ibid.

42. "an instinct against precipitousness": MM to Edward Aswell, October 29, 1935.

42. "It is difficult": MM to EB, March 14, 1936 (V).

42. "satisfactory doughtiness": MM to EB, July 11, 1936 (V).

42. "maintained unequipoise": MM to EB, June 22, 1936 (V).

43. "like one of my contemporaries": EB to MM, August 2, 1936 (R).

43. applied to Cornell: EB, interview with Ashley Brown, *Shenandoah* 17, no. 2 (Winter 1966), p. 12.

43. considered studying medicine: EB to Anne Stevenson, March 18, 1963 (W).

43. "I feel you would not be able": MM to EB, August 28, 1936 (V).

43. "a serious cause for complaint": Ibid.

43. "awful faults": EB to MM, September 15, 1936 (R).

44. "But at the length": George Herbert, "Love Unknown," lines 45–56. *The Works of George Herbert*, ed. F. E. Hutchinson (Oxford: Clarendon Press, 1941).

44. dialogue between natural and spiritual man: Joseph Summers, *George Herbert: His Religion and Art* (London: Chatto & Windus, 1968), p. 178.

45. And the sky . . . is dead: A note of David Kalstone's following this paragraph in his draft manuscript reads: "Connect to 'The Unbeliever' and Cocteau."

45. "And the poems are so fine": MM to EB, September 20, 1936 (V).

46. "tentativeness and interiorizing": MM to EB, February 14, 1938 (V).

46. "I tend to wish": MM to EB, September 25, 1936 (V).

46. "To me that word suggests": EB to MM, September 29, 1936 (R).

47. admired William Empson's: EB to MM, February 4, 1936 (R).

47. "just a sort of stunt": EB to MM, February 15, 1936 (R).

47. "A Little Miracle": EB, notebook (V).

47. "The spirit and space": Wallace Stevens, "The American Sublime," *The Collected Poems* (New York: Vintage, 1982), p. 131.

48. "sudden change of scale": MM to EB, December 1936 (V).

48. "You are no comfort": EB to MM, January 5, 1937 (R).
51. "state of good cheer": EB to MM, December 5, 1936 (R).
51. "a fabled argosy advancing": In Moore's review of Wallace Stevens's *Owl's Clover* and *Ideas of Order, Poetry* 49 (February 1937), p. 269; Moore, *Complete Prose*, p. 347.
51. "That exact portrayal": In Moore's review of *Ideas of Order, The Criterion* 15 (January 1936), p. 309; Moore, *Complete Prose*, pp. 330–31.
51. "In each clime": *Poetry* 49 (February 1937), pp. 271–72; repr. Moore, *Complete Prose*, p. 349.
52. "a linguist": *Poetry* 49 (February 1937), p. 268; repr. Moore, *Complete Prose*, p. 347.
52. "the sea- / side flowers": Moore, *Complete Poems*, pp. 5–6.
52. "Moon-vines are moon-vines": Wallace Stevens, "A Poet That Matters: A Review of *Selected Poems* by Marianne Moore," *Life and Letters Today* 13, no. 2 (December 1935), p. 63.
53. "immediate intense physical reactions": EB, notebook (V). This passage is quoted at greater length in the previous chapter, page 15.

3 / OBSERVATIONS

55. "protective apron": EB to MM, March 6, 1937 (R).
55. "I'm afraid I am quite ungracious": EB to MM, October 27, 1936 (R).
55. "I hope you may like it well enough": MM to Roger Roughton, September 25, 1936; from the copy enclosed in her letter to EB dated October 1, 1936 (V).
56. rejected the revised poem: EB to MM, October 15, 1936 (R).
56. "sorry for such conceit": EB to MM, February 4, 1937 (R).
56. "You are not a novice": MM to EB, August 9, 1937 (V).
56. She apologized: EB to MM, January 31, 1938 (R).
56. "If it is returned with a printed slip": MM to EB, February 10, 1938 (V).
56. "these horrible 'fable' ideas": EB to MM, January 31, 1938 (R).
57. "If only I could see half as clearly": EB to MM, May 5, 1938 (R).
57. "The Hanging of the Mouse": Bishop included it in the *Complete Poems* of 1969. *Complete Poems: 1927–1979*, p. 143.
57. "a heavy responsibility for you": MM to EB, February 9, 1937 (V).
57. "the insidiousness of creativeness": MM to EB, March 7, 1937 (V).
58. "the significantly detestable": MM to EB, February 14, 1938 (V).
58. "the potent retiringness": Ibid.
58. "Continuously fascinated as I am": Ibid.
59. "In Prison": Bishop, *Collected Prose*, pp. 181–91.
59. "The Sea and Its Shore": Bishop, *Collected Prose*, pp. 171–80.
59. "more like an idea of a house": Ibid., pp. 171–72.
59. "not until I am securely installed": Ibid., p. 186.
59. according to a theory: EB to MM, May 5, 1938 (R).
60. "Much as a one-eyed room": Bishop, *Collected Prose*, p. 178.
60. as part of a prior creation: See Svetlana Alpers's interpretation of Dutch art as describing a prior creation, in her *The Art of Describing: Dutch Art in the Seventeenth*

Century (Chicago: University of Chicago Press, 1983). For the camera obscura see that volume, pp. 11–13 and 27–33.

60. "Because I share with Valéry's M. Teste": Bishop, *Collected Prose*, p. 188.
60. "like a torch": Ibid., p. 173.
60. "in diligently searching": Ibid., p. 176.
61. "on the narrow hems of the wings": Ibid., pp. 178–79.
61. "Large flakes of blackened paper": Ibid., p. 179.
62. "the insanity and bliss of one's calling": Lorna Sage, review of Bishop, *Collected Prose* in the *Times Literary Supplement*, April 27, 1984, p. 461.
62. "This morning": EB to MM, January 5, 1937 (R).
62. "through swamps and turpentine camps": Ibid.
63. "about to become wild again": Ibid.
63. "It was quite a sight": EB to MM, February 4, 1937 (R).
63. "I never believed her": EB to MM, June 2, 1938 (R).
63. She and the painter Loren McIver: EB to MM, February 27, 1939 (R).
64. "The bayonet points": MM to EB, January 24, 1937 (V).
64. "heart-breaking": EB to MM, September 2, 1937 (R).
65. "Mother-love": EB to Frani Blough, August 9, 1937.
66. The inverted syntax: In Patricia Lancaster Robinson, *The Textures of Reality: A Study of the Poetry of Elizabeth Bishop*, p. 107. Doctoral thesis, Rutgers University, The State University of New Jersey (New Brunswick), 1978.
67. the bronze pinecone: EB to MM, November 24, 1937 (R).
67. "the *tides of gold*": EB, diary (V).
68. "paper streamers": EB to MM, March 29, 1939 (R).
68. "The Negroes have soft voices": EB to MM, January 31, 1938 (R).
68. "a kind of ten commandments": Quoted back to Moore by Bishop in her letter of February 19, 1940 (R).
68. "hit the Key West lighthouse": EB to MM, February 19, 1940 (R).
69. "appear to have 'sapped the strength' ": EB to MM, January 31, 1938 (R).
69. "like a rebuke": EB to MM, May 21, 1940 (R).
70. "the watchful maker": Moore, *Complete Poems*, pp. 121–22.
71. she makes us aware: See Bonnie Costello's discussion of "The Paper Nautilus" in *Marianne Moore: Imaginary Possessions*, pp. 119–20.
71. "the apparent remoteness": Bishop, *Collected Prose*, p. 54.
72. "There is no reason": Bishop, *Collected Prose*, pp. 70–71.
75. "the presence of the barbaric": R. P. Blackmur, *Language as Gesture: Essays on Poetry* (New York: Harcourt, Brace, 1952), p. 196.

4 / LOGARITHMS OF APOLOGY

76. as David Bromwich has suggested: See David Bromwich, "Elizabeth Bishop's Dream-Houses," *Raritan* 4, no. 1 (Summer 1984).
76. "that continuous uncomfortable feeling": EB to MM, September 11, 1940 (R).
77. "blackest doubts": EB to MM, February 25, 1937 (R).
77. "real respect": MM to EB, March 1, 1937 (V).
77. "an indirect blow": EB to MM, February 19, 1939 (R).
77. "Sex-Appeal": EB to MM, December 15, 1939 (R).

77. "Her idiosyncrasy": MM to James Laughlin, January 16, 1940.
78. "There are so many things here": EB to MM, September 1, 1940 (R).
78. "I make such demands": EB to MM, September 11, 1940 (R).
78. "laziness and miscalculations": EB to MM, September 1, 1940 (R).
79. "an immediate flurry of criticism": EB, Bishop, *Collected Prose*, p. 145.
79. "Do not read at mealtime": MM to EB, October 16, 1940 (V).
80. a "sizing version": EB to MM, October 20, 1940 (R).
80. "Regarding the water-closet": MM to EB, October 16, 1940 (V).
81. "because I want to emphasize": EB to MM, October 17, 1940 (R).
81. "glass-headed pins": Ibid.
82. self-reproach: David Bromwich, "Elizabeth Bishop's Dream-Houses," p. 85.
85. a biblical phrase Bishop loved: EB to MM, October 17, 1940 (R). Bishop writes, "And I wanted to keep 'to see the end' [Matt. 26:58] in quotes because, although it may not be generally recognized, I have always felt that expression used of Peter in the Bible, to be extremely poignant."
85. a "trifle": EB to MM, February 5, 1940 (R).
87. "protestant inquests": David Bromwich, "Elizabeth Bishop's Dream-Houses," p. 85.
87. "visual and instantaneous": Randall Jarrell in *Partisan Review* 12, no. 1 (Winter 1945), p. 120; Randall Jarrell, *Kipling, Auden & Co.* (New York: Farrar, Straus and Giroux, 1980), pp. 127–28.
87. "All her zoos are Egyptian": Ibid., p. 121.
88. comments and suggestions: MM to EB, November 16, 1943, and April 23, 1944 (V).
88. like Klee's *The Man of Confusion*: EB to MM, October 17, 1940 (R).
88. "It is wonderful": MM to EB, September 8, 1942 (V).
89. "I'm afraid I'll find your reasons": EB to MM, September 28, 1942 (R).
89. "don't let writing be a threat": MM to EB, May 11, 1942 (V).
89. "As for Mother": MM to EB, March 21, 1942 (V).
89. "Even just standing still": MM to EB, April 6, 1942 (V).
89. "always ironing": Ibid.
90. "why I don't feel Yeats is as wonderful": EB to MM, January 24, 1942 (R).
90. "I would be 'much disappointed' ": MM to EB, January 31, 1942, as quoted in Bishop, *Collected Prose*, pp. 146–47.
90. "his old mother-of-pearl inlaid guitar": EB to MM, January 24, 1942 (R).
90. "I too resist obliqueness": MM to EB, January 31, 1942 (V).
90. a slackening of form: MM to EB, July 20, 1943, and November 16, 1943 (V).
91. "the present terrible *generalizing*": EB to MM, July 15, 1943 (R).
91. when James Laughlin wrote: EB to MM, March 17, 1942 (R).
91. "I don't really oppose": MM to EB, March 21, 1942 (V).
91. Bishop eventually sent: EB to MM, May 23, 1942 (R).
91. "Miss Bishop does not avoid": *The Nation* 163 (September 28, 1946), p. 354; Moore, *Complete Prose*, p. 408.
92. " 'violence' of tone": EB to MM, October 17, 1940 (R).
92. "THE FISH": Marianne Moore, *Complete Poems*, p. 22.
96. "From this the poem springs": Wallace Stevens, "Notes toward a Supreme Fiction," *Collected Poems*, p. 383.

99. "unself-pity": MM to EB, April 23, 1944 (V).

99. "to finish six or seven poems": Bishop quotes this passage in her letter to Moore dated January 8, 1945 (R).

99. "assimilated beyond detection": From Moore's letter of recommendation to Houghton Mifflin for the literary fellowship, sent to Ferris Greenslet, Katherine White, and Horace Gregory—the three judges—with a copy to Bishop. MM to EB, January 5, 1945 (V).

99. Moore's review: "A Modest Expert," *The Nation* 163 (September 28, 1946), p. 354; repr. Moore, *Complete Prose*, pp. 406–8.

100. "it is my whole life": MM to EB, September 30, 1946 (V).

101. "Miss Bishop's speculation": Moore, "A Modest Expert," p. 354; *Complete Prose*, p. 408.

101. "the blackness of illness": MM to EB, November 19, 1944 (V).

101. "egotism to overcome the degradation": MM to EB, January 5, 1945 (V).

101. "I am industriously sordid": Ibid.

102. "We have not met for years": MM to EB, January 4, 1946 (V).

102. "to outgrow *torture*": MM to EB, June 1, 1946 (V).

102. "You are ill": MM to EB, April 16, 1944 (V).

102. "Dear brave Elizabeth": MM to EB, April 23, 1944 (V).

102. "I did not mention your health": MM to EB, January 5, 1945 (V).

102. "Don't conceal anything": MM to EB, September 27, 1945 (V).

103. "How touching": MM to EB, August 10, 1947 (V).

103. "I'm trying to be peaceable": MM to EB, October 15, 1947 (V).

103. "I'm not sure how much like La Fontaine": EB to RL, June 30, 1948 (H).

103. Bishop's contributions: "For M.M." and "As We Like It," *Quarterly Review of Literature* 4 (Spring 1948), pp. 127–35. Bishop later gave "For M.M." the title "Invitation to Miss Marianne Moore" (*Complete Poems*, 82).

103. "Words fail me": MM to EB, August 24, 1948 (V).

104. "and we *must*": Bishop, "As We Like It," *Quarterly Review of Literature* 4 (Spring 1948), p. 131.

104. "how it is to be *it*?": Ibid.

104. "the metaphor, when used, carries a long way": Ibid., p. 132.

105. "her individual verse forms": Ibid., p. 134.

105. " 'logarithms of apology' ": MM to EB, August 24, 1948 (V).

105. One of Bishop's best friends: Bishop reports this to Lowell in her letter dated June 30, 1948 (H).

106. "Lots of things": MM to EB, September 19, 1948 (V).

106. questions remain forever to be answered: EB, notebook (V)

ELIZABETH BISHOP AND ROBERT LOWELL

I / PRODIGAL YEARS

109. "I see us still": RL to EB, December 18, 1974 (V).

110. "Never, never was I 'tall' ": EB to RL, January 16, 1975 (H).

111. "systematically apprenticed himself": Blair Clark, "On Robert Lowell," *Harvard Advocate* 113 (November 1979), p. 10.

111. "poor symbolic, abstract creatures": Lowell, jacket blurb for Bishop's *Poems: North & South—A Cold Spring* (Boston: Houghton Mifflin, 1955); repr. Candace W. MacMahon, *Elizabeth Bishop: A Bibliography* (Charlottesville: University Press of Virginia, 1980), p. 13.

111. "a battered-up old alarm clock": EB to RL, May 1948 (H).

112. "come live in Paris": EB to RL, February 14, 1948 (H).

112. a convicted felon: RL to EB, February 25, 1948 (V).

112. would Bishop come?: RL to EB, July 2, 1948 (V).

113. "tag along": EB to RL, June 30, 1948 (H).

113. "It's my dream to maneuver": RL to EB, January 5, 1949 (V).

113. Lowell . . . accused: The incident is recounted in *The Habit of Being: Letters of Flannery O'Connor*, ed. Sally Fitzgerald (New York: Farrar, Straus and Giroux, 1979), pp. 11–12, and in Ian Hamilton, *Robert Lowell: A Biography* (New York: Random House, 1982), pp. 138–52.

114. "The clipping bureau": EB to RL, August 14, 1947 (H).

114. "Why talk *letters*": James Merrill, "Elizabeth Bishop (1911–1979)," *The New York Review of Books* 26 (December 6, 1979), p. 6; repr. *Elizabeth Bishop and Her Art*, p. 259.

115. "your stern example": EB to RL, January 1/15, 1948 (H).

115. "the proper table-level": EB to RL, May 1948 (H).

115. " 'poet by default' ": EB to RL, January 21, 1949 (H).

115. "When I think about it": EB to James Merrill, January 23, 1979.

116. "I take your remarks": EB to RL, January 1/15, 1948 (H).

118. "two poetic spigots": EB to RL, December 3, 1947 (H).

118. "all the material in this world": EB to RL, April 8, 1948 (H).

118. "minor female Wordsworth": EB to RL, July 11, 1951 (H).

118. she had forgotten how beautiful it was: EB to MM, August 29, 1946 (R).

119. "We hailed it": Ibid.

119. "My mother went off to teach": EB to Anne Stevenson, March 23, 1964 (W).

121. the "great splendor": RL to EB, August 21, 1947 (V).

122. a *dramatic* eye: Howard Moss, "The Canada-Brazil Connection," *World Literature Today* 51, no. 1 (Winter 1977), p. 30.

122. "The only intellectual life": EB to RL, January 21, 1949 (H).

123. a little time-telling refrain: RL to EB, September 7, 1948 (V); EB to RL, September 11, 1948 (H).

123. "beginning to feel like Admiral Byrd": EB to Carley Dawson, June 30, 1948.

123. "I'd 'laugh you to scorn' ": EB to RL, September 8, 1948 (H).

123. "Pain comes from the darkness": Randall Jarrell, "90 North," *Selected Poems* (New York: Atheneum, 1964), p. 104.

124. "I've really got it bad": EB to RL, September 8, 1948 (H).

124. "too much like a Lowell": EB to RL, May 1948 (H).

124. Tristan Corbière: *Poems*, tr. Walter McElroy (Pawlet, Vt.: The Banyan Press, 1947).

124. Jarrell, in a review: "Verse Chronicle," *The Nation* 165 (October 18, 1947), p. 425; Jarrell, *Poetry and the Age*, p. 162.

125. Bishop's reaction: EB to RL, late January 1948 (H).

125. "greyest New York atmosphere": EB to RL, March 18, 1948 (H).

125. "I felt with a shock": RL to EB, February 25, 1948 (V).

125. "celluloid and bargain cockatoo": Robert Lowell, "Thanksgiving's Over," *The Mills of the Kavanaughs* (New York: Harcourt, Brace, 1951), p. 51.

126. "bluebird in a tumbler": Ibid., p. 52.

126. "There is a small lobster-pond": EB to RL, September 8, 1948 (H).

126. "as your disheartened shadow tries": Lowell, *The Mills of the Kavanaughs*, p. 21.

126. *"Manque de savoir-vivre"*: Corbière, "Le Poète contumace," *Poems*, p. 46.

126. "For want of knowing": Jarrell, *Selected Poems*, p. 115.

126. "Jarrell's poetry": EB to Carley Dawson, October 1, 1948.

127. Some of the details: EB to RL, November 23, 1955 (H).

127. "There's no long struggle": Lowell, *Selected Poems*, pp. 27–28.

128. as Anthony Hecht once pointed out: In correspondence with the author.

130. "As a child": Jacket blurb for Robert Lowell, *Life Studies* (New York: Farrar, Straus and Giroux, 1959); repr. *Elizabeth Bishop and Her Art*, p. 285.

131. "black-tongued piratical vigor": Lowell uses the phrase in a letter to Bishop dated January 5, 1949 (V), saying of Randall Jarrell that he has "no black-tongued piratical vigor at all."

131. "sense of horror and panic": EB to RL, August 14, 1947 (H).

131. "one of the most harrowing": EB to RL, December 5 or 6, 1950 (H).

131. "it has so much richness": EB to RL, December 3, 1947 (H).

131. "so strongly influential": EB to RL, December 5 or 6, 1950 (H).

131. "I don't care much": EB to Anne Stevenson, March 20, 1963 (W).

131. "Most of my poems I can still abide": EB to Anne Stevenson, January 8/20, 1964 (W).

132. "entering upon the prophetic stage": EB to RL, September 11, 1948 (H).

133. Jarrell's review: in "The Poet and His Public," *Partisan Review* 13, no. 4 (September–October 1946), pp. 499–500; repr. Jarrell, *Poetry and the Age*, pp. 234–35.

133. "It's the first review I've had": EB to RL, August 14, 1947 (H).

133. "I'm a fisherman myself": RL to EB, August 21, 1947 (V).

133. "On the surface": Robert Lowell, "Thomas, Bishop, and Williams," *The Sewanee Review* 55, no. 3 (July–September 1947), p. 497; Lowell, *Collected Prose*, ed. Robert Giroux (New York: Farrar, Straus and Giroux, 1987), pp. 76–77.

2 / THE SUMMER OF 1948

136. he and she and Trumbull Stickney: RL to EB, September 7, 1948 (V).

136. "I liked *North & South*": George Santayana to RL, August 31, 1948 (H)

136. "husband that shall be monogamous": In the second of the "Songs for a Colored Singer," Bishop, *Complete Poems*, p. 48.

136. "your sense of reality": RL to EB, September 7, 1948 (V).

137. "Both poets use": *The Sewanee Review* 55 (Summer 1947), p. 498; Lowell, *Collected Prose*, p. 78.

137. "much too overpowering": EB to RL, June 30, 1948 (H).

137. "too monotonous, pathological": RL to EB, July 2, 1948 (V).

138. "You always make me feel": RL to EB, April 24, 1952 (V).

138. "You and Peter Taylor": RL to EB, January 25, 1949 (V).

138. "warm and friendly": RL to EB, June 9, 1948 (V).

138. "She has gotten a world": RL, interview with Frederick Seidel, *Paris Review* 25 (Winter–Spring 1961), p. 69; Lowell, *Collected Prose*, p. 245.

139. what might have been: RL to EB, August 15, 1957 (V).

139. "a museum town": EB to Carley Dawson, June 30, 1948.

139. "pour in like lava": RL to EB, July 2, 1948 (V).

139. called it Fatso: RL to EB, July 29, 1948 (V).

139. "a crowd of three": RL, draft (H).

139. "It's all in *Adolphe*": RL to EB, August 24, 1948 (V).

140. "An Influx of Poets": *The New Yorker* 54 (November 6, 1978), pp. 43–60.

140. like a badger: Tommy Wanning's account, in conversation with the author.

140. "My old flame": RL, draft (H).

141. "And on the next to last night": RL, draft (H).

141. "numb to the waist": EB, ms. (V).

141. "I assumed": RL to EB, August 15, 1957 (V).

141. "It seemed that our two natures blent": W. B. Yeats, "Among School Children," *Poems* (New York: Macmillan, 1983), p. 216.

142. "led to no encroachments": RL to EB, August 15, 1957 (V).

142. "My uncertain fingers": RL, draft (H).

142. "sounded a little excitable": EB to Carley Dawson, July 11, 1948.

142. "if I want to remain friends": EB to Carley Dawson, August 30, 1948.

143. "We were both somewhat embarrassed": EB to Carley Dawson, August 21, 1948.

143. "My one feeling": EB to Carley Dawson, August 30, 1948.

144. "Sordid Bohemian parties": RL to EB, August 24, 1948 (V).

144. "It has all been very tough": EB to Carley Dawson, August 21, 1948.

144. remembers the look of dismay: John Malcolm Brinnin, in conversation with the author, August 25, 1980.

145. "As far as Cal goes": EB to Carley Dawson, December 11, 1948.

145. "all the POETS": EB to Carley Dawson, November 10, 1948.

146. going home drunk: RL to EB, August 15, 1957 (V).

146. "the only sober person": EB to Carley Dawson, December 1, 1948.

146. "He must get very dull": Ibid.

146. "white & hot & exhausted": EB to Carley Dawson, November 26, 1948.

147. "more the mental aftermath": EB to Carley Dawson, December 1, 1948.

147. "I had just been doing too much": EB to Carley Dawson, November 26, 1948.

147. "avoid all intellectual excitement": EB to RL, December 5, 1948 (H).

148. resented being sexually attracted to her: Carley Dawson to EB, May 24, 1948 (V).

3 / PROSE

149. "although it is factual": EB, draft of introduction to the unfinished *Brazil-Brasil* (V). See E. Lucas Bridges, *Uttermost Part of the Earth* (New York: E. P. Dutton, 1950).

149. "a sleeping mouse": Ibid.

149. a violent allergic reaction: EB to Anne Stevenson, August 15, 1965 (W).

149. "enthralled by the Brazilian geography": Ibid.

150. "witty indeed": Elizabeth Hardwick, in correspondence with the author.

151. "uncritical affection": EB to U. T. and Joe Summers, April 21, 1953.

151. "I am extremely happy": EB to RL, July 28, 1953 (H).

151. "all fine and dandy": Ibid.

151. explains to Dr. Baumann: EB to Dr. Anny Baumann, August 5, 1948.

152. the age at which her father died: EB to Dr. Anny Baumann, January 17, 1951.

152. "I go to Rio": EB to RL, May 20, 1955 (H).

152. "I was always too shy": EB to RL, July 28, 1953 (H).

152. "a weekly institution": EB to MM, June 5, 1956 (R).

152. "carte postale beach": EB to RL, March 21, 1952 (H).

153. "magnificent and wild": Ibid.

153. "with a waterfall": Ibid.

153. all the Key West flowers: EB to MM, February 14, 1952 (R).

153. "filled with beautiful old furniture": Elizabeth Hardwick, in correspondence with the author.

153. "absolutely alone": EB to RL, July 27, 1960 (H).

154. "The most terrific storm": EB to RL, December 2, 1956 (H).

154. "electric blue eyes": EB to MM, February 14, 1952 (R).

154. "color of blueberries": EB to Dr. Anny Baumann, July 28, 1952.

154. "It started pouring": EB to RL, December 5, 1953 (H).

155. "It is sometimes necessary": W. H. Auden, speaking of Henry James at the Grolier Club, New York, October 24, 1946, as quoted by Moore in her commentary on Auden in *Predilections*, reprinted in Moore, *Complete Prose*, p. 465.

155. "There's a huge family": EB to RL, November 30, 1954 (H).

155. "a real, day-by-day diary": Introduction to *The Diary of "Helena Morley"* (New York· Farrar, Straus and Giroux, 1957), p. x; Bishop, *Collected Prose*, p. 82.

156. "Like a rheumatic old aunt". RL to EB, November 29, 1953 (V).

156. "a unique class": RL to EB, February 1952 (V).

156. "baroque, worldly, presbyterian": RL to EB, November 1951 (V).

156. "like a flayed man": RL to EB, July 18, 1955 (V).

157. "in two nights": EB, interview with Elizabeth Spires, *Paris Review* 80 (Summer 1981), p. 73.

157. "that desire to get things straight": EB to RL, May 20, 1955 (H).

157. "it starts naked": RL to EB, November 15, 1954 (V).

158. "girls' stories": RL to EB, January 1, 1954 (V).

158. "Patriquin": EB to Anne Stevenson, March 23, 1964 (W).

159. a role that "grew and grew": Bishop, "Gwendolyn," *Collected Prose*, p. 218.

159. "shut invisibly inside it": Ibid, p. 224.

160. "as fresh as paint": Introduction to "Helena Morley," p. xxxiv; Bishop, *Collected Prose*, p. 108.

160. "shoes, single shoes": Bishop, "In the Village," *Collected Prose*, p. 262.

161. "The child vanishes". Ibid, p. 253.

162. "a skein of voices": Ibid, p. 270.

162. "terrifyingly thrust upon us": "Gwendolyn," *Collected Prose*, p. 224.

162. "when one is extremely unhappy": EB, journal, 1950 (V).

163. "The pure note: pure and angelic": "In the Village," p. 253.

164. "Nate is shaping a horseshoe": Ibid, p. 274.

166. "a great ruminating Dutch landscape": RL to EB, January 1, 1954 (V).

166. "When Mother died": Lowell, "Near the Unbalanced Aquarium," *Collected Prose*, p. 350.
166. "a gruesome, vulgar, blasting surge": RL to EB, November 15, 1954 (V).
166. "I feel eccentric, antiquarian": RL to EB, November 15, 1954 (V).
167. "When I was three or four": Lowell, *Collected Prose*, p. 293.
167. "a wedding-cake": RL, draft (H).
168. "clumsy inaccurate and magical": RL to EB, May 5, 1955 (V).
168. "91 Revere Street": It appeared in *Partisan Review* 33 (Fall 1956), pp. 445–77, and as Part Two of *Life Studies* (1959); Lowell, *Collected Prose*, pp. 309–45.
168. "thin and arty": RL to EB, June 18, 1956 (V).
169. stories of childhood punishment: RL, drafts (H).
169. "a pastel-pale Huckleberry Finn": Lowell, "My Last Afternoon with Uncle Devereux Winslow," *Selected Poems*, p. 67.
170. "I was five and a half": Ibid, pp. 67–68.

4 / UNDER A READING-GLASS

172. "like prehistoric monsters": Lowell, "On 'Skunk Hour,' " *Collected Prose*, p. 227.
172. "old New Criticism religious, symbolic poems": RL, interview with Ian Hamilton, *The Review* (London) (Summer 1971), p. 26; Lowell, *Collected Prose*, p. 284.
172. "so few poems": RL to EB, March 4, 1957 (V).
173. "No poem, however, got finished": Lowell, *Collected Prose*, p. 227.
173. "like Vaughan and Traherne": RL to EB, April 29, 1957 (V).
173. "expert little stanzas . . . new kind of poetry . . . comes from the craft": RL, interview with Frederick Seidel, *Paris Review* 25 (Winter–Spring 1961), p. 70; Lowell, *Collected Prose*, p. 245.
173. "that exploring quality": *Paris Review* 25 (Winter–Spring 1961), p. 69; Lowell, *Collected Prose*, p. 245.
173. "became my test": RL, notes for "On 'Skunk Hour' " (H).
174. "I read your work with more interest": RL to EB, June 10, 1957 (V).
174. "Rereading her": RL, notes for "On 'Skunk Hour' " (H).
174. had brought more peace: RL to EB, June 10, 1957 (V).
174. to see her in Brazil: RL to EB, July 19, 1957 (V), and EB to RL, August 15, 1957 (H).
174. "slip into the monstrous": RL to EB, March 15, 1958 (V).
174. "was getting very amorous": Ian Hamilton attributes this recollection to "a friend of Robert Lowell's and Elizabeth Bishop's" with whom he spoke in 1982 (Hamilton, *Robert Lowell*, p. 238 and note, p. 491).
175. "THESE TWO VOLUMES": On the flyleaf of the first volume of Herbert's *Works*, in the Bishop archive at the Vassar Library.
175. "We should have read": EB to RL, August 9, 1957 (H).
176. "I see clearly now": RL to EB, August 8/9, 1957 (V).
176. "Gracelessly": Ibid.
176. "Maybe I shd. add": EB to RL, August 15, 1957 (H).
177. "Before she had gone": RL to Randall Jarrell, October 24, 1957, quoted in Hamilton, *Robert Lowell*, p. 236.
177. "Also I want you to know": RL to EB, August 15, 1957 (V).

Notes

179. a four-sonnet sequence: Robert Lowell, *Notebook*, 3rd ed., revised and enlarged (New York: Farrar, Straus and Giroux, 1970), pp. 234–36. The poems, further revised, are also in Robert Lowell, *History* (New York: Farrar, Straus and Giroux, 1973), pp. 196–98.

179. "It was a Maine lobster town": Lowell, *Selected Poems*, p. 99.

180. The drafts pick up her phrasing: RL, drafts (H). In the draft manuscripts, there are even closer echoes of Bishop's September 8, 1948, letter.

180. "I've just been indulging myself": EB to RL, September 8, 1948 (H).

180. "I had a dream": RL, draft (H).

180. "I want to be drowned": EB to RL, April 4–5, 1962 (H).

181. "We wished our two souls": Lowell, *Selected Poems*, p. 100.

181. "Starlike the eagle": RL, draft (H).

181. "If you ever do anything": EB to RL, December 11/14, 1957 (H).

182. "Half Nova Scotian": RL, draft (H).

182. "One reads his 'Dearest friend' ": RL, draft (H).

183. "My own father": Lowell, "Near the Unbalanced Aquarium," *Collected Prose*, p. 363.

184. a "psychiatric fieldworker": See Hamilton, *Robert Lowell*, pp. 240–43.

185. "I've been furiously writing at poems": RL to EB, September 11, 1957 (V).

185. "intent on copying its form": RL, notes for "On 'Skunk Hour' " (H).

185. "A skunk isn't much of a present": RL to EB, December 1, 1957 (V).

186. "space to breathe": Lowell, "On 'Skunk Hour,' " *New World Writing* 21 (1962), p. 158; Lowell, *Collected Prose*, p. 228.

186. Lowell's first draft: RL, notes for "On 'Skunk Hour' " (H).

187 "summery, utilitarian": RL to EB, June 21, 1958 (V).

188. "Weak and armored": RL to EB, June 10, 1957 (V).

188. "My darling receding Elizabeth": RL to EB, October 25, 1957 (V).

188. "I really glory": RL to EB, December 1, 1957 (V).

189. "Sydney Smith speaks somewhere": EB to RL, December 11/14, 1957 (H).

189. "The whole phenomena": Ibid.

189. "like a skunk": RL to Randall Jarrell, October 11, 1957, quoted in Hamilton, *Robert Lowell*, p. 234.

190. "POEMS LOVELY": EB to RL, telegram, November 1957 (H).

190. The letter is long: EB to RL, December 11/14, 1957 (H).

192. "craving something new": EB to RL, October 30, 1958 (H).

192. "that long-winded nature description": Ibid.

192. "As a child": EB, jacket blurb for Robert Lowell, *Life Studies* (1959); repr. *Elizabeth Bishop and Her Art*, p. 285.

5/QUESTIONS OF TRAVEL

194. "Jungle into picture": RL to EB, January 4, 1959 (V).

194. "a bit artificial": EB to RL, February 15, 1960 (H).

195. "studying the stones of Florence": EB to Howard Moss, May 10, 1960. Mary McCarthy's *The Stones of Florence* had been published the year before.

196. See Charles Wagley, *Amazon Town: A Study of Man in the Tropics* (New York: Macmillan, 1953), pp. 224–33.

196. "the best fairy story": RL to EB, April 28, 1960 (V).

197. "The more I read the book": Introduction to *The Diary of "Helena Morley,"* p. x; Bishop, *Collected Prose*, p. 82.

197. "I'm sure I've heard": EB to MM, April 10, 1958 (R).

198. "Memories of Uncle Neddy": Bishop, *Collected Prose*, pp. 227–50. First published in *The Southern Review* 13 (Fall 1977), pp. 786–803.

198. "Uncle Neddy will continue": Bishop, *Collected Prose*, p. 250.

198. In the real Uncle Artie: EB to RL, December 11/14, 1957 (H).

198. "not a violent, active Devil": Bishop, *Collected Prose*, p. 228.

199. "like Great Village in 1920": EB to RL, April 4–5, 1962 (H).

199. a short stanzaic version: "The Scream," *For the Union Dead*, p. 8. It does not appear in the *Selected Poems*.

199. "I don't know why I bother": EB to RL, April 4–5, 1962 (H).

199. just a footnote: RL to EB, April 14, 1962 (V).

199. "NO—I was very pleased": EB to RL, April 26, 1962 (H).

200. "more romantic and gray": RL to EB, March 10, 1962 (V).

200. "larger, gayer": Ibid.

200. he claims to have heard: Ibid.

200. "A scream!": "The Scream," *For the Union Dead*, p. 9.

200. "Are they too frail": "In the Village," Bishop, *Collected Prose*, p. 274.

201. "never climbed / Mount Sion": Lowell, "Middle Age," *Selected Poems*, p. 103.

201. "sounding like you": EB to RL, April 4–5, 1962 (H).

202. "no one else I can talk to": RL to EB, April 7, 1959 (V).

202. "rewriting *everything*": RL to EB, July 24, 1959 (V).

202. "left strangely dumb": RL to EB, March 15, 1958 (V).

202. "I don't seem able to use": RL to EB, March 18, 1962 (V).

202. "I think his tone": Ibid.

203. "like living in someone else's house": RL to EB, August 25, 1960 (V).

203. Lowell's translations: See the poems in Robert Lowell, *Imitations* (New York: Farrar, Straus and Giroux, 1961) and his introduction, pp. xi–xiii, which is reprinted in Lowell, *Collected Prose*, pp. 232–34.

203. "ABSOLUTELY STUNNING": EB to RL, telegram, January 26, 1961 (H).

203. she finally sent off a letter: EB to RL, March 1, 1961 (H).

204. In an earlier letter: EB quotes from a draft of the lost letter—"dated New Years!" she writes—in EB to RL, March 1, 1961 (H).

205. "At the Green Cabaret": Lowell, *Imitations*, pp. 87–88.

205. "On the Road": Ibid., pp. 86–87.

205. "A Malicious Girl": Ibid., p. 88.

206. "But it was terrific": Ibid., p. 87.

206. "The Sleeper in the Valley": Ibid., p. 89.

206. "partly self-sufficient": Lowell, *Imitations*, p. xi; Lowell, *Collected Prose*, p. 232.

207. also *his*-story: Stephen Yenser, *Circle to Circle: The Poetry of Robert Lowell* (Berkeley: University of California Press, 1975), p. 306.

207. The attempt to be all-inclusive: EB, draft note on Lowell's style, particularly in *Day by Day* (V).

207. "distinct from the lived one": James Merrill, "Elizabeth Bishop (1911–1979)";

The New York Review of Books 26 (December 6, 1979), p. 6; repr. *Elizabeth Bishop and Her Art*, p. 259.

208. "I seek leave": "Shifting Colors," Robert Lowell, *Day by Day* (New York: Farrar, Straus and Giroux, 1977), pp. 119–20.
208. found the last lines "weird": EB, draft note on Lowell's style, particularly in *Day by Day* (V).
208. She disliked: EB to RL, June 15, 1961 (H).
209. "That Anne Sexton": EB to RL, July 27, 1960 (H).
209. "You *tell* things": EB to RL, June 15, 1961 (H).
209. "She's more inspired": RL to EB, July 12, 1960 (V).
209. "good in spots": EB to RL, January 22–23, 1962 (H).
209. "intensely *interesting*": EB to RL, May 19, 1960 (H).
209. "Fall 1961": Lowell, *Selected Poems*, p. 105.
209. "Your poem is haunting me": EB to RL, May 19, 1960 (H).
210. "tough, red-headed, illegitimate": EB to RL, August 26, 1963 (H).
210. "The Drinker": Lowell, *Selected Poems*, p. 116.
210. Bishop asked specially: EB to RL, April 22, 1960 (H).
210. "most awful line": EB to RL, July 27, 1960 (H). Bishop's comments on "The Drinker" are from this letter.
210. "the weight of drinking": Elizabeth Hardwick, review of Bishop, *Collected Prose* in *The New Republic* 190 (March 19, 1984), p. 34.
211. "A Drunkard": EB, draft (V).
212. "I have a poem": EB to RL, July 27, 1960 (H).
213. "My passion for accuracy": EB to RL, August 27, 1964 (H).
213. "Please don't age yourself": Ibid.
218. "My Last Afternoon with Uncle Devereux Winslow": Lowell, *Selected Poems*, pp. 66–71.
218. "best thing in the language": RL to EB, October 3, 1961 (V).

6/QUESTIONS OF MEMORY

222. "with the steady excellence": RL to EB, October 28, 1965 (V).
222. "a very powerful initiation poem": Ibid.
222. "Please never stop writing me letters": EB to RL, July 27, 1960 (H).
222. "You have no idea": EB to RL, January 22–23, 1962 (H).
223. "Oh so many poets": EB to RL, July 30, 1964 (H).
223. "utterly spooky": RL to EB, April 14, 1962 (V).
224. "one has the feeling": EB to RL, April 26, 1962 (H).
224. "I'm pretty much at sea": EB to RL, October 1, 1964 (H).
224. "the voice of the man": RL, review of 77 *Dream Songs*, *The New York Review of Books*, May 28, 1964, p. 3; Lowell, *Collected Prose*, p. 110.
224. since about 1948: Jarrell sent Bishop "The Night before the Night before Christmas" with his letter dated November 1948. *Randall Jarrell's Letters*, ed. Mary Jarrell (Boston: Houghton Mifflin, 1985), p. 210.
224. Much of it seemed limp to her: EB to RL, December 31, 1948 (H).

224. "I was vexed": Randall Jarrell to EB, September 1956. *Randall Jarrell's Letters*, p. 413.

224. "neurotic behavior": Ibid.

225. "I like your poetry better": Randall Jarrell to EB, February 1957. Ibid, p. 420.

225. "But life beats art": Randall Jarrell to EB, April 1957. Ibid, p. 422.

225. thanked Jarrell: Jarrell mentions this in his letter to Bishop dated April 1957. Ibid.

225. "really in his way": RL to EB, May 8, 1963 (V).

225. "One can talk more easily": RL to EB, February 25, 1965 (V).

226. "all the compliments I could truthfully pay": EB to RL, March 11, 1965 (H).

226. "where he *gets* these women": Ibid.

226. "His worst flaw": RL to EB, October 28, 1965 (V).

226. "I just never did like": EB to RL, March 20, 1973 (H).

226. "Perhaps I shouldn't say this": EB to RL, February 10, 1972 (H).

226. "one of the unhealthier jobs": EB to RL, August 26, 1963 (H).

226. "I think suicide": RL to EB, undated, written after Randall Jarrell's funeral on October 17, 1965 (V).

227. "so absolutely gifted": RL to EB, October 28, 1965 (V).

227. "I felt awful about Randall": EB to RL, November 18, 1965 (H).

227. "reasonable doubt about its being a suicide": See *Randall Jarrell's Letters*, pp. 519–21, for Mary Jarrell's account, which treats the circumstances of Jarrell's death and the coroner's report in detail.

227. "I know my drinking": EB to RL, October 11, 1963 (H). The sentence of Roethke's reads "From a burnt pine the sharp speech of a crow / Tells me my drinking breeds a will to die.": Theodore Roethke, "The Mallow," *The Complete Poems* (Garden City, N.Y.: Doubleday, 1966), p. 266.

228. "the same life": "For John Berryman," *Day by Day*, p. 27.

228. "I feel we must beware": EB to RL, April 23, 1967 (H).

228. a book on Brazil: *Brazil*, by Elizabeth Bishop with the editors of *Life* (New York: Time-Life Books, 1962).

228. "change very fast very soon": EB to RL, July 6, 1965 (H).

229. "To the Botequim & Back" and "A Trip to Vigia": Unpublished in Bishop's lifetime; they are included in Bishop, *Collected Prose*.

229. "I like Ouro Prêto": EB to RL, November 18, 1965 (H).

229. "in this Robinson Crusoe atmosphere": EB, notebook (V).

229. As early as the mid-sixties: EB to Howard Moss, March 25, 1965.

229. "suspense of strangeness": EB, draft of introduction to the unfinished *Brazil-Brasil* (V). See E. Lucas Bridges, *Uttermost Part of the Earth* (New York: E. P. Dutton, 1950).

230. "a mixture": EB to Howard Moss, January 29, 1964.

230. " 'Bravo for the new park' ": EB to Anne Stevenson, February 7, 1965 (W).

230. "back to the Brazilian madhouse": EB to RL, July 30, 1964 (H).

230. "what they used to call a 'nervous breakdown' ": EB to RL, September 25, 1966 (H).

230. "She has had this breakdown coming on": EB to RL, March 3, 1967 (H).

231. her "most spectacular" attack of asthma in years: Ibid.

231. "I suppose I had Lota": EB to RL, December 15–16, 1969 (H).

231. "I miss her more": EB to RL, February 27, 1970 (H).
232. "too much like my own early days": EB to RL, May 13, 1970 (H).
232. leave the Ouro Prêto house: EB to RL, February 27, 1970 (H).
232. "I lost my mother": EB to RL, June 15, 1970 (H).
233. "Don't let the academic stuffiness": EB to RL, October 26, 1972 (H).
233. "It's been a joy": RL to EB, October 9, 1967 (V).
234. "Well, you are right to worry": EB to RL, February 27, 1970 (H).
234. included in his revised *Notebook*: Robert Lowell, *Notebook*, 3rd ed., pp. 234–36.
234. "I hope they roll up to": RL to EB, February 20, 1970 (V).
234. then revised all four again two years later for *History*: Robert Lowell, *History*, pp. 196–98.
235. "for versing one of your letters": RL to EB, December 1970 (V).
235. Bishop's letter: EB to RL, February 27, 1970 (H).
236. "You are right to worry": Lowell, *History*, p. 197.
237. "Accident threw up subjects": "Afterthought," in Lowell, *Notebook* (1970), p. 262.
237. it wasn't a "memory bath": Peter Taylor, "Robert Trail Spence Lowell: 1917–1977," *Ploughshares* 5, no. 2 (1979), p. 79.
238. "casual in tone and form": John Berryman, "Waiting for the End, Boys," *Partisan Review* 15 (February 1948), p. 254; John Berryman, *The Freedom of the Poet* (New York: Farrar, Straus and Giroux, 1976), p. 297.
238. "Do you still hang your words in air": Lowell, *History*, p. 198.
239. "unerring Muse": Ibid.
240. "DOLPHIN is magnificent poetry": EB to RL, March 21, 1972 (H).
241. "Hopkins' marvelous letter to Bridges": The letter is dated February 3/10, 1887. Bishop quotes a portion of it in her memoir of Marianne Moore (Bishop, *Collected Prose*, pp. 155–56).
242. "perhaps it's as simple as that": EB to RL, March 21, 1972 (H).
242. "I feel like Bridges": RL to EB, March 28, 1972 (V).
242. "a kind of masterpiece": RL to Frank Bidart, April 10, 1972.
243. "no hurry for time": RL to EB, March 28, 1972 (V).
243. "It's the revelations": RL to EB, Easter [April 2], 1972 (V).
243. "making the poem unwounding": Ibid.
243. she objected to the title "Burden": EB to RL, March 21, 1972 (H).
243. "rather serenely gracious": RL to EB, Easter [April 2], 1972 (V).
244. "Now the book must still be painful": RL to Frank Bidart, May 15, 1972.
244. Lee Edelman: See Lee Edelman, "The Geography of Gender: Elizabeth Bishop's 'In the Waiting Room,' " *Contemporary Literature* 26, no. 2 (Summer 1985), pp. 179–96.
245. "The Country Mouse": Bishop, *Collected Prose*, pp. 13–33.
247. "I deplore the 'confessional' ": EB to RL, March 21, 1972 (H).
247. "My immorality": RL to EB, July 12, 1973 (V).
247. "One life, one writing!": Lowell, "Night Sweat," *Selected Poems*, p. 134.
247. "irreparable and awful actions": EB to RL, July 22, 1973 (H).
248. "The room itself is spacious": EB to Elizabeth Spires, September 14, 1978.
249. "instinctive, modest": James Merrill, "Elizabeth Bishop (1911–1979)," p. 6.

249. "Talking with you in Cambridge": RL to EB, May 1, 1974 (V).
249. "passed out of some shadow": RL to EB, June 18, 1974 (V).
250. "Of course, it's different for a writer": EB to RL, January 16, 1975 (H).

AFTERWORD

251. "Her 'questions of travel' ": This and the succeeding quotations from David Kalstone in this afterword are to be found in the essays on Elizabeth Bishop and Robert Lowell in his *Five Temperaments* (New York: Oxford University Press, 1977).
258. "not land possessed": Svetlana Alpers, *The Art of Describing: Dutch Art in the Seventeenth Century* (Chicago: University of Chicago Press, 1983), p. 149.
258. "with its hordes of angry soldiers": Ibid, p. xxi.

Index

Index

Index

Index

Index